Y0-BRR-865

THE FUTURE
OF META-ANALYSIS

THE FUTURE
OF META-ANALYSIS

Kenneth W. Wachter

AND

Miron L. Straf

EDITORS

A project of the
Committee on National Statistics,
Commission on Behavioral and Social Sciences
and Education, National Research Council

RUSSELL SAGE FOUNDATION   NEW YORK

NATIONAL RESEARCH COUNCIL

The National Research Council was established by the National Academy of Sciences in 1916 to associate the broad community of science and technology with the Academy's purposes of furthering knowledge and of advising the federal government. The Council operates in accordance with general policies determined by the Academy under the authority of its congressional charter of 1863, which establishes the Academy as a private, nonprofit, self-governing membership corporation. The Council has become the principal operating agency of both the National Academy of Sciences and the National Academy of Engineering in the conduct of their services to the government, the public, and the scientific and engineering communities. It is administered jointly by both Academies of Engineering and the Institute of Medicine. The National Academy of Engineering and the Institute of Medicine were established in 1964 and 1970, respectively, under the charter of the National Academy of Sciences.

NOTICE: The project that is the subject of this report was approved by the Governing Board of the National Research Council, whose members are drawn from the Councils of the National Academy of Sciences, the National Academy of Engineering, and the Institute of Medicine. The members were chosen for their special competencies and with regard for appropriate balance.

This report has been reviewed by a group other than the authors according to procedures approved by a Report Review Committee consisting of members of the National Academy of Sciences, the National Academy of Engineering, and the Institute of Medicine.

Library of Congress Cataloging-in-Publication Data

The Future of meta-analysis / Kenneth W. Wachter and Miron L. Straf, editors.
    p.   cm.
Includes bibliographical references.
ISBN 0-87154-890-9
   1. Social sciences—Research—Evaluation. 2. Meta-analysis. 3. School integration—United States—Case studies. 4. Aphasics—Rehabilitation—Case studies.   I. Wachter, Kenneth W. II. Straf, Miron L.
H62.F88   1990
300'.72—dc20   90-8372
                                                 CIP

Workshop on the Future of Meta-Analysis

Kenneth W. Wachter (Chair)
Graduate Group in Demography and Department of Statistics,
University of California–Berkeley

Norman M. Bradburn
Provost, University of Chicago

Harris M. Cooper
Center for Research in Social Behavior, University of Missouri–Columbia

David S. Cordray
Department of Human Resources and Department of Psychology,
George Peabody College, Vanderbilt University

Stephen E. Fienberg
Department of Statistics, Carnegie Mellon University

Davida Fromm
Alzheimer's Disease Research Center, University of Pittsburgh

Joel B. Greenhouse
Department of Statistics, Carnegie Mellon University

Larry V. Hedges
Department of Education, University of Chicago

Nan M. Laird
Department of Biostatistics, Harvard School of Public Health

Frederick Mosteller
Department of Statistics and Technology Assessment Group,
Harvard University

Ingram Olkin
Department of Statistics and School of Edu   Stanford University

S. James Press
Department of Statistics, University of California–Riverside

Robert Rosenthal
Department of Psychology, Harvard University

Donald B. Rubin
Department of Statistics, Harvard University

Jeffrey M. Schneider
Instruction and Professional Development, National Education Association

Burton H. Singer
Department of Epidemiology and Public Health,
Yale University School of Medicine

Judith Tanur
Department of Sociology, State University of New York at Stony Brook

Fredric M. Wolf
Department of Postgraduate Medicine and Health Professions Education,
University of Michigan

Miron L. Straf Director
Linda Ingram Consultant
Satish Iyengar Consultant
Barbara A. Busey Secretary

Acknowledgments

We especially appreciate the encouragement of Murray Aborn, of the National Science Foundation, at every stage of this project and the aid of Judith Tanur, formerly a member of the Committee on National Statistics, in bringing the ideas to fruition. Ann Marie Ross helped to prepare this volume for publication, and Barbara Busey helped to make the workshop a success. We are also grateful to Linda Ingram and Satish Iyengar, who served on the staff of the workshop; to Evelyn Simeon and Michele Zinn, also on the Committee on National Statistics staff; and to Eugenia Grohman, of the Commission on Behavioral and Social Sciences and Education. Finally, we are grateful to the Russell Sage Foundation for its support to produce this volume and especially to its President, Eric Wanner, for his valuable assistance and advice.

Contents

Introduction

Kenneth W. Wachter / Miron L. Straf

In October 1986 the Committee on National Statistics (CNSTAT) of the National Research Council convened a workshop on the future of meta-analysis. The goal of the workshop was to assess the role actually played by meta-analytic methodologies in current practice and, in particular, to assess their applicability to policy-relevant research, identifying strengths and limitations and suggesting priorities for future research. The presentations at that workshop, the transcript of key parts of the discussion, and the subsequent comments by workshop members on new ideas from the workshop form the basis for the present volume.

Meta-analysis refers to the application of quantitative methods to the problem of combining results from different analytic studies. Typically, a statistical analysis is made of numerical summaries of each study. Meta-analysis is not a statistical method per se, but rather an orientation toward research synthesis that uses many techniques of measurement and data analysis.

This volume comes at a time when existing approaches to meta-analysis have been summed up in several acclaimed books, including Cooper (1984); Glass, McGaw, and Smith (1981); Hedges and Olkin (1985); Hunter, Schmidt, and Jackson (1982); Light and Pillemer (1984); Rosenthal (1984); and Wolf (1986). A repertory of techniques and a variety of perspectives have now been developed, made accessible, and even codified. But controversy between enthusiasts and skeptics continues and, even as the previous progress is being assimilated, the subject seems to be growing beyond the bounds marked out by these works. It is a natural time to ask, "What next?"

We and many other participants went to the CNSTAT workshop with definite ideas as to what issues would come to the fore. These expectations centered on questions of mismatch between the methods that methodologists were advancing and the methods that users were actually using or could use. They also centered on a set of unsolved statistical problems. We expected action on the technical frontier. And, indeed, such issues figured prominently in the discussions and figure prominently in this volume. But we found at the workshop, and the reader will find in these pages, a different set of issues taking center stage. These are conceptual issues, having to do with the nature and goals of meta-analysis in the service of research synthesis. We have found no short rubric or catch phrase with which to point toward the issues that we mean. They are reflected in tensions within the field concerning the justification for pursuing or forgoing a complete versus selected representation of prior studies in a meta-analysis and concerning the primacy of main effects versus mediating influences and covariates in meta-analyses. The concluding pages of this introduction return to these issues. Although they cannot be tied together into one neat bundle, they hold together at a basic level, and they indicate that the field is moving now in new directions.

The implication of the workshop, then, and the argument of this book, is that the future of meta-analysis will be very little like its past.

An Overview of the Volume

Part I introduces meta-analysis with a survey of its past and a tally of aspirations for its future. These chapters are not meant to be a textbook explanation of what meta-analysis is or how it can be applied. That function is already admirably served by the books we have cited. We assume that readers have already encountered some basic concepts of meta-analysis, either in theory or in practice, and we assume that the encounters have left them, like us, curious about where the subject stands today and where it may be headed.

We take up the present state of meta-analysis, including its problems and possibilities, with two specific case studies that are made the basis for critique and commentary. The first, in Part II, a meta-analysis prepared especially for this volume, examines effects of rehabilitation therapy for aphasia. The second, in Part III, is an important earlier investigation of effects of school desegregation on the academic achievement of black children.

Meta-analysis has close affinities with many areas of statistics, and these areas provide, in Part IV, vantage points for broader views of meta-analytic techniques and assumptions. Attention then turns, in Part V, explicitly toward the future, toward possible new paradigms for the subject, toward the tension over basic concepts and directions that we have already mentioned, and toward priorities for further reflection and action.

Methodological Imperatives

We now consider in more detail the salient issues that arise in each of the parts of the volume. We begin with the health of meta-analysis on the technical side as it figures in Part I.

The early discussions at the workshop that led to this volume were characterized by a mixture of exuberance and anxiety. It is no easy matter as far as methodological developments are concerned to assess the present health and future prospects of the field. There is no doubt that some of the procedures of meta-analysis are in widespread use, with applications so various that they are venturing beyond the original conditions required by the formal methodologies. Other procedures with extensive formal development and investment of theoretical effort have not been finding their way at all into users' repertories. And little headway has been made on some of the oldest and most widely recognized problems faced by reviewers of research, such as lack of independence among studies, incomparability of measurement scales, and coding schemes for study quality.

What do the success stories of the methods that have been taken up on every side have to say about the failure of others to diffuse into practice or about the targeting of new methodological initiatives? What are the prospects for built-in safeguards to head off foolhardy application of methods when the minimum assumptions to sustain them are not satisfied? Are there any ideas that might finally allow progress on the recalcitrant technical issues that have hampered meta-analysis?

In Chapter 1, Ingram Olkin sets the stage with reflections on the history and goals of meta-analysis and a summary of problems and recommendations. In Chapter 2, Larry Hedges takes up nine specific methodological imperatives.

Case Studies

The two case studies in Parts II and III give contrasting examples of meta-analytic practice. The aphasia study is a case close to the traditional sort of scientific setting in which research results from separate teams are to be combined. The desegregation study is a remarkable unpublished compilation of six meta-analyses of the same set of primary studies, undertaken within a framework of public policy interests and exhibiting the special difficulties that attend meta-analysis in contexts of this kind.

The aphasia example was prepared with an eye to presentation at the workshop by Joel Greenhouse, of Carnegie Mellon University, Davida Fromm, of the Western Psychiatric Institute and Clinics, and four of their colleagues. In Chapter 3, the authors chronicle the problems encountered by first-time meta-analysts as they attempt to draw on the existing repertory of approaches. They escort the reader through the process, step by step, commenting on the decisions they found themselves making along the way and on the needs for further methodological guidance to inform those decisions. The emphasis is not on presenting statistical detail but rather on becoming self-conscious about the actual practice of meta-analysis. Further statistical results from the aphasia study can be found in Iyengar and Greenhouse (1988). The standpoint is that of an informed newcomer. A commentary by Nan Laird on this second case study, from the standpoint of an experienced practitioner, is found in Chapter 4. She draws attention to the particular problems of practice that make the questions of completeness of literature search and choice of summary statistics pivotal, and she relates the lessons of this case study to the enterprise of research reviewing throughout clinical and public health research.

The desegregation example in Part III originated in 1982 when the National Institute of Education (NIE), in a project under the direction of Jeffrey Schneider, put together a desegregation studies team of social scientists. Two of them worked as a pair and the other five worked singly. They were charged with analyzing 19 of the best-conducted of the generally poor studies of desegregation then available, selected from 157 known empirical studies. Most of the researchers had prior experience studying the relationship of desegregation to achievement. They had found different effects and had drawn different conclusions from their own analyses. The NIE posed a single question to them: Does school desegregation lead to improved black student academic achievement as measured by standardized tests? The NIE wanted to identify the similarities and differences in the analyses of scientists who worked with the same data under similar conditions and common constraints. Jeffrey Schneider explains the desegregation project in Chapter 5. (The studies themselves have not been published, but contributors to this volume were generously permitted to examine relevant drafts.) Linda Ingram gives an overview of this unpublished background material in Chapter 6.

The original project included a comparative study by Thomas Cook of the six meta-analyses commissioned by the NIE, which is discussed by

James Press in Chapter 7. In tandem with the project, Harris Cooper gathered empirical data on the changing beliefs of the authors of the six analyses as they prepared their submissions and on the changing beliefs of readers perusing the final products. He presents a revised version of his report on his results in Chapter 8 and amplifies it in Chapter 9 with a discussion of needs for new methods and practices as shown by this case study. In Chapter 10, David Cordray rounds off Part III by drawing lessons from the case study about the advantages and limitations of meta-analysis for policy analysis, how the advantages can be enhanced, and how the limitations can be overcome.

CNSTAT has a particular interest in the promise of meta-analysis for policy-oriented research, and we would have liked to include in this volume an expanded treatment of the kinds of questions that David Cordray touches on. But it appears that there is not yet enough experience with applications of meta-analysis to policy for a full account. We hope that the next few years will provide opportunities for such a more extensive treatment.

It is commonplace for those attempting meta-analyses to find too little information given in published papers or reports to allow computation of effect sizes or proper coding of features of design. This problem rears its head in both our case studies, and it may be particularly troublesome for research that appears in journals read by those with interests in policy. CNSTAT, in its report *Sharing Research Data* (Fienberg, Martin, and Straf 1985), has recommended strong standards for ensuring the availability of data from primary studies to scholars attempting reanalyses. If these standards come to be widely obeyed, the prospects for meta-analyses could be much enhanced.

Just as meta-analysis may prove valuable for policy-oriented research, so the demands of policy-oriented research may prove a valuable stimulus to meta-analysis. Combining results from a number of experiments has a long history in astronomy, agriculture, bioassay, and high-precision measurements in physics, but such endeavors in the social and behavioral sciences are recent and controversial. Their use in aid of policy formulation and decision-making is only beginning, and it calls for new attitudes. In scientific work, single studies are, in principle, capable of providing definitive conclusions on some problems, obviating the need for meta-analysis. But rarely, if ever, can a single study provide definitive conclusions on which to base policy; some synthesis of multiple studies is almost always called for.

There is an honorable place in reviews of literature on scientific problems for hunches about mechanisms. Sometimes the right insight can sweep away previous disagreements. But stakeholders with competing interests in a policy are rarely going to be helped to reach convergence of views, considering the merits of conflicting studies, by subjective assessment, however wise. But it is just as true that no systematized methodology for research reviews can substitute for wisdom. The public policy arena is one in which the tension between subjectivity and objectivity in research synthesis comes most sharply into view.

Other Vantage Points

Drawing back from specific cases to the general picture, Part IV contains reactions to meta-analysis from vantage points informed by other sectors of the statistical sciences. In Chapter 11, Robert Rosenthal offers answers to criticisms repeatedly raised against meta-analysis. In Chapter 12, Norman Bradburn compares the work of designing a meta-analysis to the work of designing a survey, and assesses the scale of the challenge that both enterprises pose. In Chapter 13, Fred Wolf takes as his starting point ideas from the philosophy of science and analyzes the problem of bias and the many forms it takes.

Looking Toward the Future

Part V is an attempt at synthesis, explicitly focused on the future. In Chapter 14, Don Rubin sketches a new theoretical framework for meta-analysis which, if accepted, would settle a number of the questions about which leaders in the field are presently divided. Chapter 15 presents excerpts from the discussions that took place at the workshop, transcribed from tapes and edited with reference to notes taken at the meetings. Here the reader will find the broader conceptual issues taking shape, the issues to which we return at the end of this introduction. In Chapter 16, Frederick Mosteller pulls together, from all the chapters of this volume and the discussions of the workshop, suggestions for kinds of action that could lead to an even brighter future for meta-analysis.

Central Questions

We now turn from our preview of the volume to our own reflections on the intellectual issues at stake, some of which are only hinted at and some of which are fully debated in the chapters that follow.

The readers of this book will not be left with a consensus of views as to what the future of meta-analysis will be. What stands out more than anything else is a set of friendly tensions beginning to divide the field. As we have said, technical issues involving the relationship between existing methodology and existing practice might have been expected to be paramount themes, but they turn out not to be the worries that loom behind these commentaries and critiques. The dominant concerns are, instead, about the rationale behind the everyday decisions of meta-analysts, which are illustrated very clearly in the two case studies. The discussion about these decisions reveals uncertainty or disagreement about the conceptual basis for meta-analysis.

We focus on three of these practical questions that raise deeper conceptual issues. They are questions that arise throughout the chapters and permeate the discussion. The views here are our own, and doubtless none of the other authors would phrase the questions in quite our way or see quite the same implications. But we think all would agree that these are central questions, and the ways in which the field treats them will be crucial in shaping the future of meta-analysis.

The three specific questions are: (1) Should a scientist conducting a meta-analysis strive to recover all relevant research, pursuing a complete representation of the universe of research results on the question, or should a strategy of selection be adopted, such as restricting the collection to good studies, to studies that are published and readily available, or to studies retrieved under some other rules? (2) Should a meta-analysis focus on a single measure of a main effect or should it investigate patterns of response to covariates, intervening variables, and features of study design for their own sake and not just as they relate to estimates of main effects? (3) Is there any formal basis for choosing among different proposals as to how the results of different studies should be combined?

Completeness

Must a meta-analyst systematically strive to locate all available research that bears on the chosen question? Many of the authors of this volume believe a complete search to be fundamental. They discuss ways to improve searches, to find relevant theses, to ferret out papers that go unpublished because of negative or statistically nonsignificant findings. Some encourage journals to show more willingness to publish studies that fail to reject a null hypothesis. Concerned with problems of location and retrieval, they urge journals to include more descriptive titles and better key words or phrases in articles, however hard it may be to describe a paper or title in terms that will be meaningful years later, when meta-analysts come to do their work. There are other authors, however, who see this preoccupation with complete search as a mistake, diverting scarce time away from other aspects of the analysis of more importance to the final outcome, or even distorting the nature of the meta-analytic enterprise.

Completeness of search is one issue of completeness. Completeness of the subset of studies analyzed is a second issue. Once the task of location is over, should a meta-analyst include in the analysis essentially all those located studies which give enough information to calculate basic measures? Or should a more elite subset of studies be preselected on grounds of caliber or centrality? Should ratings of study quality serve as admissions criteria, excluding studies from the sample prior to statistical work, or should they figure as coded variables, entering into the statistical analysis itself?

On the first issue, our case studies are alike in that they undertook initial searches that aimed at being comprehensive. The desegregation project collected 157 studies of black achievement in desegregated schools, a large number of which were unpublished and hard to find. The aphasia project collected 114 articles on treatment, including grant reports and conference proceedings as well as articles. In both projects, the target universe was broadly defined.

On the issue of preselection before analysis, the teams conducting the two case studies both ended up analyzing small preselected subsets. But they did so with very different points of view. In the desegregation project, the selection of a small subset of higher-quality studies was conceived to be one of its salient features. The 19 studies analyzed were selected by reviewers for the sponsoring agency on the basis of explicit and largely objective criteria of coverage, reporting, and design (set out in detail by Jeffrey Schneider in Chapter 5). This preselection proved controversial and not fully tenable: some analysts did not use some of the 19 studies, and others added to the set. There may have been objective criteria for selection, but in practice the criteria were subjectively applied.

The aphasia study, in contrast, tried to obtain every relevant article. The selection of a subset for analysis was conceived to be a temporary practical expedient, to be remedied by analysis of the full collection at a later time. The early pages of Chapter 3 give a lively account of the pitfalls in compiling the universe of relevant literature. At the meetings, this account led to advice on every side. The authors were admonished not to lose heart and to go on looking for the literature in every nook and cranny. What more devastating criticism of a meta-analysis can there be than that it misses some important segment of the literature?

Commenting on this endeavor in Chapter 4, Nan Laird takes a stand against the pursuit of completeness, calling it "one of life's mistakes that we only make once." Emphasizing the trade-off between search time and coding time and the importance of duplicate coding for quality by coders blinded to study outcome, she writes that "a narrow focus facilitates a more reliable result." Like Laird, most of the contributors to this volume take it for granted that including all relevant studies is generally impractical. In discussion, Harris Cooper wryly noted: "Nobody's out there searching forever. If they are, they're certainly not the folks who are here. They're still at the library and have never published."

Those who see the motivation for limiting search as primarily a practical one predictably enough hold a variety of views on how to limit it. In discussion, some compared the search for studies to sequential sampling and were inclined to seek ways to assess the marginal benefit from obtaining one more study or conducting one more search. Some thought that search might just as well be limited by arbitrary constraints, such as a fixed span of years or a fixed set of initial journals or computerized indices plus fixed protocols for reference follow-up. Are the characteristics that correlate with readiness of retrieval principally aspects of quality, so that more exhaustive search turns up material of limited value? Or is there so likely to be a correlation between study outcome (for instance, significance of p-values) and readiness of retrieval that less exhaustive searches spell greater dangers of bias? A truly exhaustive search has the shining advantage of producing a universe of studies for later selection or sampling that has a clear characterization. With a limited search, how does one characterize the population from which studies selected for analysis form a sample or defined subgroup?

Some see the completeness of search as largely irrelevant. For them, it is important that the universe be broad enough to include the "important" papers. Important papers have influence on the scientific literature (either by definition or as a fact, with rare exceptions) and any reasonable search will unearth them. This view fits well with the view that studies actually included in the analysis should be selected by strict criteria of quality from the collection of all those retrieved.

Like the search process, the selection process, as all authors agree, should be formally specified and clearly described in any meta-analysis. The disagreement comes as to whether stringent preselection, from among the retrieved studies before analysis, is to be deemed theoretically desirable, as in the desegregation project, or is to be made merely a practical recourse, as in the aphasia project, to be minimized and as far as possible avoided.

Although cognizant of the practical limitations, some authors insist, as an ideal, on the ethic of comprehensiveness. After all, if selection for quality is carried to its logical extreme, then what room is left for the statistical side of meta-analysis? The stricter the criteria, the smaller the selected subset, and a small enough subset can be inspected directly, with no need of statistical methods for combination, summarization, and exposure. In the desegregation project, fairly basic criteria excluded all but 19 of the 157 retrieved studies, and the analyses were already hampered (as Chapters 6 and 7 show) by the smallness of the "sample" size. Stricter criteria would have left a number too meager for any meaningful graphs or summary statistics. Of course, for many questions a great deal can be learned from a handful of good studies, but these, it would be claimed from this point of view, are not the questions amenable to meta- analysis. What would happen on a given question if that will-o'-the-wisp, the definitive study, could be found? It would let us do without meta-analysis.

Some preselection is always required; meta-analysis cannot proceed without reports of basic outcome statistics and some semblance of scientific design. It is also true that the distinction between preselecting by quality, on the one hand, and coding and weighting for quality, on the other hand, can be called an artificial distinction. But there remains a philosophical issue. It often happens that features of statistically superior design are to be found concentrated among studies that share other characteristics of target population or scientific orientation. Meta-analysis has gone far beyond vote counting, but there is always a sense in which the selected studies can be likened to an electorate. Preselecting (or heavily weighting) for more than minimal standards of quality can, in effect, deny some sectors of research opinion the vote. Is this troubling? Or is it the *sine qua non* of scientific research synthesis?

Despite such longstanding arguments in favor of the ethic of comprehensiveness, it appears to us that a shift toward an opposite point of view is to be found in many of the exchanges of Chapter 15 and in many of the chapters in this volume. This stance is consistent with a different goal of meta-analysis, one that is not to summarize the results of varied studies, but rather to understand the basic science. With this goal, making inferences from a meta-analysis can be likened to making inferences from a regression model: It is not necessary to sample all values of the independent, carrier variables. Scientists can base their opinions on mutually exclusive reference lists and still reach the same conclusions. The further meta-analysis leaves vote-counting behind and the more it embraces structural modeling of study outcomes, the weaker the imperative for completeness becomes.

Main Effects

Should the focus of a meta-analysis be on a single measure of a main effect? Or should the analysis take into account covariates, intervening variables, features of study design, and other complexity?

The arguments for the first point of view are well known. The initial appeal of meta-analysis, especially to policymakers who prefer usable generalizations, is as a process to cut through the complexity of research literature. With enough studies, details of design may fade into the background and broad generalizations may emerge. If studies are categorized by many different factors of their design and many intervening variables, too few studies may fall into each of the categories to sustain persuasive inference. If, instead, the focus is on the broadest common denominator—the main effect—a larger pool of studies is available to bolster inference. Studies are pooled with the hope that effects of differences in their designs tend on the whole to cancel each other out.

These well-established arguments for concentration on main effects, as it turns out, find few supporters in the chapters of this book. Instead, there is strong belief that meta-analysis in the future should leave behind its concentration on main effects and take up more and more subcategorization and the modeling of interaction and complexity.

Three reasons for this view stand out. First, primary studies themselves are becoming more complex. As David Cordray notes in Chapter 10, in evaluation research "simple pre-test versus post-test assessments are being replaced with structural models that emphasize mediational mechanisms, implementation issues, estimates of the influence of exogenous factors, and so on." In Chapter 13, Wolf quotes John Tukey: "Science . . . does not begin with a tidy question. Nor does it end with a tidy answer." Second, once policymakers are satisfied with a simple generalization, they become more sophisticated. Psychotherapy may be effective, but what is the uncertainty of the conclusion? Is two hours per week better than one? Third, conclusions from an analysis are more credible when known complexity is taken into account.

But taking account of complexity in a meta-analysis could entail excluding all but the few particular studies that give sufficient information about interactions. This point brings up again the question of completeness from the last section. If research synthesis comes to be confined to a few studies, however much better than all the rest, and gives short shrift to the simplistic inferences that might be drawn from the rest, is it a meta-analysis at all?

Such an apparent contradiction arises if the goal of meta-analysis is taken to be the summarization of a measured outcome across many different studies. The contradiction evaporates if the goal of meta-analysis is not summarization, but rather, development of a new hypothesis or a new theory that is consistent with past observations and that explains matters further.

This latter goal for meta-analysis necessitates mining studies for information about complex relationships, to develop further theory to account for the spectrum of differing and sometimes conflicting outcomes. In such an enterprise, analysis is not confined wholly to the few studies that take all important factors into account or that exemplify the soundest of feasible research designs, for new theory should as far as possible seek to be consistent with all prior credible outcomes. Some studies may sharply improve theory. For example, they may indicate important explanatory variables that may be used to improve the effect of a treatment. Other studies may contribute marginally, serving only as additional observations explained within an expanded existing theory.

When research studies are placed in perspective, we always learn something about what next steps to take, what new studies to conduct, what variables to accommodate in their design, or what factors to look to for improvements. This is a point underlined by Ingram Olkin in Chapter 1: "Meta-analysis should help us to understand the structure of the phenomenon being studied by clarifying the areas where subsequent experimentation will be most informative." To the extent that this goal— always one of the goals of meta-analysis—becomes the primary goal, the levels of complexity treated in future meta-analyses will show a rapid rise.

Combining Results

How should the results of different studies be combined? As Olkin describes in Chapter 1, the earliest important procedure, developed by R. A. Fisher, was based on combining p-values of different experiments. Over 100 papers have been written on this method. It is not surprising that the p-value has become the *sine qua non* of research studies in the social and behavioral sciences. Its ubiquity, however, can misguide us. In Olkin's words:

> The exclusive use of p-values has become a disease. It is fostered by journals and by granting agencies. It is not at all unusual to see one, two, or three stars in every article of most journals in the social and psychological sciences. This is a form of statistical Star Wars. It has the effect of misdirecting attention from trying to understand the structure of the phenomenon to a decision format that is not often the goal.

The common use of p-values provides direct opportunity for results from many sources to be combined. But meta-analysis itself is more like an observational study than an experiment, and observational studies rarely satisfy the assumptions for the methods based on p-values that experimental studies do. In Chapter 2, Larry Hedges argues that meta-analysis must pay more attention to the lack of independence among studies, to modeling between-studies variation, to missing data, to biases, and to study quality. All of these problems, he says, can be approached with greater statistical rigor. In the discussion, however, concern was expressed that in practice the quality of the statistical procedures seems to be of less import to the final conclusions from a meta-analysis than are the choices governing selection of studies for inclusion, especially when a small group of studies are being preselected for analysis.

The desegregation project—in which only 19 studies were preselected for analysis from a collection of 157—illustrates the influence of study selection. As Linda Ingram makes clear in her summaries of the six separate meta-analyses of this one data base, inclusion or exclusion of a few further studies, deviating from the original list of 19, accounts in large measure for the differences in final conclusions that the meta-analysts reached. In Chapter 5, Jeffrey Schneider points out that there may have been objective selection criteria in this case at the outset, but they were subjectively applied and maintained. "How do you bring together," he wonders, "a group of people who know the literature, know the outcomes of what all the research says, and then use selective criteria to judge it?"

Statisticians know that once data have been used to develop a theory, the same data cannot be used to test it. Yet sometimes meta-analysis appears to be used in this way. Hypotheses of how desegregation improves the academic achievement of black students are formulated by knowledge of many studies that are then used in meta-analyses to evaluate or test those hypotheses.

Even setting aside the problems surrounding selection of studies for consideration, disagreements remain over how to combine them, disagreements already touched on under the heading of "completeness." Should better studies be treated differently from the others? Some would give the better studies greater weight; some would focus exclusively on them.

Are there technical guidelines for conducting meta-analyses that would help to resolve these problems? Wolf notes that some guidelines have been published, but that imposing them is fraught with problems. He quotes from Cook's paper in the desegregation project:

In meta-analysis, varying the assumptions underlying an analysis is desirable because it makes heterogeneous those facets of research where no "right" answer is available and fallible human judgment is required. To attempt to legislate a single "right" way either to compute effect size or to sample studies would be counter productive so long as none of the analysts is clearly wrong.

Certainly, as Cook says, we cannot legislate a right way of doing meta-analysis. Even in the legal sphere, little of life is ever governed by legislation. Much more is settled implicitly with reference to general principles, expressed in common law. For meta-analysis, what are the general principles that play this role? Despite the spirit of cooperation that pervades the field, there seems to be much less of a shared picture of the basic nature of the subject than one would have thought.

Is There a Method to This Meta-Analysis?

Stimulated by discussions at the workshop, Donald Rubin in Chapter 14 articulates one possible conceptual framework for the subject, not so much in its past or present incarnations but in terms of what it may develop. Rubin represents meta-analysis with the help of the formal construct of response-surface analysis, in which the outcomes of different treatments being compared are a function of factors X of scientific interest (gender, age, etc.) and features Z of the design (type of laboratory, whether or not randomization was used, etc.). The goal of meta-analysis, according to Rubin, is not to estimate the average outcomes for different design features, but rather to estimate the outcomes as a function of the scientific factors X for an ideal experiment Z_0. By regression or other means, the outcomes would be expressed as a function of (X,Z) and then extrapolated to the ideal Z_0.

In discussion, Straf suggested that, instead of extrapolating to an ideal, one could use the response surface just to indicate the directions for improved outcomes. Such a use is akin to the method of evolutionary operation. The ideal experiment, Z_0, to which Rubin would extrapolate, is very much the same kind of entity as a new scientific theory or hypothesis emerging from a meta-analysis. The picture matches well with a view of meta-analysis that discounts the goal of summarization of a body of literature and highlights the goal of more detailed construction of scientific hypotheses.

Within Rubin's picture, completeness of search and selection of studies are relegated to the status of very secondary issues. They affect the efficiency of estimates formed as extrapolations, but any contributions to bias are corrected away in the estimation process. This approach appears to assume that one has a scheme for coding those aspects of study design that affect outcome. It also appears to assume that one can represent these aspects of design, and of intervening variables, within a space of possibilities on which we can define a metric and can locate the position or direction of an ideal best experiment relative to the data points for the studies being analyzed. Under such circumstances, certainly, problems of bias can be solved at the stage of analysis and conclusions conditioned on whatever studies one happens to have or choose.

Conclusion

Many of us came to the workshop, as we mentioned at the outset, believing the future of meta-analysis to lie in methodological research on certain technical problems. Our minds were filled with possibilities like tree structures to describe dependencies among studies, protocols for sequential search and assessment of marginal benefit in retrieving studies, schemes for the multidimensional coding of design quality, weighting schemes as alternatives to preselection, and bootstraps and resampling algorithms for describing variability inherent in conclusions. Some expected that new technical guidelines or a new technical agenda might emerge for this volume.

Instead, the chief issues in this volume revolve around the nature and purpose of meta-analysis itself. Some of the hallmarks of meta-analysis in the 1970s and 1980s are not now taken for granted by many leaders of the field. These include the painstaking systematic search and retrieval of studies, the focus on single central questions, and the primacy of one or a few numerical summary measures combining the outcomes of the separate studies. While not on the verge of abandonment, these preoccupations are certainly up for debate and critique.

Alongside the goal of summarization and synthesis of an existing body of findings, the goal of extrapolation to new hypotheses is gaining prominence. For the first goal in an ideal setting, the quality of the data points, their representative character, and the accuracy of coding make all the difference: when assembled and brought suitably to view, the data may speak for themselves. For the second goal in an ideal setting, the data, representative or not, may sustain a modeling enterprise; a full repertory of statistical modeling techniques comes into use.

The latter goal accords closely with Sir Karl Popper's views of how science advances. Meta-analysis aims at the development of new theory consistent with past observations, accounting for the variety of outcomes of previous studies, and making testable, falsifiable predictions in its prescriptions for further studies. With the goal of better understanding the basic science inherent, for instance, in Rubin's formal construct for meta-analysis, many issues recede: what studies to select and how; whether selected studies are representative, and, if so, of what; whether they are independent. Other issues take the stage: how to characterize features of design and dimensions of quality; how to model the effects of intervening variables; how to control for the effects of the arbitrary choices that the models interject.

There is now in the field tension about the relative importance of these goals and about the relative primacy of these different sets of issues. It is not our purpose here to adjudicate between the different points of view. Each of the tendencies represented in these pages will have a part in shaping the future of meta-analysis. The chapters of this volume leave little room for doubt that meta-analyses will come to be much more complex and varied than they have been in the past. In the short run, the spotlight is on sorting out conceptual stances rather than on solving technical problems. Fortunately these conceptual stances affect questions of emphasis rather than questions of validity or credibility, and meta-analysis seems well suited, as these debates continue, to make a larger and larger contribution to the social and behavioral as well as the medical and natural sciences, and to a broad range of policy-relevant research.

PART I

Prospects

1

History and Goals

Ingram Olkin

> Science is built up with fact, as a house is with stone.
> But a collection of facts is no more a science
> than a heap of stones is a house.
>
> *Jules Henri Poincaré*

We have reached a point where psychologists, sociologists, educators, and medical researchers are all of the opinion that meta-analysis was first developed in their particular discipline. It is well known that as soon as you say that you are first, you are bound to be wrong. So I start with some history.

I suspect that the integration of results of independent evidence is quite old. Certainly, there is synthesis in every jury trial, in the deliberations of a committee in awarding a prize, and in the formulation of policy. Scientists have also required synthesis, and it may be of interest to see how some early scientists grappled with the problem of amalgamating evidence. The following is an example from physics in which experiments were conducted by Heyl in 1930 in the determination of the gravitational constant. Heyl used three media—gold, platinum, and glass—in his experiments. The results of his experiments are given in Table 1.1.

Heyl first argued that since the range for platinum and glass were the same, and considerably smaller than that of gold, the overall average value should be the mean of these two, namely:

$$(1/2)\ (6.664) + (1/2)\ (6.674) = 6.669.$$

He subsequently argued that the data from the experiments with gold should not be discounted and should be included. However, he suggested that they should be weighted less than the others. He then obtained a weighted mean:

$$(1/7) (6.678) + (3/7) (6.664) + (3/7) (6.674) = 6.670.$$

Although carried out in a subjective manner, we see here an early example in what is usually termed a "hard science," the problem of weighing of evidence.

It is really the inclusion of a *quantification* of the evidence that distinguishes meta-analysis from other integrative procedures. One of the earliest quantifications was by Sir Ronald A. Fisher in the late 1920s. He states this most clearly in the following quotation from *Statistical Methods for Research Workers* (4th ed., 1932, p. 99):

> When a number of quite independent tests of significance have been made, it sometimes happens that although few or none can be claimed individually as significant, yet the aggregate gives an impression that the probabilities are on the whole lower than would often have been obtained by chance. It is sometimes desired, taking account only of these probabilities, and not of the detailed composition of the data from which they are derived, which may be of very different kinds, to obtain a single test of the significance of the aggregate, based on the product of the probabilities individually observed.

The method that Fisher proposed was based on combining p-values. A bibliography of over 100 papers written since Fisher's proposal dealing with the problem of combining p-values was compiled by S. Rahman, of

Table 1.1   Measuring Gravitational Force

	Gold	Platinum	Glass
	6.683	6.661	6.678
	6.681	6.661	6.671
	6.676	6.667	6.675
	6.678	6.667	6.672
	6.679	6.664	6.674
	6.672		
Mean	6.678	6.664	6.674
Mean Absolute Deviation	.003	.002	.002
Range	.011	.006	.006

the University of Toronto. I cite a few of the titles that appeared prior to 1960.

1931 Tippett, L. H. C. The method of statistics.
1937 Cochran, W. G. Problems arising in the analysis of a series of similar experiments.
1938 David, F. N. On the p-test for randomness.
1942 Wallis, W. A. Compounding probabilities from independent significance tests.
1949 Lancaster, H. O. The combination of probabilities arising from data in discrete distributions.
1950 Pearson, E. S. On questions raised by the combination of tests based on discontinuous distributions.
1951 Wilkinson, B. A statistical consideration in psychological research.
1952 Baker, P. C. Combining tests of significance in cross validation.
1952 Brozek, J., and Tiede, K. Reliable and questionable significance in a series of statistical tests.
1953 Jones, L. V., and Fiske, D. Models for testing the significance of combined results.
1954 Birnbaum, A. Combining independent tests of significance.
1954 Mosteller, F., and Bush, R. R. Selected quantitative techniques.
1954 Sakoda, J. M.; Cohen, B. H.; and Beall, F. Tests of significance for a series of statistical tests.
1955 Good, I. J. On the weighted combination of significance.
1958 Liptak, T. On the combination of independent tests.
1959 Sterling, T. C. Publication decisions and their possible effects of inference drawn from tests of significance or vice versa.
1959 Zelen, M., and Joel, L. S. On the weighted compounding of the two independent significance tests.

The exclusive use of p-values has become a disease. It is fostered by journals and by granting agencies. It is not at all unusual to see one, two, or three stars in every article of most journals in the social and psychological sciences. This is a form of statistical Star Wars. It has the effect of misdirecting attention from understanding the structure of the phenomenon to a decision format that is not often the goal.

This brings me to an important point, namely that journals be urged to engage in more meaningful data reporting, to include a sufficient amount of data that subsequent researchers will be able to fully evaluate the results of the experiment.

Our history continues. Although the literature contains a number of examples that focused on the synthesis of results of independent studies, they were rather sporadic.

Between 1969 and 1980, the field consolidated, as illustrated by the following studies:

1969 Glass, G. V., and Hakstian, A. R. Measures of association in comparative experiments: Their development and interpretation.
1971 Light, R. J., and Smith, P. V. Accumulating evidence: Procedures for resolving contradictions among different research studies.
1972 Glass, G. V.; Peckham, P. D.; and Sanders, J. R. Consequences of failure to meet assumptions underlying fixed effects analysis of variance and covariance.
1976 Glass, G. V. Primary, secondary and meta-analysis of research.
1977 Smith, M. L., and Glass, G. V. Meta-analysis of class size and its relationship to attitudes of instruction.
1977 Glass, G. V. Integrating findings: The meta-analysis of research.
1979 Glass, G. V., and Smith, M. L. Meta-analysis of the relationship between class size and achievements.
1980 Pillemer, D. B., and Light, R. J. Synthesizing outcomes: How to use research evidence from many studies.

In 1976 Gene Glass gave the subject its name: meta-analysis. His central methodological contribution was the introduction of an effect size on which to base an integration. Glass used "effect size" to mean a standardized mean difference. Since this term became entrenched in the literature, Hedges and I used, in our book, *Statistical Methods for Meta-Analysis*, the term "effect magnitude" for differences other than mean differences. However, I believe that effect size is now being used as a generic term to indicate standardized differences between the control and experimental groups, whether the differences are means, correlations, proportions, and so on.

The introduction of an effect size had the positive effect of moving us away from p-values and vote counts to parameters and models. This was a critical step forward. However, at times combinations of estimates were made when the underlying populations were different, thereby leading to a variety of biased results.

The methodology of meta-analysis is rather straightforward and has often been attempted by novices both in the substantive field and in statistics. This led to an overuse, often accompanied by abuse. As a consequence there was a swell of opposition to meta-analytic techniques. Abuses in statistical analyses are rather common and occur even with very standard statistical procedures, such as analysis of variance and covariance, loglinear analysis, and multivariate analysis.

What we should focus on are the insights that meta-analysis might provide. I like to think of the meta-analytic process as similar to being in a helicopter. On the ground individual trees are visible with high resolution. This resolution diminishes as the helicopter rises, and in its place we begin to see patterns not visible from the ground. Indeed, astronauts have stated that the earth's beauty is unimaginable from ground level!

Let me illustrate the point of pattern recognition with a simple example. Consider a set of comparisons made by three researchers, each one comparing two grades.

Experiments	Grades	Means	S.D.	Results
I	6 vs. 9	10, 16	3.7, 3.0	Significant
II	7 vs. 10	12, 18	3.5, 3.4	Significant
III	8 vs. 11	14, 20	3.9, 3.2	Significant

Here we have three comparisons, each leading to a significant result. Suppose that three other comparisons are made:

Experiments	Grades	Means	S.D.	Results
I	6 vs. 7	10, 12	3.7, 3.5	Nonsignificant
II	8 vs. 9	14, 16	3.9, 3.0	Nonsignificant
III	10 vs. 11	18, 20	3.4, 3.2	Nonsignificant

With these comparisons, we obtain three nonsignificant results. Finally, a third set of comparisons:

Experiments	Grades	Means	S.D	Results
I	6 vs. 11	10, 20	3.7, 3.2	Significant
II	7 vs. 10	12, 18	3.5, 3.4	Significant
III	8 vs. 9	14, 16	3.9, 3.0	Nonsignificant

Now the results are mixed. The point to note is that a nondiscriminating synthesizing analysis, such as vote counts, might yield quite conflicting impressions.

On the other hand, if we graph the results, as in Figure 1.1, we see how the means vary by grade.

Perhaps more important, we can also see whether a particular point is an outlier, as in Figure 1.2. Here, grade 9 is behaving quite differently from the other grades. This would not be visible from the simpler analyses.

Meta-analysis has served to generate some new research questions. For example, within the class of tests based on p-values, such as minus twice the sum of log p's or the rth largest p-value, which tests are admissible and for what alternatives do particular tests have good power? These are

**Figure 1.1   Plot of Hypothetical Data
from Three Studies with Grade Level as a Covariate**

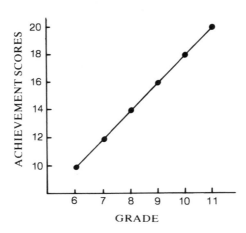

**Figure 1.2.   Plot of Alternative Hypothetical Data
from Three Studies with Grade Level as a Covariate**

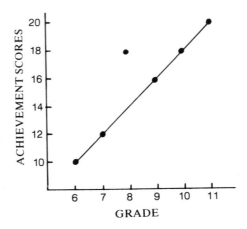

questions that have recently been resolved but arose from meta-analytic considerations.

In terms of effect sizes there has been considerable study of the case of a single control (C) and a single experimental (E) group:

	C	E
means	μ_C	μ_E
variances	σ_C^2	σ_E^2
effect	$\delta = (\mu_E - \mu_C)/\sigma_C$	

But we could have a number, m, of experimental groups, as in the case of each of m laboratories conducting an experiment:

	C	E_1	E_2	$\ldots$	E_m
means	μ_C	μ_1	μ_2	$\ldots$	μ_m
variances	σ_C^2	σ_1^2	σ_2^2	$\ldots$	σ_m^2

When $\mu_1 = \ldots = \mu_m = \mu_E$, we wish to estimate $\delta = (\mu_E - \mu_C)/\sigma_C$. However, the estimator used would be different in the case when $\sigma_{1}, \ldots, \sigma_m$ differ from the case when $\sigma_1 = \ldots = \sigma_m$. If the same laboratory conducted m experiments, the results might be correlated, with a common correlation and with a common variance. However, it may also be the case that the variances differ. This leads to two different covariance structures.

In other models, we may have more complicated covariance structures. Also, alternative linear structures may be appropriate in different situations.

A Summary of Problems and Recommendations:

1. It is imperative, if we are to take advantage of the large number of studies being conducted, that complete descriptions of the experiment and more detailed summary statistics be published.
2. Meta-analysis should help us to understand the structure of the phenomenon being studied by clarifying the areas where subsequent experimentation will be most informative.
3. Results may be screened in a variety of ways:
   (a) Only the best—that is, the most significant—results in repeated experiments are reported.
   (b) Results that have a high surprise factor, in the sense of being contrary to folklore or expectations, are reported. (An example is the study that reported that taller people have higher IQs.)

(c) Experiments performed sequentially permit stopping as soon as significance appears.

In order to reduce screening, I recommend that a scientific repository be established for the reporting of all studies, whether significant, nonsignificant, or indecisive. The adoption of standards for sharing research data, as recommended in Fienberg, Martin, and Straf, *Sharing Research Data*, would enhance the possibility of extracting usable measures from a wider range of studies.

4. Seminars for editors of technical journals, newspaper science editors, book editors, and popular magazine editors should be held to help them understand the interpretation of data. There is often an indiscriminate reporting of results. (Illustrative is a newspaper report that "more than 75 percent of the group had an income less than the median"!)

Meta-analysis is designed to deal with a goal that is important in many fields. Our task is to help set standards for data collection and reporting and subsequently to carry out the necessary research to improve the methodology.

I hope that this volume will be one of many focused on meta-analysis.

2

Directions for Future Methodology

Larry V. Hedges

I believe that the most significant contribution of meta-analysis is to have focused attention on methodological *rigor* in research reviewing. Methodological standards in original research help ensure the validity of the research. They exist because it is known that some methodological procedures are subject to biases that render research results invalid or at least uninterpretable. For example, some methods of problem formulation (e.g., post hoc hypothesis formulation), data collection (e.g., purposefully biased or nonrandom sampling), data evaluation (e.g., eliminating subjects whose behavior contradicts the research hypothesis), data analysis (e.g., failure to use statistical methods to evaluate stochastic evidence), and reporting (e.g., failure to describe procedures clearly) may lead to difficulties in interpretation or to invalid research results. The methodological standards which are familiar to most researchers are an attempt to constrain variations in procedure in order to control biases and improve the validity of original research studies.

Research reviews involve many of the same procedures as original research, including problem formulation, sampling, data evaluation, data analysis, and reporting. It seems obvious that some variations of these procedures can lead to biases which may reduce the validity of the conclusions of a research review (Cooper 1982, 1984). That is, methodological standards serve the same function (of helping to ensure validity) in research reviews as they do in original research. Given the importance of methodological standards in ensuring the validity of the results of research reviews and given the importance of literature reviews in the generation of scientific knowledge, it is astonishing that there was an almost complete lack of attention to methodological standards for procedure in social science literature reviews prior to 1976 when Gene Glass coined the term "meta-analysis."

In this chapter I examine aspects of statistical and methodological procedure in meta-analysis that deserve more attention in future research. I define statistical procedure rather broadly to include many aspects of research that are not explicitly part of the formal data analysis. The assumption here is that statisticians have a crucial role in helping substantive experts frame questions and develop rigorous procedures. It should be emphasized, however, that statisticians can only help. Research syntheses require the careful conceptualization of both subject matter and primary research that is usually possessed by only the most sophisticated substantive researchers. Good research syntheses are likely to require a partnership of good subject-matter experts with thoughtful statisticians.

This chapter is organized around nine major issues for research synthesis. General issues are presented first. More specific issues are presented in an order that roughly corresponds to Cooper's five stages of a research synthesis (1982): problem formulation, data collection, data evaluation, data analysis and interpretation, and presentation of results. I have attempted to identify issues that have important implications for the practice of research synthesis and to draw analogies to primary research which may suggest methods of addressing these issues. In many cases the need is not so much for new methods as for better applications and adaptations of existing statistical methods to the context of research synthesis.

Research Syntheses Should Make Better Use of Existing Methodology

One of the most significant problems with current research synthesis (and probably the easiest to remedy) is failure to use existing methods. An example is the prevalent failure to recognize that estimates of the effect size (the standardized mean difference) from different studies may have different precisions. The variance (conditional on the population effect size for that study) of the estimated effect size is proportional to the reciprocal of the within-study sample size. Consequently, when sample sizes vary across studies, so do the (conditional) standard errors of the estimated effect sizes. Within-study sample sizes vary in all meta-analyses, often by as much as 100 to 1. Neglecting such a huge variation in precision is unwise.

Some of the earliest work on meta-analysis in social science journals suggested simple procedures for handling variations in precision across studies (e.g., Hedges 1981, 1982; Rosenthal and Rubin 1982; Kraemer 1983). Yet the predominant mode of analysis remains the ordinary unweighted analysis of variance or regression analysis that ignores differences in precision. Use of correct methods is increasing, but diffusion of innovations is taking more time than it should.

Research Syntheses Should Have a Written Plan or Protocol to Guide Procedures and Constrain Procedural Variations

Research syntheses are much like primary research studies or clinical trials. There are many subjective steps lurking among the details of problem formulation, data collection, data evaluation, data analysis, and reporting of results. Minor variations in question or construct definition may alter the body of evidence subjected to statistical analysis. Similarly, slight changes in the definition of which studies are relevant or of "high enough" quality for inclusion may have a profound impact on the eventual body of evidence produced. Obviously, the choice of analyses has an effect on what may be revealed by the data analysis. If the procedure is not constrained before the data collection, biases (self-serving or otherwise) may be introduced. Protocols or advance plans for data collection and analysis are used in clinical trials to control variations in procedure. It seems highly desirable for research syntheses to use carefully detailed plans for data collection, data evaluation, data analysis, and presentation of results. Such plans should be constructed in advance of data collection. Deviations from the plan and the reasons for such deviations should be reported along with the results of the synthesis.

Research Syntheses Should Have a Prospective as Well as Retrospective Function

Research syntheses provide a survey of the available research evidence relevant to a specific problem. As such, they serve a retrospective function. Research syntheses also have a prospective function that has been largely ignored. By identifying inadequacies in the research literature, syntheses may suggest efficient allocation of resources for future research.

Two sorts of inadequacy may be revealed. The first arises when there are too few relevant studies with adequate controls to permit precise estimation of an overall average treatment effect or its variation across studies. This often happens when studies of high quality are difficult to execute and have small sample sizes. Large between-studies variations in treatment effect (among any well-controlled studies) may suggest that resources should be divided among several new studies, rather than allocated to a single large study.

A second sort of inadequacy arises when variations in study characteristics are too highly correlated to permit independent assessment of their association with treatment effects. A paradigm example is a research area with both laboratory studies and field studies of a similar treatment. The laboratory studies have excellent control over treatment and assignment (high internal validity) but are removed from context and hence have low external validity. The field studies have less control over treatment and assignment (low internal validity) but are representative of the context in which the treatment is expected to be used (i.e., have high external validity). In this example, control and setting are highly correlated in the existing research and the existing data cannot help us to sort out association of treatment effects with control from the association of treatment effects with setting. More such studies will not resolve the ambiguity. However, a single, well-controlled field experiment might reduce the ambiguity. The situation is analogous to the problem in experimental design of the selection of new design points to produce the greatest increase in information (see, e.g., Evans 1979). Knowledge of existing ambiguities helps suggest both the limitations of existing research and the characteristics of studies that could reduce those ambiguities.

Research Syntheses Should More Carefully Consider the Limitations of Empirical Data

One of the advantages of meta-analysis is that many judgments about the potential effects of study characteristics can be empirically tested (Glass, McGaw, and Smith 1981). For example, one may test whether study quality is related to study effect size. Similarly, questions about study design, procedure, and measurement can be tested. However, empirical testing is sometimes abused, often because of a failure to recognize the limitations of empirical methods based on a given set of data.

Not All Propositions Can Be Tested in a Given Set of Data

The very ubiquity of empirical tests has sometimes constituted an abuse of testing procedures. A very large number of study characteristics may be examined, and the number of tests may even exceed the number of independent effect size estimates. With such large numbers of tests, the meta-analyst runs a great risk of capitalizing on chance. Simultaneous test procedures that control adequately for this source of error reduce the power of the tests, and power decreases with an increasing number of tests. There is a limit to the number of tests that can be supported by a given collection of studies, and this limit is usually far less than the number of possible main-effect and interaction hypotheses that could arise from a modest list of study characteristics. The responsible meta-analyst must therefore recognize the limitations of the data available and test only a subset of all *possible* propositions.

Propositions Are Not Independent of One Another

A second abuse of empirical testing stems from study characteristics that are not independent of one another. Then it is difficult to disentangle the effects of various study characteristics. The problem of interpreting the relationships between study characteristics and effect size is essentially like that of interpreting a correlational (nonexperimental or observational) study. Relationships are confounded and many rival hypotheses are possible. In this situation technical (statistical) methods are unlikely to lead to credible conclusions because, as in any instance of multicollinearity, the data alone are insufficient to distinguish all relationships of interest.

The alternative is one used in other highly confounded situations, such as the interpretation of quasi-experiments. Patterns of results from the data analysis and other evidence in addition to the data can be used to argue for the credibility of a proposition (see Cook and Campbell 1979). Rival hypotheses can be posed and perhaps eliminated by various means. Sometimes, of course, rival hypotheses cannot be eliminated and therefore weaken the conclusion to the extent that they are plausible as explanations. Once again, considerations outside the data at hand are essential for interpretation.

Research Syntheses Should Pay Greater Attention to Sampling Issues

Assembling a collection of studies is often viewed as a sampling problem: the problem of obtaining a representative sample of all studies that have actually been conducted. Because the adequacy of samples necessarily determines the range of valid generalizations that are possible, the procedures used to locate studies in meta-analysis have been regarded as crucially important. Much of the discussion on sampling in meta-analysis (e.g., Cooper 1984; Glass, McGaw, and Smith 1981; Hunter, Schmidt, and Jackson 1982; Rosenthal 1984) concentrates on the problem of obtaining a representative or exhaustive sample of the studies that have actually been conducted. However, this is not the only or even the most crucial aspect of sampling in meta-analysis. Another equally important sampling question is whether the samples of subjects and treatments in the individual studies are representative of the subject populations and treatment populations of interest.

The importance of representative sampling of subjects is obvious. The importance of representative sampling of treatments is more subtle. The question is whether the treatments that occur in studies are representative of the situations about which the reviewer seeks knowledge (Bracht and Glass 1968). For example, one criticism (Slavin 1984) of Glass and Smith's meta-analysis (1979) of the effects of school class size is that many of the class sizes represented in the studies (e.g., of the effects of tutoring) were too small to be representative of school settings. A representative sample of studies, each of which involves a nonrepresentative sample of subjects or treatments, brings us no closer to the truth about the subjects or treatments that we care about.

Thus, there are two levels of sampling to be concerned about in meta-analysis: the sampling of studies actually conducted, and the sampling by those studies of the phenomenon of interest to the reviewer. The situation is much like that of two-stage samples in sample surveys. The reviewer samples clusters or secondary sampling units first (i.e., studies); then the individual subjects or primary sampling units are sampled from the clusters.

Strategies for obtaining representative or exhaustive samples of studies have been discussed by Glass, McGaw, and Smith (1981) and by Cooper (1984). The problem of obtaining representative samples of subjects and treatments is constrained by the sampling of studies and, consequently, is not under the complete control of the reviewer. The reviewer can, however, present descriptions of the samples of subjects and treatments and examine the relationship between characteristics of these samples and study outcomes.

Missing Data in Meta-Analysis

Missing data is a problem that plagues many forms of applied research. Survey researchers are well aware that the best sampling design is ineffective if the information sought cannot be extracted from the units that are sampled. Of course, missing data is not a substantial problem if the data are "missing at random" (Rubin 1976), but missing data in meta-analysis are rarely missing at random. On the contrary, the causes of the data being missing are often systematically related to effect size or to characteristics of studies. Missing data then pose a serious threat to the validity of conclusions in meta-analysis.

MISSING DATA ON EFFECT SIZE. Studies (such as single case studies) that do not use statistical analyses are one source of missing data on effect size. Other studies use statistics but do not provide enough information to allow the calculation of an effect size estimate. Sometimes this is a failure to report relevant statistics. More often it is a consequence of the researcher's use of a complex design that makes difficult or impossible the construction of an effect size estimate using the proper metric (see Glass, McGaw, and Smith 1981) or standard deviation. Unfortunately, both the sparse reporting of statistics and the use of complex designs are plausibly related to study outcomes. Both result at least in part from the editorial policies of some of the most selective journals in psychology and education, which often discourage reporting of all but the most essential statistics. Perhaps the most pernicious sources of missing data are studies which *selectively* report statistical information. Such studies typically report only information on effects that are statistically significant, exhibiting what has been called reporting bias (Hedges 1984). Effect size data missing from studies that report complete data on only significant effects can lead to serious biases, like those caused by selective publication, discussed below.

The most common response to incomplete effect size data is to ignore the problem. This is a bad strategy. It reduces the credibility of the meta-analysis because the missing data are obvious to knowledgeable readers. Another problematic strategy is to replace all missing values by the same imputed value (usually zero). Although this strategy usually leads to a conservative estimate of the overall average effect size, it creates serious problems in any attempt to study the variability of effect sizes and the relationship of study characteristics to effect size. A better strategy is to extract from the study any available information about effect size. The direction of the effect (the sign of the effect size) can often be deduced even when an effect size cannot be calculated. A tabulation of these directions of effects can supplement the effect size analysis (e.g., Gianconia and Hedges 1982; Crain and Mahard 1983) or form a part of an analysis that includes this information in an estimate of effect size (see Hedges and Olkin 1980, 1985).

Perhaps the most promising strategy for dealing with missing effect size data is to use the many new analytic techniques that have been developed for handling general missing data problems (e.g., Dempster, Laird, and Rubin 1977; Little and Rubin 1987). Many examples of work in this tradition can be found in applications to sample surveys (Madow, Nisselson, and Olkin 1983; Madow, Olkin, and Rubin 1983; Madow and Olkin 1983; Rubin 1987). These strategies, as applied to research synthesis, would involve using the available information (including study characteristics) to estimate the structure of the effect size data and the relationships among study characteristics and effect sizes (see Hedges 1988 for an example). They can also be used to study the sensitivity of conclusions to the possible effects of missing data. Although these strategies have much to recommend them, they have not been used in meta-analysis.

MISSING DATA ON STUDY CHARACTERISTICS.   Another less obvious form of missing data is missing data on study characteristics, which result from incompletely detailed descriptions of the treatment, controls, experimental procedure, or the outcome measures. In fact, the generally sketchy descriptions of studies in the published literature often constrain the degree of specificity possible in schemes used to code between-studies differences.

The problem of missing data about study characteristics is related to the problem of breadth of constructs and operations for study characteristics. Coding schemes that use a high degree of detail (and have higher fidelity) generally result in a greater degree of missing data. Consequently, vague study characteristics are often coded for all studies, or more specific characteristics are coded for relatively few studies (see Orwin and Cordray 1985). Neither procedure alone inspires confidence.

One strategy for dealing with missing information about study characteristics is to have two levels of specificity: a broad level which can be coded for nearly all studies and a narrower level which can be coded for only a subset of the studies. A more elegant solution is to use the more refined analytic methods for handling missing data in sample surveys, discussed previously.

Two other strategies are little used and deserve more attention. One is the collection of relevant information from other sources, such as technical reports, test reviews or articles that describe a program, treatment, or measurement method. The appropriate references are often published in research reports. Direct examination of published tests is a good way to get information on those instruments. A second and often neglected source of information is the direct collection of new data. For example, in a meta-analysis of sex differences in helping behaviors, Eagly and

Crowley (1986) surveyed a new sample of subjects to determine the degree of perceived danger in the helping situations examined in the studies. This rating of degree of perceived danger to the helper was a valuable factor in explaining the variability of results across studies.

Publication Bias

An important axiom of survey-sample design is that an excellent sample design cannot guarantee a representative sample if it is drawn from an incomplete enumeration of the population. The analogue in meta-analysis is that an apparently good sampling plan may be thwarted by applying the plan to an incomplete and unrepresentative subset of the studies that were actually conducted.

The published literature is particularly susceptible to the claim that it is unrepresentative of all studies that may have been conducted (the so-called publication bias problem). There is considerable empirical evidence that the published literature contains fewer statistically insignificant results than would be expected from the complete collection of all studies actually conducted (Bozarth and Roberts 1972; Sterling 1959). There is also direct evidence that journal editors and reviewers intentionally include statistical significance among their criteria for selecting manuscripts for publication (Bakan 1966; Greenwald 1975; Melton 1962). The tendency of the published literature to overrepresent statistically significant findings leads to biased overestimates of effect magnitudes from published literature (Lane and Dunlap 1978; Hedges 1984b), a phenomenon that was confirmed empirically by Smith's study (1980) of ten meta-analyses, each of which presented average effect size estimates for both published and unpublished sources.

Reporting bias is related to publication bias based on statistical significance. Reporting bias creates missing data when researchers fail to report the details of results of some statistical analyses, such as those that do not yield statistically significant results. The effect of reporting bias is identical to that of publication bias: Some effect size estimates are unavailable (e.g., those that correspond to statistically insignificant results).

Publication or reporting bias may not always be severe enough to invalidate meta-analyses based solely on published articles (see Light and Pillemer 1984; Hedges 1984b). Theoretical analysis of the potential effects of publication bias showed that even when nonsignificant results are never published (the most severe form of publication bias), the effect on estimation of effect size may not be large unless both the within-study sample sizes and the underlying effect size are small. However, if both the sample sizes in the studies and the underlying effect sizes are small, the effect on estimation can be substantial.

The possibility that publication or reporting bias may inflate effect size estimates suggests that reviewers should consider investigating the possible impact of this bias. One method is to compare the effect size estimates derived from published sources (e.g., books, journal articles) and unpublished sources (e.g., conference presentations, contract reports, ERIC documents, or doctoral dissertations). Such comparisons, however, are often problematic because the source of the study is often confounded with many other study characteristics. An alternative is to use estimation procedures such as maximum likelihood estimation of effect size under publication bias (see Hedges 1984b; Hedges and Olkin 1985). If these corrections produce a negligible effect, it suggests that publication and reporting bias are negligible. Another less specific alternative is to use Rosenthal's file-drawer number (1979a), but the reader may want to examine the discussion of the limitations of this technique in Hedges and Olkin (1985).

There have been relatively few serious attempts to explicitly model the effects of publication or reporting bias on the outcomes of research syntheses. More attention needs to be given to analyzing the sensitivity of the results of research syntheses to the possible effects of publication bias.

Research Syntheses Should Pay More Attention to Study Quality

The quality of the primary research studies that provide information to a research synthesis necessarily limits the generalizability of the results of that synthesis. It is very difficult, if not impossible, to obtain valid conclusions from a collection of highly flawed studies. Moreover, the inclusion of highly flawed studies in a research synthesis may decrease the *credibility* of that synthesis among researchers. Consequently, most meta-analysts attempt to set standards of minimal quality for inclusion in research syntheses. Many researchers also make some assessment of the variations in the quality of research studies that are included in the meta-analysis.

Two predominant methods for assessing study quality are the "threats-to-validity" approach and the "study methods" approach (Cooper 1984). In the threats-to-validity approach, study quality is treated as an "absolute," and each study is rated according to the threats to validity (sources of bias) to which it is vulnerable. In the study-methods approach, relative study quality is rated by the grouping of studies with similar methodology. Both procedures have great generality in handling the systematic evaluation of study quality, but both are problematic if not explicitly adapted to the context of the research that is under review. The threats-to-validity approach has the advantage that it rates studies on an absolute scale. The disadvantage is that the importance of a particular threat to validity (i.e., a potential source of bias) depends on the research context. For example, the effects of maturation may be an important source of bias in some kinds of long-term quasi-experiments, but relatively unimportant in short-term studies. Naive assessments of study quality that do not weight sources of bias according to their likely importance in particular research contexts are likely to be misleading. The principal disadvantage of study-method approaches to assessment of study quality is that they are inherently relative, comparing only relative quality of the studies under review. Such a scheme makes it difficult or impossible to render the conclusion that all of the studies are of such poor quality as to be inadequate.

There has been relatively little sophisticated research in the social sciences on the effects of design flaws on study results. Some early research by Glass, McGaw, and Smith (1981) suggested that global quality ratings were rarely related to effect size. Many of my own analyses have suggested that studies with poor experimental control exhibit much larger variability in results (i.e., larger effect size variance components) than do studies with randomization or other evidence of control for preexisting differences. Such work is barely the beginning of what is needed.

We need better methods for accumulating evidence from studies that may be flawed. One strategy is outright exclusion of flawed studies. *Empirical* research that might suggest when research studies are so flawed as to be worthless is badly needed. An alternative strategy is to find ways of extracting some information from flawed studies. Research on the best ways to utilize imperfect evidence is also badly needed. We need to know the ways in which flawed studies might be made to contribute evidence. For example, are corrections for bias sometimes feasible? Can flawed studies still contribute useful evidence on variation in treatments or controls?

Research Syntheses Should Examine Variations in Treatments and Controls Across Studies

In almost all applied research there is variation in the treatments (and controls) that are implemented in different sites. The problem of treatment fidelity and variations in implementation of treatments is an important topic in evaluation research. Research syntheses should expect to find variations in the treatments implemented in different studies. Indeed, research syntheses are sometimes perceived to provide stronger results than single studies precisely because they incorporate many variations in treatments. One goal of any research synthesis should be to assess the variations in treatment across studies and to attempt to quantify variations in effect magnitude that may be related to variations in treatment (the nature of control groups). Both fixed- and random-effects approaches to this problem are likely to be useful. The random-effects approach is to estimate a treatment effect size variance component that quantifies the variation in treatment effect sizes across studies. The fixed-effects approach involves attempts to specify important dimensions of variation in treatment implementation and determine how these dimensions of treatment covary with treatment effects. Better methods for characterizing both variation in treatments and the relationship of variations in treatment to variations in their effects would be useful.

Research Syntheses Should Pay More Attention to Modeling Between-Studies Variation in Effects

One of the most crucial aspects of research synthesis is the choice of model for between-studies variation in effect magnitude. There are basically three approaches to modeling between-studies variation, which might be called fixed-, random-, and mixed-effects models. Let $\Theta_1, \ldots, \Theta_k$ be the treatment effect parameters (the true or population values of treatment effects) from k studies and let $T_1, \ldots, T_k$ be the corresponding estimates from the k studies.

In fixed-effects models, $\Theta_1, \ldots, \Theta_k$ are fixed but unknown constants. By studying the relationship between study characteristics and treatment effects, the data analyst may try to deduce stable relationships that explain the variability in study results except for that attributable to within-study sampling variability. The evaluation of particular explanatory models is part of this process. However, fixed-effect models are not the only way to conceptualize data analysis in meta-analysis.

The random-effects conception arises from a model in which the treatment effect parameters are *not* functions of fixed study characteristics. In this model, the Θ_i's vary randomly from study to study, as if they were sampled from a universe of possible treatment effects. Sometimes a parametric form for the distribution of Θ_i's is given (e.g., $\Theta_i \sim N(\mu, \sigma^2)$) and sometimes the form of the distribution is unspecified. The random-effects conceptualization is consistent with Cronbach's proposal (1980) that evaluation studies should consider a model in which each treatment site (or study) is a sample realization from a universe of related treatments. The primary difference between the interpretation of fixed- and random-effects models is that between-studies variation in treatment effects is conceived to be the result of sampling of *studies* in random-effects models. The data analyst usually seeks to quantify this variation by estimating a "variance component" σ^2_θ: an index of the variability of population treatment effects across studies.

Mixed models involve a combination of the ideas involved in fixed- and random-effects models. In these models, some of the variation between treatment effects is fixed (i.e., explainable) and some is random. Consequently, the data analyst seeks to explain some of the variation between study results via fixed study characteristics and then to quantify the remainder by estimating a variance component (see, e.g., DerSimonian and Laird 1983; Raudenbush and Bryk 1985). Such models have considerable promise as data analytic tools for situations in which it is useful to treat some of the variability between study results as random. Further development of such methods is definitely needed.

It might seem obvious that in complicated situations such as modeling between-study variation, fixed-effects models are unlikely to be realistic. Yet fixed-effects models for research synthesis have passionate defenders and far more users than random or mixed models. A very large proportion of the work on combining the results of clinical trials or biomedical studies rely on the Mantel-Haenzel statistic and other techniques which are essentially fixed-effects models. Moreover, fixed-effects models sometimes provide an excellent fit to the data, suggesting that essentially no additional variation is present (see, e.g., Linn and Petersen 1985; Becker 1986; Raudenbush and Bryk 1985).

Purely random-effects models also have their defenders and some impressive applications (e.g., Rubin 1980, 1981; Hunter, Schmidt, and Jackson 1982). Yet the application of random-effects models to many research synthesis problems is unsatisfying. Researchers expect systematic differences between study results because they *plan* their studies to be systematically different. Attempts to treat what may seem to be major systematic differences as "random effects" are viewed as intolerable oversimplifications. However, the between-studies variance component as a descriptive index of variation of study results is extremely useful.

Mixed models combine the advantages of fixed and random effects. They can represent both systematic variation and random effects within the same analysis. Moreover, mixed models reduce to either fixed- or random-effects models if the data demonstrate that such models are appropriate.

A major problem, however, with either random or mixed models is the realistic specification of the distribution of the random effects. Most statisticians have excellent insight about distributional assumptions for replicates within experiments. The problem of specifying the distribution of between-studies effects is more difficult. The studies are *not* simple replicates. Fixed effects are often lurking in between-studies variation. Censoring and truncation effects may be present. Outliers are not uncommon. None of these problems is unprecedented or inherently intractable. However, the realistic specification of random effects is difficult, and it is a problem about which few of us have a great deal of experience and about which there is too little collective wisdom.

Before we routinely resort to simple specifications like $\Theta_i \sim N(\mu, \sigma^2)$, we need to know more about how realistic such specifications are and how sensitive the results of analyses may be to the choice of distributional specification. Some work in progress by my colleague Wing Wong suggests that there may be real reasons to worry about sensitivity of random-effects analyses to choice of specification. More work is clearly needed in this area. Another promising direction for further research is the attempt to avoid a priori specifications by using the empirical distribution of the random effects via bootstrapping or adaptive estimation. Recent work by Laird and Louis (Laird 1978, 1982; Laird and Louis 1987) is a useful beginning, but more work is needed.

Research Syntheses Should Pay More Attention to Problems of Dependence

One of the most persistent statistical issues raised in discussions of meta-analysis is the potential lack of statistical independence among effect size estimates. Such statistical dependence can arise in at least four ways. First, several different effect size estimates may be calculated from different measurements on the same subjects. This situation typically arises in meta-analysis when a study uses measures of several different outcome constructs or several different measures of the same construct. The second sort of dependence arises from calculation of several effect sizes in a study, each of which uses the same control group or the same treatment group. For example, in a study with one control group and two treatment groups, the two effect sizes computed with reference to the single control group are correlated. A third sort of dependence arises because several different samples in the same study are used to calculate effect size estimates. The fourth type of dependence arises because a series of studies conducted by the same investigator or research team may not give results that are completely independent.

The first type of dependence (that arising from multiple effect sizes calculated on different measures from the same subjects) has received the most explicit attention (e.g., Rosenthal and Rubin 1986). One of the reasons that such dependence arises is that many meta-analysts (e.g., Glass, McGaw, and Smith 1981) choose to code every possible effect size estimate to avoid "loss of information." The rationale is that if each different measurement provides additional information, then effect size estimates based on those measurements provide additional information about the underlying effect size. However, analytic study of the situation (see Hedges and Olkin 1985) suggests that the actual amount of additional information (measured by increased precision of the estimate making optimal use of all information) is often quite modest. For example, using two or three correlated effect sizes based on measures of the same construct is unlikely to increase statistical precision by more than 10–20 percent.

Dependence arising when several effect size estimates make use of the same control group (or, conceivably, the same treatment group) poses different problems. In this situation the additional effect sizes may add substantially to the precision of estimation. Because the correlation between the estimates can be calculated exactly in this situation, multivariate procedures (see Hedges and Olkin 1985) can be used to provide a statistical analysis that takes into account the dependence of the estimates.

The other two forms of dependence, arising from multiple samples within studies and arising from a series of studies conducted by the same investigators, are more difficult to accommodate. The implication of these sorts of dependence is that the underlying (population) effect sizes within studies or from a series of studies by the same investigator are less variable than are the other effect sizes. Such dependence can attenuate relationships in fixed-effects models and should lead to difficulties in obtaining adequate model specification. The strong tests for model misspecification can help to detect such problems in fixed-effects models. The effects of this sort of dependence in random- and mixed-effects models may be more serious, for two reasons. First, the dependence results in a serious misspecification of the error structure of the model. Second, there is no obvious way to detect problems of dependence *that have not been anticipated*. Because misspecification may lead to biases in parameter estimates, undetected dependence in random- and mixed-effects models may lead to serious biases in inference. Specific dependencies that are anticipated can be incorporated and even tested as hypotheses in both fixed-effects models (by appropriate coding strategies) and in random- or mixed-effects models by proper parameterization of error covariance matrices and estimation of covariance components (see Dempster, Rubin, and Tsutakowa 1981).

More explicit attention to the nature and magnitude of dependencies in research synthesis is badly needed. More experience in modeling dependencies is needed, as are better methods for detecting potential dependencies.

Conclusion

There is a great deal of room for improvement in the methodology used in meta-analysis. Existing techniques are not used as effectively as they could be. Clearer conceptions of statistical models and their use in research synthesis are needed. Methodological developments in related areas need to be adapted and used in research synthesis. However, we should not lose perspective in a critique such as this. Few areas of primary research in the social sciences could escape unscathed from the careful scrutiny of sophisticated critics. With all its defects, meta-analysis can, and often does, lead to more rigorous reviews of research than are possible with conventional techniques. Improvements in the methodology for meta-analysis promise to increase the rigor and credibility of this technique.

PART II

Case Study:
The Effects of
Rehabilitation Therapy
for Aphasia

3

The Making of a Meta-Analysis: A Quantitative Review of the Aphasia Treatment Literature

*Joel B. Greenhouse / Davida Fromm
Satish Iyengar / Mary Amanda Dew
Audrey L. Holland / Robert E. Kass*

Introduction

The project described here began in 1985, when Audrey Holland and Davida Fromm, of the Western Psychiatric Institute and Clinic, University of Pittsburgh, who had become interested in meta-analysis as a primary research tool, invited Joel Greenhouse, of the Statistics Department at Carnegie Mellon University, to collaborate with them on a quantitative review of the aphasia treatment literature. A working group consisting of three statisticians (Joel Greenhouse, Satish Iyengar, and Robert Kass), two speech pathologists (Davida Fromm and Audrey Holland), and a social psychologist (Mary Amanda Dew) was already formed and meeting when Stephen Fienberg and Kenneth Wachter, of the Committee on National Statistics, persuaded them to coordinate their project with the committee's study of the future of meta-analysis. A case study was sought in which a novice, or at least someone not strongly influenced by the previous literature nor committed to existing schools or approaches, would conduct a meta-analysis, report on the process, and reflect on the experience and the methods. This then became our charge from the committee.

We were guided by two objectives: (1) to conduct a systematic quantitative review of the aphasia treatment literature to gain insight into the unresolved issues regarding the efficacy of treatment and (2) to step back, observe, and reflect on all aspects of the process of conducting a meta-analysis. To accomplish both goals, we took an inefficient approach.

29

Initially, at each step of our investigation, we ignored the available meta-analytic literature until after we had discussed among ourselves how to proceed. We each kept notes of this process. This report is based on the synthesis of the chronology of our experience with this meta-analysis.

Before giving an overview of our investigation, we should make two comments. First, our meta-analysis is still incomplete. A quantitative literature review is a time-consuming endeavor. We do have some early results, however, and we will use them to illustrate various points. Second, we have found the current literature on meta-analysis to be not only thorough and thoughtful but also readable and helpful for the novice (e.g., Glass, McGaw, and Smith 1981; Hedges and Olkin 1985; Light and Pillemer 1984; Rosenthal 1984).

Overview

We will focus primarily on the practice of meta-analysis. Using our meta-analysis of the efficacy of treatment of aphasia as a case study, we shall go through the steps we followed in this quantitative review, highlighting the issues, decisions, and judgments made and indicating the difficulties we encountered.

A theme that recurs throughout this chapter concerns the role of the statistician in a meta-analysis. In our investigation, the role of the speech pathologist was always clear. From the outset, Dr. Holland and Dr. Fromm were the critical players in the investigation. At every step, there were substantive questions, decisions, and judgments required from individuals knowledgeable about aphasia. Given this critical role of the subject matter specialists, what role remains for the statistician? We find the role much the same as in a single study investigation: to ask questions that sharpen issues, to guide the analysis, and to assess the impact of various decisions and judgments on the results, that is, to evaluate the sensitivity and robustness of the inferences.

We begin in the next section with an introduction to the issues involved in treatment studies of aphasia and ask why a meta-analysis is needed. This question deals as much with the sociology of the discipline as it does with the science. Next, we describe the retrieval of the research results. We then describe the process of reducing and organizing the data base. We proceed to carry out an illustrative meta-analysis on a portion of our data, obtaining estimates of the combined treatment effect and evaluating the sensitivity of our inferences to different assumptions. We conclude with reflections on the "file-drawer" problem and on our overall experience in conducting this meta-analysis.

Why Do a Meta-Analysis
of the Efficacy of Treatment for Aphasia?

Aphasia is an impairment, as a result of brain damage, of the ability to interpret and formulate language. The majority of aphasic patients have suffered strokes in the left cerebral hemisphere; the other possible causes are trauma, neoplasm, and infection. Aphasic patients may demonstrate difficulties in understanding, reading, speaking, and writing. We note that the problems of aphasic individuals are not the result of generalized intellectual impairment like dementia or of significant motor or muscle programming dysfunction.

One school of thought, dating back to the nineteenth century, believes that language therapy for chronic aphasic patients is of little value. The "classical" anatomic approach to the classification of aphasia syndromes assumes a one-to-one correspondence between certain areas of the brain and specific language functions. If auditory comprehension, oral expression, and reading are exclusively localized in different areas of the adult left hemisphere, destruction of a specific language center must then result in isolated, often disassociated defects of a single language component and produce predictable aphasia syndromes. According to this approach, attempts to rehabilitate aphasic patients with specific language defects would appear hopeless, as these centers of the brain cannot be restored. This reasoning has led to the belief that language therapy for chronic aphasic patients is of little value except for providing psychological support.

On the other hand, many clinicians, based on their clinical experience, believe that the "classical" anatomic approach is not dynamic enough to account for brain/behavior relationships and that aphasia therapy does work. Clinical researchers have produced more studies of efficacy of aphasia therapy than exist for therapy for any other speech or language disorder. The literature includes large group studies, single-subject research designs, and case reports. Although there are some influential studies suggesting that speech therapy makes no significant contribution to recovery, most attest to the efficacy of treatment. Between the two schools the question is still unresolved. We believe that there are three primary reasons for this: (1) poorly designed research, (2) a cumulation problem, and (3) contradictory belief systems.

The first reason the question is unresolved is that there has been a failure by both clinical investigators and uncritical readers to appreciate the elements of rigorous experimental design. For example, assessing the efficacy of treatment is complicated by spontaneous recovery. During the first three months immediately following a stroke or insult, patients often improve as a result of physical and physiological recovery in the brain itself. But studies of the effects of treatment in the early period following stroke often lack a control group for estimating spontaneous restitution of function. Nor is random assignment to treatment groups universal, despite the many biological, medical, and behavioral variables which may influence response to treatment. Further, selection criteria are not always explicit and treatment regimens are not always carefully specified or controlled.

A second reason is the difficulty in assimilating results from the many studies using small group and single-subject designs. Approximately 40 percent of the literature on efficacy of treatment in aphasia employs single-subject designs. A third and potent reason is the natural reluctance to abandon traditional, widely held beliefs, such as that language and cognitive recovery following stroke results only from spontaneous recovery. Thus, studies that fail to find a significant treatment effect are disproportionately more influential among professionals with such a belief system.

It appears timely to apply the techniques of meta-analysis to this literature, not only to address the primary question, Does aphasia therapy work? but also to ask:

1. Is treatment for aphasia efficacious, as assessed by measures of overall speech and language performance?
2. Does aphasia therapy substantially improve patients' verbal skills?
3. Does aphasia therapy substantially improve patients' auditory comprehension abilities?
4. Does aphasia therapy substantially improve patients' functional communication or pragmatic skills?
5. How is the outcome of aphasia therapy influenced by the following factors: etiology, severity of aphasia, type of treatment, duration of treatment, concentration of treatment, time of initiation of treatment?

Collecting the Data:
Retrieval of Research Results

In setting out to retrieve the relevant literature, our educated guess was that we would be searching for 40 to 50 articles, but our database grew, in fact, to 114 articles. First, we retrieved all articles from our own and from a colleague's collections of reprints, proceedings, and books, and from these generated lists of additional references. In addition, we did an exhaustive review, for the last ten years, of the *Index Medicus* under "aphasia."

Before long we were wrestling with difficult decisions. The first criterion for inclusion was obvious—a study had to involve treatment. But then we had to decide on criteria for scientific rigor. Should we include articles without control groups? Should we include studies without explicit subject-selection criteria, or studies of right-brain-damaged patients, trauma patients, and tumor patients? Should we include single case studies and studies that employed single-subject designs? Should we include studies that did not provide relevant numerical data in the text or tables— that is, studies with data available only in figures or graphs? Should we include studies with no quantitative outcome?

At first, we decided to include only studies that had at least five subjects, yielding 56 articles in all. But after a meeting of the entire working group, and after much discussion, we decided to abandon the arbitrary cutoff of five subjects, adding 33 more studies to the total, and to continue our search focusing on abstracts rather than titles alone. It became clear that we had overlooked an entire subset of articles that we had mentally filed under the heading *recovery articles*, such as "Sex Differences in Recovery from Aphasia," which in nine cases turned out to include some treatment.

Although the retrieval process was extremely labor intensive, there was good motivation to proceed rapidly. New articles on the topic continued to be published with each journal issue. Dr. Fromm grew to dread the arrival of the *Journal of Speech and Hearing Disorders*, hoping for the first time in her life that there would be no articles on aphasia! In the June issue an aphasia treatment study referred to eight aphasia treatment articles that she had not found previously. This was a psychological setback, and it led us to a re-review of the reference lists of all articles in our database, yielding 8 more, for a total of 114 journal articles, book chapters, grant reports, and conference proceedings. We had already uncovered a startling fact—the literature was at least twice as large as commonly thought, and *more* than twice as large as the literature covered in any published qualitative review.

Although we believed that the search was exhaustive, we were still concerned with the possibility of having missed relevant literature. We considered designing a sampling scheme, based on our experiences at retrieval so far, to estimate the number of additional published studies still unretrieved. We did not pursue this idea to completion, but we believe that it might be a useful one.

Each article retrieved was summarized; the one-page summary included (along with the authors, title, and year of publication):

1. information about subjects—mean age, time post-onset, etiology, and type of aphasia, when available;
2. therapy information—type of treatment, and its duration and intensity;
3. design information—sample size, presence of a control group; and
4. notes on the nature of the data available in the results section and how they were displayed.

Finding the articles took about 15 minutes per article and preparing the summaries took an average of 45 minutes per article, plus time for abstracting numerical results. The total time for the 114 articles was about 115 hours.

Just as data collection is the most critical phase of a single study, the retrieval of research results seems the most critical phase in a quantitative literature review. It became obvious that this phase could be completed only by a subject matter specialist, that is, a person knowledgeable about aphasia, in our case Dr. Fromm. She felt, however, that a measure of reliability would have been added to the project by having two experts, rather than one, involved in this stage.

Focus Phase: Substantive Issues

Although our original objectives had seemed clear, we seemed to lose our sense of direction and focus when confronted with this vast amount of data. The original questions regarding the efficacy of treatment for aphasia were too general and needed to be sharpened. For example, how should we define outcome? Some of the 114 studies used standardized tests of aphasia, of which there are over a dozen; some reported overall scores as well as subtest scores; some reported only subtest scores. Some studies selected certain subtests from standardized tests, while others used rating scales, homemade tasks, and all possible combinations thereof.

Having identified outcome measure as an important study characteristic, we considered other characteristics. Types of treatment were divided into individual language therapy (the majority involving one-on-one work with a speech pathologist), group language therapy (one pathologist with a small group of patients), and indirect therapy (social and commu-

TABLE 3.1 *(continued)*

Study Number	Sample Size	Outcome Measure	Pre-treatment		Post-treatment		t-Statistic	p-Value	Comments
			Mean	S.D.	Mean	S.D.			
54+10	18 individuals	Pica-0 %ile	Difference Score		$\bar{x}=20$	s.d.= 2.30		<.05	Conservative approximation
	16 group	Pica-0 %ile	"	"	$\bar{x}=15.75$	s.d.= 6.02		<.05	Used 24-week completers Stats are anova's on 3 groups Time × group × time
55	29	Pica-0	11.63	1.66	12.23	1.40			
	29	(Pica-0 %ile)	64.07	19.26	70.93	17.03			
62	13	Pica-0	9.48	1.98	12.72	1.50	11.66	<.01	My s.d. calculation only
SS3	2	Pica-0 %ile	45.00	0.63	46.00	1.41	0.07	.25	All my calculations
SS4	2	WAB-AQ	66.00	7.07	70.15	5.16	3.074	.1	All my calculations
SS11	2	Pica-0 %ile	36.00	26.87	43.00	16.97	1.00	.25	All my calculations

Notes: Table is reproduced from Dr. Fromm's notes; s.e. = standard error; s.d. = standard deviation.

discuss only the steps involved in obtaining a combined estimate of treatment effect from these studies. In the meta-analysis literature (see, e.g., Rosenthal 1984), there is often a choice of how to measure an effect size, the difference among measures usually being in the use of a pooled estimate of variability from the two groups or the use of the control group or pre-treatment group measure of variability. Below we consider two measures of effect size as an illustration of how the answers might differ based on the choice of measure.

The first measure of effect size we consider, ES1, is the difference between the post- and pre-treatment scores, divided by the *pre-treatment* standard deviation. It is argued that since these patients are beyond the period of spontaneous recovery and it is unlikely that they will improve in the absence of treatment, the pre-treatment scores can be used as a surrogate for a control group. Unfortunately, the raw data needed to estimate ES1 for study 54/10 were not available, although the authors did report the paired-t-statistic. To impute ES1 for study 54/10, we used an estimated standard deviation derived from the other studies (with N's > 2) that measured outcome using the PICA-overall percentile score. Since the pre-treatment standard deviations for studies 1, 6, 11, 37, and 55 were relatively stable, we took the average standard deviation from these studies, 18.3, for the estimated standard deviation for study 54/10.

Alternatively, we also considered a measure of effect size, ES2, based on the paired-t-statistic. It is the mean within-subject difference divided by the standard deviation of the differences. Studies 32, 38, and 55 did not report a paired-t-statistic, although we do have pre- and post-treatment means and standard deviations for them. To compute an estimate of the standard deviation of the differences for each of these studies, we first found the average correlation (r) between pre- and post-treatment scores for the other studies having N > 2 that did report the paired-t-statistic. This value was 0.74, which we then used to impute ES2 for studies 32, 38, and 55. The values for both ES1 and ES2 for each study may be found in Table 3.2 along with the relevant estimated quantities, indicated by a *, used to compute them.

A combined estimate of treatment effect can be obtained as a simple average of the individual effect sizes across the 13 independent studies. Based on ES1, the average effect size is $\overline{\text{ES1}} = 0.80$, with an approximate 95 percent confidence interval of (0.50, 1.10). Based on ES2, the average effect size is $\overline{\text{ES2}} = 1.37$, with an approximate 95 percent confidence interval of (0.73, 2.03). Taking a weighted average of the individual effect sizes weighted by the individual study's sample size yields an average weighted effect size of $w\overline{\text{ES1}}=0.77$ and $w\overline{\text{ES2}}=1.38$.

Table 3.2   Summary Statistics and Estimates of Effect Size for Studies Using a Pre-treatment and Post-treatment Design

Study Number	Sample Size	Pre-treatment Mean	S.D.	Post-treatment Mean	r	ES1	ES2
1	7	54.30	14.50	52.90	0.74	− 0.10	− 0.14
6	14	60.00	19.27	71.10	0.92	0.58	1.50
11	45	37.60	18.76	66.51	0.70	1.54	1.92
14	15	9.42	1.78	11.24	0.42	1.02	0.94
32	104	8.90	2.24	9.90	0.74*	0.45	0.62*
37	17	56.65	19.45	73.18	0.79	0.85	1.19
38	36	9.23	1.51	10.25	0.74*	0.68	1.00*
54	34	0.00	18.30*	18.00	0.74*	0.98*	4.04
55	29	64.07	19.26	70.93	0.74*	0.36	0.52*
62	13	9.48	1.98	12.72	0.87	1.64	3.23
SS3	2	45.00	0.63	46.00	0.74*	1.59	0.05
SS4	2	66.00	7.07	70.15	0.74*	0.59	2.18
SS11	2	36.00	26.87	43.00	0.74*	0.26	0.71

For the purposes of this illustration, the remainder of this discussion will consider only estimates based on ES1. According to Cohen's "rough guidelines" (1977), our average effect size of 0.80 (0.77 weighted) represents a medium to large effect. Cohen (1977) also suggests a more practical interpretation of effect size. That is, the average patient receiving therapy for aphasia approximately three months post-stroke would have an overall improvement score greater than 78.8 percent of the patients who did not receive treatment. To put these results into a clinical context, recall that aphasia is a disorder of listening, speaking, reading, and writing. However, not all patients are equally impaired in all areas. Therefore, treatment is usually tailored to the specific patient's deficit. As a result, an overall measure of outcome, such as the PICA-overall, may not be very sensitive. So an effect size of .80 based on an overall measure of outcome seems important clinically as well as statistically, especially when one considers the diverse nature of both the disorder and its therapy. Of equal importance, however, is an analysis of the mediating variables, in this case type of treatment and its influence on the various outcomes of interest.

We next considered two analyses which reflect on the sensitivity of the combined measure of treatment effect. We anticipated that the single-subject studies might yield, on the average, larger effect sizes than the group studies given the individualized nature of the therapy. However, the average effect size for the group studies (N's > 2) is 0.80 compared

TABLE 3.3   Assessment of the Influence of Each
Study on the Average Effect Size

Study Number (i)	$\overline{ES1}$	$\overline{wES1}$
1	0.878	0.794
6	0.848	0.696
11	0.742	0.649
14	0.785	0.692
32	0.833	0.930
37	0.799	0.770
38	0.813	0.786
54/10	0.788	0.750
55	0.840	0.815
62	0.733	0.737
SS3	0.738	0.769
SS4	0.821	0.777
SS11	0.837	0.737
median	0.813	0.770

with the average effect size of 0.81 for the single-subject studies (average weighted effect sizes, .77 versus 0.81, respectively). This result suggests a stability of the treatment effect across different study designs.

We again found stability of the treatment effect across studies when we investigated the influence of each individual study on the average effect size. Let $\overline{ES1}(i)$ ($\overline{wES1}(i)$) be the average unweighted (weighted) effect size computed from all the studies except study i. Table 3.3 presents the values for $\overline{ES1}(i)$ and for $\overline{wES1}(i)$, respectively. The median average unweighted effect size is again 0.81, and the median average weighted effect size is 0.77. Study 1, the only study with a negative effect size, is the most influential study in the unweighted analysis, and study 32, the largest study in the group, is the most influential study in the weighted analysis.

Reflections on the File-Drawer Problem

A nagging problem in meta-analysis arises out of the concern that the retrieved studies form a biased sample of all studies that were done and that some adjustment is needed to compensate for this bias. One source of bias is editorial policy that discourages the publication of studies which do not yield results that are statistically significant at the traditional levels (e.g., $p < 0.05$). Even the perception of such a policy can send the results of a study into a file drawer (or worse, a garbage can). See Hedges and Olkin (1985) and Rosenthal (1984) for further discussion. Some researchers in meta-analysis have concentrated on this type of bias and have proposed various methods of adjustment for it.

These methods are limited in their scope, however, because of another possible source of bias that Rosenthal's own research on expectancy effects has suggested to us. Namely, if after analyzing the results of a study, a researcher finds the results contrary to his expectations or his beliefs, he may seek reasons to dismiss the study. Finding fault with the study's design is one way of doing that. Furthermore, after the publication of a study that makes a certain claim, other investigators will try to replicate that study. Such an investigator's previous experience may then lead him to try to either further substantiate or disprove the original claim, and this intent could be the source of the bias.

Based on our experience with the meta-analysis described here, we have considered two approaches to the file-drawer problem. The first, the "fail-safe-sample-size" approach, calculates ". . . the number of studies averaging null results that must be in the file drawers before the overall probability of a type I error can be just brought to any desired level of significance . . ." (Rosenthal 1984, p. 108). See also Hedges and Olkin (1985). The second approach explicitly models the selection process by incorporating a weight function into the likelihood function and yields a maximum likelihood estimate of the effect size; see also Hedges and Olkin (1985) and Bayarri and DeGroot (1987). We discuss and analyze these two approaches in detail elsewhere in a paper entitled, "Selection Models and the File-Drawer Problem" (Iyengar and Greenhouse 1988).

Reflections on Meta-Analysis

We conclude this report with some observations about the process of meta-analysis and some remarks about its future. Having had this opportunity to participate in a meta-analysis and to reflect on the methods, we summarize our observations as follows:

1. The subject matter specialist plays a central role in a meta-analysis. In a meta-analysis, there are major substantive questions, decisions, and judgments that can be made only by individuals knowledgeable about the problem area.
2. Just as in a single-study investigation, research questions in a meta-analysis must be carefully articulated. A clear and carefully thought-

out research agenda is critical in proceeding smoothly through the various steps of a meta-analysis.
3. An important role of the statistician in a quantitative literature review is to ask relevant questions which help sharpen and clarify issues, to guide the analysis, and to assess the impact of the various decisions, judgments, and assumptions on the results of the meta-analysis.

With respect to the future of meta-analysis, we believe that "meta-analysis is here to stay." We have some reservations and concerns, however, about the direction of future developments. As we mentioned in the introduction, meta-analysts have already considered many of the basic issues that occurred to us and have devised a variety of methods for dealing with them. We fear misuse, however, and perceive the danger, which is ever-present with mass dissemination of methodology, as greater than the developers seem to find it. Rosenthal's rebuttal (1984, p. 17) that nonquantitative review is even more likely to be applied inappropriately is certainly an important point, but it begs the question: What substantially could be done to improve literature review? Meta-analysis, with its current packaging and emphasis, can be only part of the answer. The other part involves important aspects of the review process, which have been addressed by Rosenthal, Glass, Light and Pillemer, and others, but which seem to have received less emphasis than the formal technical developments in their work.

A literature review can have two closely related, yet rather different goals. It may tell us what we may conclude about a phenomenon, based on a collection of studies, or it may summarize what the studies contribute to our knowledge of the phenomenon. Thus, we could try to answer the question, Does aphasia therapy work? Or we could instead describe the manner in which our collection of studies alters our knowledge of aphasia therapy. The distinction is one of emphasis. A good literature review should include both kinds of statements. This is an issue of how best to report reports. We would value most highly those reviews that not only summarize results but also usefully summarize the nature of the information contained in the results. A careful identification and classification of relevant features of design could often be more informative than the summaries of results themselves.

We are especially concerned about the problem of using results and reporting on studies that are of different qualities. Differing quality may be accommodated within the meta-analytic formalism, as Rosenthal points out (1984, p. 55), by assigning appropriate weights to each study. Summaries, such as overall effect size, may then be computed. This process, however, deserves as much attention as the final result. Thus, it seems to us, it is most informative to report an assessment of the quality of the studies and to specify the criteria according to which that assessment has been made.

Although it may be quite useful to have widely available the step-by-step methodology for quantitative summary produced by Rosenthal, Glass, and others, we suspect that even greater advances would come from an equal effort in articulating the steps that should be followed in determining good quality studies from bad. To have each study evaluated by several excellent methodologists, and then to assess these assessors for their reliability, is an ideal solution (Rosenthal 1984, p. 55), not only in the good sense that it is a good suggestion but also in the bad sense that it is sufficiently difficult to implement that, we fear, few practitioners will use it. Certainly it is far more demanding than the simple methods for combining results from studies.

Furthermore, it is not only *relative* quality and its relationship to effect size that matters. *Absolute* quality is even more important: In a large literature there may be only a few really good studies. These need to be singled out and discussed separately, since they provide most of the information in the literature—again, an informative review would discuss what makes those studies good. The observation that poor studies tend to lead to similar conclusions is neither good nor bad; it is simply irrelevant. Assessing quality can be difficult. Our point is that tools for assessing quality (e.g., step-by-step procedures) would be helpful and that quality assessments, and other descriptions of study variability, should be an essential part of the reporting of scientific reports.

In addition to quality heterogeneity, there are other important heterogeneities, and these, too, deserve special attention in a careful review. Within homogeneous groups of studies, though, there remains variability, and a summary should include an estimate of variability. We can perhaps say what we mean about this matter more easily by introducing a simple conceptualization. Suppose we have k homogeneous studies with sample sizes n_i, effect sizes δ_i, and estimated effect sizes Y_i, $i = 1, \ldots, k$, and suppose further that, conditionally on δ_i and σ, the Y_i's are i.i.d. Normal $(\delta_i, \sigma^2/n_i)$ and the δ_i's are i.i.d. Normal (μ, τ^2). In this setting, one goal of meta-analysis would be to learn about μ, but another would be to learn about τ. We believe it is no less important to report knowledge about τ than to report knowledge about μ. This is an instance of our general preference for reporting the manner in which studies contribute to knowledge: We could obtain precise knowledge of μ when studies are either quite consistent in their results, or disparate, and it is important to know which.

It is useful to keep this simple framework in mind, since we regard it as generating justification for some formal procedures, such as overall effect size estimation (the weighted mean is, of course, the maximum likelihood estimator of μ). From this point of view, we may succinctly express our reservations about the applicability of certain meta-analytic procedures in particular settings: The assumption that the effect sizes are normally distributed is quite arbitrary. Sometimes we might wish to consider some heavy-tailed or skewed distribution instead. More worrisome, however, is the situation in which there is such gross heterogeneity that it is unclear how the effect sizes should be related—so unclear that some alternative but dramatically different assumption would seem equally plausible. This would often be the case when the various studies have different outcome measures. Although one may assert that such effect sizes will have some distribution, so that mixing apples and oranges becomes possible, it is a delicate matter to accurately model the distribution so that useful results will be obtained. This, too, is a matter that deserves more attention.

4

A Discussion of the Aphasia Study

Nan M. Laird

The original Committee on National Statistics (CNSTAT) idea in planning the workshop on the future of meta-analysis was to involve a number of methodologists and experienced meta-analysts by asking them to prepare meta-analysis case studies. My position on this plan was that we were naive to expect these people to donate their time, not to mention that of their students and colleagues. In the beginning, my opinion did not receive much support; however, subsequent CNSTAT meetings generally bore out my predictions. In the end, only one group of researchers was willing to undertake the project, and probably only because they had independently been planning to conduct a similar project. This group had no prior experience as meta-analysts; they proceeded as novices, first letting judgment guide the direction of their analyses and subsequently referring to literature on the subject.

Having at least partially completed one meta-analysis, they now qualify as what I would call experienced meta-analysts. I suspect that they would also fall into the category of methodologists probably unwilling to repeat the experience except under very special circumstances and even then not without easy access to unlimited slave labor. Their report has, for me, raised some new ideas as well as reinforced many prior prejudices.

The magnitude of the task of identifying, reviewing, and abstracting data from the literature cannot be overemphasized in my view, and it is generally understated in the literature on meta-analysis. Most researchers are familiar with the process of reviewing the literature, and it is tempting to suppose that reviewing the literature for the purpose of a meta-analysis would be only modestly more difficult and time-consuming. Nothing could be further from the truth. Two distinctions are immediately obvious—first is the need to be completely comprehensive in the search process and second is the extreme difficulty of abstracting usable data from a published paper.

The first step in the process is to clearly define goals and set out inclusion criteria. This enables one to define the target population for the search. Our novice meta-analysts "decided our first objective was simple—include all studies." This is one of life's mistakes that we only make once. It is tempting at the outset to assume that it is best to collect all possible information early in a project on the grounds that it will be easier to narrow, rather than broaden, the focus at a later date. The opposite has been my experience, both in primary and secondary data collection. Overambition at the data collection phase often leads to one's becoming overwhelmed by the enormity and complexity of the database, so that even a simple analysis of a specific issue becomes elusive. My own thinking on this issue has been greatly influenced by both Fred Mosteller and Tom Chalmers, a physician turned meta-analyst, whose work show great skill in the art of problem definition.

The authors comment on the desirability of duplicate reviews. My own work leads me to feel that the process of reviewing the articles for quality and for content must be independently duplicated and that much of the review process should be done in blinded fashion. In the medical literature several authors have put forth rating schemes which allow reviewers to develop a quantitative measure of study quality. If possible, assessment of quality should be blinded to study outcome. Since blinding and duplication can considerably lengthen the review process, a narrow focus facilitates a more reliable result. The authors comment on the need for subject matter specialists to review the article for quality content, but it would be equally desirable to have the statistician involved in the process of data abstracting and the data collection process validated by an additional independent review.

The procedure of searching the literature is very important. Tom Chalmers' work suggests that even the most careful and sophisticated computerized literature searches yield only about 50 percent of the relevant published literature in the area of clinical trials in medicine. The authors' discussion of their own experience underscores the difficulty of carrying out an exhaustive search and of documenting the completeness of the search. While much meta-analytic literature focuses on the failure to consider unpublished studies, more thoughtful research on methods of improving the yield of published studies that are actually found would be useful.

Table 4.1   **Studies Reporting PICA Percentiles**

Study Number	Sample Size	Pre	Post	%
1	7	54.30	52.90	−1.40
6	14	60.00	71.10	11.10
11	45	37.60	66.51	28.91
37	17	56.65	73.18	16.53
54	34	—	—	18.00
55	29	64.07	70.93	6.86
SS3	2	45.00	46.00	1.00
SS11	2	36.00	43.00	7.00
Average		50.50	60.50	11.02
(weighted)		50.80	67.30	17.03

Having collected all the relevant studies, the authors organize the studies by type of outcome, type of treatment, and study design. A prototype analysis is presented using 13 studies with single group pre- and post-test designs and an overall measure of outcome. The authors use effect sizes to summarize the results. In my view, effect sizes are necessary evils which are sometimes unavoidable but which should be used only when all else fails. This view is not well represented in the meta-analysis literature. I believe that the present analysis is a good example of why this is true. The authors find that this group of studies yields an overall effect size of .8, which is fairly insensitive to weighting scheme and various exclusions. Following Cohen (1977) they conclude that this indicates that the "average patient receiving therapy for aphasia approximately three months post-stroke would have an overall improvement score greater than 78.8 percent of patients who did not." The authors note that in clinical context this is an impressive achievement for the therapy. But is it?

Ken Wachter suggests an alternative interpretation for an effect size of .8, which seems more realistic in view of the data. If two patients are randomly selected from the population of aphasia patients, one treated and one not, the treated patient is likely to be better off than the untreated one only about 71 percent of the time ($P(Z < .8/\sqrt{2})$, where Z is a standard normal), which is a considerably less impressive statement about therapy, especially in view of the fact that they are better off 50 percent of the time when therapy is completely ineffective.

However, in this case a much more direct assessment is possible. All but one of the 13 studies use the same outcome measure, the PICA score. Eight of the 12 give the PICA score as a percentile, which can be interpreted as where a patient stands in relation to a large group of aphasia patients. One could possibly convert the average PICA scores to approximate average PICA percentiles for the other four studies.

The 8 studies reporting percentile scores have an average effect size of .76 and thus do not differ systematically from the group as a whole. For 7 of these studies the average mean percentile prior to treatment was 50.5 percent (50.8 percent weighted by sample size). I interpret this to mean that the patients are representative of aphasia patients on the whole. The average gain for all 8 studies was 11.02 percent (17.03 percent weighted), yielding an average post mean of something between 61 and 67 percent. By this measure, the effect of therapy is to raise one's percentile standing by something between 11 and 17 percent, a result which again seems far less impressive and much more easily communicated than Cohen's interpretation of the .8 effect size. The authors also report that the pooled estimate of the pretest percentile score is 18.3 percent; multiplying this by .8 gives yet another way of assessing the magnitude of the effect. This gives an estimated mean gain of 14.6 percent, which agrees well with the average percentile change.

The way the data are arrayed in Table 4.1 clearly shows that one study contributes a lot to the result. This underscores the desirability of measuring and reporting the variation in treatment effects.

In my view, the data analysis phase of the meta-analysis should be quite different from that of an experiment where data dredging and hypothesis generation are suspect. I feel that confirmatory hypothesis testing has been overemphasized in the meta-analysis literature, and more descriptive analyses should be emphasized. A very important first step in this process is arraying the results in a clear and informative fashion. The strength of the tables presented by the authors is that they do give much original detail on the studies, but their serious weakness is that this method of display confuses the reader and makes direct assessment of results difficult. The abstracted data represent an enormous and valuable contribution of any meta-analysis. More serious time and attention should be given to the problem of displaying the data in useful and informative ways.

Because of lack of analysis time, the results of the controlled and randomized studies are not reported. The authors wisely keep these studies separate, and we look forward to seeing whether or not their analyses confirm the present findings. The remaining analyses center on the file-drawer problem, and they suggest some imaginative improvements to Rosenthal's method for handling this problem. In summary, the authors are to be congratulated for undertaking their task and providing us with a useful documentation of what the novice meta-analysts can expect.

The following are additional points from the medical and public health perspective:

1.   Effect sizes are not used much in either clinical therapy or epidemiological meta-analyses because most studies use the same measure of endpoint, normally a rate or proportion. The meta-analysis literature on analytic techniques for combining rate differences, ratios, or odds ratios is relatively small but central in medicine and public health. This is one area where we could benefit from much additional statistical work.

2.   In studies of clinical therapy especially, meta-analysis is very valuable in assessing the significance of secondary endpoints. This was borne out during my recent collaboration with Drs. Hine and Chalmers on the meta-analysis of the effects of lidocaine prophylactic treatment for prevention of ventricular arrhythmias following acute myocardial infarction (AMI) (Hine et al. 1986). A previous meta-analysis and numerous individual studies have demonstrated beyond a doubt that lidocaine treatment does reduce ventricular fibrillation following AMI. Indeed, so successful is the therapy that a recent study in the *New England Journal of Medicine* proclaims that dramatic increases in numbers of deaths prevented can be attributed to lidocaine treatment. However, no study has actually shown any significant mortality effect; this is generally attributed to small sample sizes, small effects, and thus low power. We set out to see if a meta-analysis could demonstrate a treatment effect on mortality. To our surprise, we did demonstrate a statistically significant effect on early mortality, but in the opposite direction: the combined evidence suggests that lidocaine therapy may actually increase the death rate! The potential implications of this finding are enormous. The power of any individual study to detect a difference equal to the observed magnitude (a difference in death rates of only about 3 percent) is well under .20. However, considering the prevalence of AMI, a 3 percent increase in death rates is important.

In the meta-analyses of clinical therapy it is common practice to include only randomly controlled trials (RCT's). A rationale for this practice is that comparisons between RCT's and studies using historical (HCT) or alternate (ACT) controls generally show that HCT's or ACT's overstate the effect of therapy, presumably because of biased selection. A view sometimes expressed in clinical literature is that the difference in results for RCT's, HCT's, and ACT's may in fact be attributable to an intervention being tested in RCT's which is of poorer quality. RCT's are often lengthy to carry out and thus may not be implementing current therapies by the end of the trial; they are often multicenter and involve clinical groups without appropriate skill and/or enthusiasm for the therapy; therapies may need modification when subjected to a strict protocol, and so on. These opinions about RCT's are not limited to the medical arena.

I believe that meta-analysis may be able to play an important role in confirming or laying to rest the hypothesis that the treatments differ in RCT's and HCT's or ACT's. If the two effects (namely, randomization and treatment quality) are completely confounded, it is of course hopeless, but I suspect that some area of clinical research, probably surgery, would yield a fruitful area for testing this hypothesis.

The effect of media coverage of meta-analysis in medicine is another distinct area which seems to have no clear counterpart in the behavioral sciences. A recent case in point are two independent meta-analyses showing significant benefit for some chemotherapy treatments of breast cancer (Himel et al. 1986). The effect of the large media coverage of these findings on ongoing RCT's in this area has not yet been determined, but it cannot help but be real. Meta-analysis has the potential for changing research directions in important ways, and I believe that it would be useful to document this potential.

Finally, with regard to the "representativeness" of the results of meta-analysis. Few would argue that studies included in a meta-analysis are really random samples from a population of studies, although it may be useful to regard them as such from the point of view of summarization. In some areas of medicine it may be possible to take a very different approach. For example, for many diseases we can make good estimates of the eligible patient population, and we may be reasonably certain that all patients receive some form of therapy. We may even know the distribution of therapies. Thus the patients included in the meta-analysis can be put into the context of sampling from a finite population. It seems to me that this perspective may lead to more useful ways of dealing with the file-drawer problem. One related approach has been suggested by Begg (1985), and more work in this direction may pay good dividends.

PART III

Case Study: The Effects of School Desegregation on the Academic Achievement of Black Children

5

Research, Meta-Analysis, and Desegregation Policy

Jeffrey M. Schneider

Although much of the research literature on school desegregation has focused specifically on determining the effects of desegregation on academic performance of black students, no one has conclusively answered the question. Reputable social scientists do find statistically significant relationships (positive and negative) which persist even after controlling for socioeconomic status (SES), sex, and other relevant factors, but inconclusive research findings have led to differing conceptions of the size and impact of the effect. Perhaps desegregation has important effects on black student achievement, but the nature of these effects may vary with type of student, type of school, type of community, SES, sex, and other factors. Perhaps desegregation does not have a single effect, positive or negative, on the academic achievement of black students, but rather some strategies help, some hurt, and still others make no difference. In order to clarify the state of research knowledge about desegregation on the academic achievement of black students and, if at all possible, to identify areas of consensus and reconcile differences of interpretation, the National Institute of Education (NIE) commissioned a set of papers and a conference on this topic.

Because of the controversy and confusion surrounding the topic, NIE had previously not earmarked a large portion of its budget for studying the desegregation–achievement relationship. It had historically been the NIE contention that asking if desegregation improves minority achievement was an inappropriate educational question, for abandonment of desegregation was not an education issue. For that matter NIE never considered desegregation to be an education treatment, but a legal requirement. The important education question is one of effectiveness. School desegregation remedies should remedy the effects of past inequalities, as measured by educational progress. Thus, NIE encouraged researchers to ask useful questions—what works under what conditions—and not to assume that desegregation is an identical process whenever it occurs. It was the NIE contention that only by asking these questions could policymakers find that social scientists would offer some helpful answers (Henderson, von Euler, and Schneider 1982). The hope was that once the desegregation–achievement question was answered, researchers would be better able to concern themselves with the essential educational questions surrounding quality education, effective schools, and good race relations.

Previous Attempts at Reconciliation

There had been two basic types of research investigation into the effects of school desegregation on the academic achievement of black students. The first approach had been the large-scale national study based on simultaneous achievement testing in a large number of schools. This approach had been taken by Coleman et al. (1966) who, while finding a small amount of gain, concluded that other factors (e.g., SES) were more important. A variant of this approach was the Bridge, Judd, and Moock (1979) attempt to synthesize desegregation research. They concluded that minority students attending predominantly white, high SES schools score higher on achievement tests. While this approach gave us much valuable information, it also lost any differences which may have existed within individual districts. Much of the early discussion about the desegregation–achievement relationship grew out of the use of single studies or variation within a small number of studies (e.g., Armor 1972, 1973; Pettigrew 1973).

The second approach to studying desegregation had been to compile a large number of small published and unpublished studies, each dealing with a single school district. The first major attempt to use this approach was Weinberg's review of the literature (1970). In both this project and his later reexamination (1972), Weinberg included an amazingly comp'ete review of the research literature on minority achievement but made little or no attempt to select studies according to how adequate they were methodologically or how well they led to causal inference. A second comprehensive review by St. John (1975) included 43 studies classified according to research design, thus allowing her to observe the relationship between methodology and the impact of desegregation. St. John concluded that while the quality of the studies was too uncertain and the results too mixed to lead to any definitive statements, more studies than not showed that school desegregation improved the achievement of black students. In 1977 Bradley and Bradley also reviewed the research literature and found so many methodological problems that they concluded it was impossible to draw accurate generalizations about the effects of desegregation on the academic achievement of black students. Their procedures, however, did not attempt to expand knowledge of research methodology beyond the St. John analysis. In 1980, Krol reviewed 71 studies using formal meta-analysis as his analysis strategy. This ensured that individual studies were screened for minimum adequacy and that results were converted to standardized estimates based on a ratio of test means to their standard deviations, thus allowing researchers to better estimate the magnitude of desegregation effects. As a result of his meta-analysis, Krol concluded that desegregation had a very small positive (but statistically non-significant) effect on the academic achievement of black students of about .16 standard deviations, which amounts to between 1 1/2 and 3 months of progress during an academic year.

In 1978, Robert Crain and Rita Mahard had found that desegregation raised the achievement test scores of black students in desegregated schools. Crain and Mahard updated their review in 1981, using meta-analysis as their methodology for examining 93 research studies. They intentionally included studies with weaker designs in order to test the impact of design on the desegregation effects found. They concluded that the overall effect size mean was a nonsignificant .065 standard deviations. However, a significant positive effect of .3 standard deviations was found under two conditions—if a plan were implemented before first grade and on a metropolitan basis. The Crain-Mahard meta-analysis used a traditional approach, including all available studies. Paul Wortman (1982) felt that the Crain and Mahard approach was inappropriate because it allowed for the inclusion of many studies which were flawed by methodological weaknesses and others which were "cross sectional surveys," lacking the necessary statistical information to analyze desegregation effects. Wortman, instead, undertook his meta-analysis using 31 studies which met his requirements concerning minimum methodological quality and concluded that desegregation had a definite positive effect on the achievement of black youths.

The Purpose of This Effort

NIE knew from the beginning of the project that much of the available research on school desegregation and its effect on black students' academic achievement suffered from design flaws and raised more questions than it answered. It was not known, however, whether desegregation suffered from this in any greater measure than any other research areas, nor was it known why so many reputable scholars disagreed in their interpretation of analytical results.

In 1981, the new administration of NIE publicly raised serious questions about desegregation as a public policy and about the quality of desegregation research. NIE commissioned a set of papers in an effort to obtain the views of six reputable scholars who had previously reported opposing conclusions in this area and one research methodologist who had not been identified as a desegregation specialist. NIE wanted to find if there was a reason to continue funding desegregation research and to determine whether, with the same data set and common ground rules, similarities and differences in scholarly analysis could be identified and clarified.

The participants were selected because of their previous research findings. A major criterion used for selection was that participants be respected for their skills as researchers and for their knowledge of research methodology. Robert Crain and Paul Wortman had previously found desegregation to have a positive effect on black student achievement. David Armor and Norman Miller had previously questioned the value of desegregation as a method of increasing the achievement of black students. Walter Stephan and Herbert Walberg had previously been neutral about the desegregation–achievement relationship. A methodologist, Thomas Cook, was added to the expert panel to review the work of the other experts and to discuss technical questions that might arise concerning the results of the synthesis effort.

These seven scholars met in July 1982 and agreed on the use of comprehensive criteria in selecting the studies to be analyzed. The criteria for the rejection of a study, listed below, were based on Paul Wortman's prior analysis:

1. Type of study
   a. nonempirical
   b. summary report
2. Location
   a. outside USA
   b. geography nonspecific

3. Comparisons
   a. not a study of achievement of desegregated blacks (except in cases which used white comparisons)
   b. multiethnic combined
   c. comparisons across ethnics only
   d. heterogeneous proportions of minorities in a desegregated condition
   e. no control data
   f. no pre-desegregation data
   g. control measures not contemporaneous
   h. excessive attrition (review must provide specific justification for the inclusion of studies with excessive attrition, but amount was not specific)
   i. majority black in a desegregated condition (review must provide specific justification for the inclusion of black in a desegregated condition, unless the reviewer provides specific justification)
   j. varied exposure to desegregation (unless the reviewer provides a specific justification demonstrating that the variation in exposure time is not meaningful)
   k. groups are initially noncomparable (unless the reviewer provides a specific justification that the amount of divergence is not meaningful)
4. Study desegregation
   a. cross-sectional survey
   b. sampling procedure unknown
   c. separate noncomparable samples at each observation
5. Measures
   a. unreliable and/or unstandardized instruments
   b. test content and/or instrument unknown
   c. dates of administration unknown
   d. different tests used in pre-tests and post-tests
   e. test of IQ or verbal ability
6. Data analysis
   a. no pre-test means
   b. no post-test means, unless the author reported pre-test scores and gains
   c. no data presented
   d. N's not discernible

Of the total of 157 empirical studies of black student academic achievement in desegregated schools identified, a "core" of 19 studies met the criteria. Panel members, however, agreed that individual reviewers would be allowed to add or delete studies from the "core," with specific justification.

Findings

The panel presented its findings in December 1982. Overall, it concluded that, based on the 19 studies, black students make slight gains in reading when they are taught in desegregated schools, while gains in mathematics are near zero. While this was interesting it was neither unexpected nor of major importance.

However, the process of this analytical effort accomplished much. First, it graphically demonstrated the poor quality of much of the desegregation research. Second, a comprehensive set of "accept-reject" criteria for research in this area had been developed. These criteria were agreed to by nationally respected scholars who had (before this project) differed in their assessment of the desegregation literature. Third, a comparative meta-analysis was a significant and inexpensive tool for acquiring new insights and perspectives. Fourth, while the results were as political as any previous study, the political nature of the research was understood by all participants from the onset, and the procedure did attain movement toward finding agreement.

In addition, several interesting facts about desegregation research were uncovered as a result of the process:

1. After quality standards were agreed on, only 19 of the studies of all those previously undertaken met the minimum qualifications.
2. Most of the qualified studies (12 of 19) were at least a decade old at the time of the meta-analysis.
3. Nine of the 19 qualified studies were either unpublished doctoral dissertations or master's theses. It became clear that the funding of dissertation research is a very inexpensive way to achieve high quality results.
4. Equally valuable and almost as inexpensive is research done by school districts for their own use (5 of the 19 studies).

6

An Overview
of the Desegregation Meta-Analyses

Linda Ingram

This chapter summarizes the findings of the scholars selected by the National Institute of Education (NIE) to review desegregation research (U.S. Department of Education 1984) in order to make the methodological discussions of this case study in Chapters 7 to 10 more comprehensible. A full account of the studies is beyond our scope, but a few brief remarks should be useful. Jeffrey Schneider has described the process by which these scholars were selected and how they went about selecting a common set of studies to review. Here, the work of each team of researchers is summarized, along with Thomas Cook's commentary on the researchers' methods and conclusions at the end.

David J. Armor

David J. Armor, of David Armor and Associates, asked, in "The Evidence on Desegregation and Black Achievement," whether the resource investment in improving racial balance in schools is justified by education payoffs. Black parents' support for busing may decline if desegregation is found to have minimal impact on their children's learning. He reviewed previous reviews of desegregation and achievement and found remaining disagreement among the experts about the effects, largely, he thought, because they were all looking at different sets of studies which vary greatly as to their adequacy for making causal inference.

THE SELECTION OF STUDIES.   Armor felt that the selected studies *do* fulfill certain requirements: quasi-experimental designs, with pre- and post-tests, and segregated (50 percent or more black) control groups. He eliminated two of the selected studies for various methodological reasons. However, he found that there are still some problems in the selected studies:

1. More voluntary than mandatory programs were selected, which possibly reduces generalizability (but may provide a hypothesis-testing opportunity).
2. The longest term study is only three years, complicating inference to desegregation experience, which spans all 12 school attendance years.
3. Only one of the studies is a randomized experiment, and therefore the control groups are not generally equivalent to the treatment groups prior to the start of desegregation.
4. Study selection did not require equivalent pre- and post-tests, only that the content be similar and that the same test be used for treatment and control groups.
5. Not all control groups fulfilled the 50 percent black requirement.

ANALYSIS PROCEDURES.   Armor adjusted post-test scores for pre-test group differences and then followed procedures outlined by Wortman (1982), with some refinements. For example, he pooled standard deviations wherever possible to improve the reliability of the standard deviation estimate. He increased the number of adjusted effect estimates that would ordinarily be available by, for example, using standard deviation estimates from other studies in the data set, providing they were based on the same test. Armor felt that this was critical since many otherwise good studies lacked only standard deviation estimates.

DISCUSSION.   Armor felt that the overwhelming majority of 47 different tests by grade possible in the selected studies showed no significant effects of desegregation on black achievement. Only 11 of these tests were found to be significant at an acceptable level, and two of these were negative "effects."

Averaging across studies and grade levels and using alternative methods, he found an average effect of .06 of a standard deviation for reading and .01 for math, neither statistically significant. His extrapolated results showed that desegregation could only nominally close the gap between black and white students' reading achievement. Other tests showed that the effects were not cumulative over time, that early desegregation did not have greater effects than later desegregation, and that the overall average reading effect was not a consistent one. Armor concluded that the best studies available demonstrated no significant and consistent effect of desegregation on black reading achievement and *no* effect on black math achievement. Finally, he suggested that the gains shown in some of the studies may be caused by unique educational programs available in a few schools.

Robert L. Crain

Robert L. Crain, of the Rand Corporation and the Center for the Social Organization of Schools, Johns Hopkins University, suggested in "Is Nineteen Really Better than Ninety-Three?" that ideology did show up in the panelists' essays (including his), but that it tended to show up in the conclusions and interpretations rather than in the data analysis—it is very difficult for contemporary social scientists to disagree about methodology.

THE SELECTION OF STUDIES.   Crain thought that the biggest difference among panel members was on the methodological issue of whether to include only the better studies or review all the studies available. He suggested that among the panelists there was a correlation between the number of studies looked at and the effect of desegregation on black achievement: that is, when more studies were looked at, higher effects were found. Denying that the methodological criteria which define a good study can be known in advance, he decided that the selection of only 19 studies was a serious error and that the two selection methods—all the studies versus a few of the better studies—should be tested empirically.

Crain's criterion for study selection would have been that the desegregation experience begin in kindergarten or first grade; the selection of any other time period will systematically underestimate the effects of desegregation. However, the panel elimated most of these early desegregation studies because of the difficulty of pre-testing very young children for the required longitudinal analysis, whereas Crain felt that cohort analysis should be equally acceptable or superior in this situation. Therefore he reanalyzed the previous Crain and Mahard (1982) analysis of 93 studies and selected the 20 best designs which analyzed children desegregated in kindergarten or first grade. These 20 studies included 5 studies which used a randomized experimental design, 8 studies which used cohort (or historical control group) comparisons, and 7 studies which were longitudinal with nonrandom assignment.

The 20 studies were selected not as models for research but because they would give the least biased estimates of the effects of desegregation on black achievement. Crain noted that his requirements for methodology and the amount of material reported by the authors were less demanding than the panel's requirements.

ANALYSIS.   The results of these 20 studies showed consistently positive effects, with a median effect size of 0.12 standard deviations. Crain noted that if the principal function of selecting a superior subgroup of studies is to find consistent results which are masked by error in a random sample of studies, he performed this function and the panel did not.

Norman Miller and Michael Carlson

Norman Miller and Michael Carlson, of the University of Southern California, provided a historical context to the desegregation question in "School Desegregation as a Social Reform: A Meta-Analysis of Its Effects on Black Academic Achievement."

THE SELECTION OF STUDIES.   Miller and Carlson required that control groups be over 50 percent black, and thus eliminated 2 of the 19 preselected studies. In addition, they established several criteria for the inclusion of comparisons within studies:

1. N's must be larger than 10 for both segregated and desegregated conditions.
2. Segregated control groups must not receive any special treatments which extend beyond typical classroom experience.
3. Dependent variable must be a verbal, math, or other major content area achievement test (excluding, e.g., "work study skills").
4. Pre-tests and post-tests must measure an identical construct.
5. Post-test standard deviations, along with pre-test and post-test mean differences for segregated and desegregated conditions, must be present (or there must be an analysis of covariance table with similar information).

ANALYSIS.   The authors defined effect size as the post-test desegregated versus segregated difference in means (as expressed in pooled post-test standard units) minus the pre-test desegregated versus segregated difference in means (as expressed in pooled pre-test standard units). Weighting study outcomes equally, not by sample size, and correcting for measurement unreliability, they found an overall mean effect size of +.159.

Miller and Carlson also examined three potential moderator variables: (1) The year of the desegregation program had a moderate negative relation to effect size; (2) the region (North versus South) was unassociated with effect size; (3) the percentage of blacks in the classroom had a small negative effect on verbal effect size and a small positive effect on math effect size.

SUMMARY. The authors found that black gains relative to white gains were small, and that black gains were not attributable to the presence of white classmates per se. Instead, they interpreted black gains as being caused by the more general improvements in schools or districts that occurred during the implementation of desegregation. Also, while the mean effect size is "average" for various kinds of education interventions, desegregation is not an education program in the sense that, for example, computer-based instruction is; the underlying psychological processes are unknown. Overall, Miller and Carlson argue that whatever the academic effects found, they are due to teachers and schools and only attributable to percentage changes in the numbers of black versus white students to the extent that such changes go along with teacher and school changes. In conclusion, Miller and Carlson suggest that if there are other compelling reasons to desegregate schools, considerations of academic achievement should not be a deterrent.

Walter Stephan

Walter Stephan, of New Mexico State University, began "Blacks and *Brown*: The Effects of School Desegregation on Black Students" with a section on the problems with achievement tests, as a precautionary note on the interpretation of the selected studies. To the extent that desegregation has an effect on achievement scores, it may be caused by the quality of instruction, the quality of the student body, or the students' motivation. Also, the testing situation may have an effect.

ANALYSIS. After eliminating four studies from the set because the segregated control groups were not 50 percent black or were attending desegregated schools, Stephan used the Glass (1977) formulas to calculate effect sizes. He calculated the effect of desegregation by year for each study on the assumption that desegregation has linear effects over time, at least over the first three years. Using study or grade as the unit of analysis, he found approximately +.15 effect size for reading and .00 for math. However, the effect sizes may be unreliable because of small sample sizes, nonrandom sampling, unreliability of measures, varying quality of achievement measures, attrition, and uncertain comparability of control groups. The main threat to external validity was the nonrepresentativeness of the black students, and the fact that most of the studies covered voluntary situations in large cities. In addition to grade, Stephan analyzed the effects on scores of duration of desegregation program, city size, region, and voluntary/mandatory desegregation, but felt that all results were inconclusive because the effect sizes themselves were unreliable.

DISCUSSION.   Stephan suggested that a major problem with desegregation research is that it covers only the first few years of desegregation and does not look at effects on whites or on communities. In addition, the research has not isolated the factors associated with successful programs. Overall, public policy decisions on desegregation will have to continue to be made on the basis of competing values rather than on scientific evidence.

Herbert J. Walberg

Herbert J. Walberg, of the University of Illinois at Chicago, in "Desegregation and Education Productivity" compared the effects of desegregation with those of other factors in the process of school learning that have been recently synthesized. He reviewed several studies of the effects of various teaching processes on student outcomes done in the last 15 years and, despite some methodological problems with the primary studies, he felt that the studies showed that five broad teaching constructs—cognitive cues, motivational incentives, engagement, reinforcement, and management and climate—are positively associated with student learning outcomes. Walberg felt that recent research points even more definitively to manipulable factors that affect educational achievement. He noted that nearly all this research has been carried out in natural settings such as homes and schools, and most of it shows generalizability across student characteristics, subjects, and research methods.

Walberg then compared the effect sizes of these research syntheses with those of three meta-analyses of busing studies: Krol (1978), Crain and Mahard (1982), and his own synthesis of the studies selected by the NIE panel. He found that the results of the desegregation meta-analyses had a smaller percentage of positive studies than reviews of other education factors. Busing studies as a set were indeterminate with respect to significance, in contrast with other education factors.

He concluded that a wide variety of experimental and education conditions, such as the amount and quality of instruction, constructive classroom morale, and stimulation in the home environment, have been consistently effective under a wide variety of conditions. School desegregation, in contrast, does not appear to prove promising in the size or consistency of its effects on the learning of black students.

Paul M. Wortman

Paul M. Wortman, of the University of Michigan, began "School Desegregation and Black Achievement: An Integrated View" by noting the special problems that the desegregation-achievement literature poses for meta-analysis: the literature is almost entirely quasi-experimental, and this is susceptible to several rival hypotheses. Major threats to validity include the use of students with extreme scores ("selection") and the differential rates of intellectual growth displayed by whites versus blacks ("maturation"). Wortman then discussed several types of quasi-experimental research designs that are found in the literature, because of the influence that design has on the estimate of effect size.

He did his own review of all available studies, building on the Crain and Mahard (1978) and Krol (1978) reviews, but he excluded many studies because they did not meet specific methodological criteria. A set of 31 studies was analyzed, along with the smaller set of 19 NIE core studies. He found similar effect sizes, approximately .14 for both sets of studies, representing about a two-month gain for the desegregated students. Wortman noted that actual details of the programs are not reported, making it impossible to determine effective or ineffective programs. Subsidiary analyses comparing type of achievement, duration of desegregation, grade level, and difference in percentage black for segregated and desegregated students were also done, with mostly inconclusive results.

Thomas Cook

Thomas Cook's assignment was to comment on the other six analyses. His comments dealt primarily with the meta-analytic work of Armor, Miller, Stephan, and Wortman because Crain and Walberg adopted different formats for their presentations. Crain, instead of conducting a meta-analysis, critically discussed some of the assumptions behind the others' efforts and concluded that he would stand by the results of his own prior meta-analytic work (Crain and Mahard 1983). Walberg devoted most of his paper to a review of factors other than desegregation that raise academic achievement, to make the point that more effective means than desegregation exist to raise the achievement of black children.

Cook commented on the most important points and assumptions made by the authors and did not comprehensively analyze any single person's work. He briefly discussed the studies examined, noting that individual panel members considered different subsets of the 19 studies to be methodologically adequate.

Cook was impressed by the degree of correspondence obtained: there were no negative estimates, the estimates for reading gain were all larger than the estimates for math, and even the largest differences represent only a month or so difference in gain. Cook found that the range of reading effect sizes in the four meta-analyses he considered in depth was from .06 to .26 standard deviation units, and the range of math effect sizes was from .00 to .08. He used the rule of thumb of associating a gain of one-tenth of a standard deviation with one month's gain in knowledge. Concerning these differences, Cook noted that the small discrepancies between the panelists in mean estimates "principally reflect differences in (1) the studies included for review; (2) the way effect sizes were computed; and (3) a preference for some types of control groups over others within a few studies." He cautioned that there is no single "right" way either to compute effect sizes or to sample studies, and suggested that it is more reasonable to expect "convergence" as a range than a point.

Cook next examined the panelists' final measures of central tendency. The panelists chose different units of analysis to report (sometimes one effect size for a whole study, sometimes several effect sizes for various comparisons within a study when, e.g., more than one grade was examined). While Cook preferred reporting both sorts of computation, if forced to choose he would opt for the study as the unit so as not to weight the results toward school districts where desegregation was tested using several grades.

While Cook presented frequency distributions of reading effect sizes for Armor, Miller, Stephen, and Wortman based on the studies they chose to analyze, he noted that not much confidence could be put in these distributions—several new cases might radically alter the estimate of central tendency. The distributions prepared using these authors' results tend to be roughly bimodal, with most cases at the zero level of effect size, but with several cases around the +.50 level of standard deviation units (this would be a gain of five months using Cook's rule of thumb of associating a gain of one-tenth of a standard deviation with one month's gain in knowledge).

Cook also prepared tables comparing the mean and median of the four authors' analyses of the reading and math scores in the 17 common core studies. These comparisons were rough because common N's were not available for all the authors. Each author had rejected at least one of the common core studies. Also, for some authors data for whole studies were used, while for others data for grade comparisons within studies were used. The mean increase in reading scores ranged from .13 (Stephan and Armor) to .26 (Wortman) standard deviations; the median (when studies rather than comparisons were used for all four authors) ranged from 0 (Armor) to .08 (Stephan).

Thus, Cook found that the measures of central tendency diverged from each other, with the means higher than the medians, and the medians higher than the modes. Cook cautioned that the central tendency analyses should not be interpreted to mean that desegregation has had no effect in most schools. He puts forward two reasons for a low level of confidence in the results:

1. The underlying distribution of mean effect sizes (however computed) for the population of school districts that have already desegregated is unknown; and
2. with so few comparisons and studies, it is difficult to have much confidence in the sample distributions; a dozen new cases could radically alter the estimates of central tendency.

If the population of effect sizes is indeed skewed, it is not clear which measure of central tendency is to be preferred. The mean represents national impact at some abstract, aggregate level, while the mode represents what should happen to the typical school.

Because the mean may be a misleading measure of central tendency, Cook next examined the reasons why some school districts are outliers. He concluded that while some districts may have benefited more from desegregation than others, it is not clear whether they are outliers for methodological reasons (such as small sample size, unstable measures, or initial group achievement differences) or substantive reasons (such as child's age at desegregation, number of years of desegregation, voluntary versus mandatory desegregation, or percentage of whites in the class).

Cook also commented more generally on the use of meta-analysis to examine the desegregation studies. Meta-analytic techniques depend heavily on the assumption that the average bias is zero with respect to threats to internal, external, or construct validity. Cook suggested that desegregation research is problematic for the meta-analyst since the need for control groups to eliminate bias ensures that few studies will meet minimal methodological criteria. The sample of studies will also tend to be highly variable, given the wide range of desegregation activities, children, grades, and times studied. Another problem with meta-analysis is that the method is not strong on explanation. Explanation of outliers requires extensive measurement of the treatment and of causal mediating processes (e.g., dominant language patterns). While various potential explanatory forces were isolated in these studies, they could not be separated out from each other.

In summary, Cook offered the following conclusions, among others, from his analysis of the panelists' work:

1. Desegregation did not cause any decrease in black achievement.

2. On the average, desegregation did not cause an increase in achievement in mathematics.

3. Desegregation increased mean reading levels. The gain reliably differed from zero and was estimated to be between two and six weeks across the studies examined.

6. Studies with the largest reading gains can be tentatively characterized along a number of methodological and substantive dimensions, including small sample sizes; the study of two or more years of desegregation; desegregated children who outperformed their segregated counterparts even before desegregation began; and desegregation that occurred earlier in time, involved younger students, was voluntary, had larger percentages of whites per school, and was associated with enrichment programs.

8. The panel examined only 19 studies of desegregation, with most panelists rejecting at least two of them on methodological grounds. When the results for each study (or each comparison) are plotted for reading or mathematics, the distributions are based on so few observations that . . . the assumption that the obtained distributions closely approximate what the underlying population distributions are [is not acceptable].

7

Comments on
the Desegregation Summary Analysis

S. James Press

Thomas Cook presented an interesting summary of several distinct meta-analyses of school desegregation studies carried out by Armor, Crain, Miller, Stephan, Walbert, and Wortman. He found positive and neutral effects of school desegregation on black student achievement. But let us examine the bases of his conclusions.

The author focused on measures of central tendency of effect sizes in the various meta-analyses. He examined means, medians, and modes of effect sizes in the analyses; and that may be all that can be done given the information available to him. Nevertheless, it is hard to find any discussion of quantitative inference being used in these meta-analyses.

The basis for quantitative inference in meta-analysis was laid by Glass, in 1976, when he suggested that we evaluate "effect size" for each study in a meta-analysis. In the following year, Gilbert, McPeek, and Mosteller (see Bunker, Barnes, and Mosteller 1977, Chapter 9) did an empirical Bayesian analysis of the benefits of various surgical techniques. There was a profusion of books on the subject of meta-analysis, from Glass et al. in 1981 to Hunter et al. 1982, Light and Pillemer 1984, Yeaton et al. 1984, and Hedges and Olkin 1985. There has also been an extensive literature

Note: These comments are based on Thomas Cook's full examination of the meta-analytic evidence, not on the summary of his paper contained in Chapter 6 of this volume.

developed in the professional journals in education, psychology, and other fields. But the author focused on the qualitative analyses used for research synthesis in the various meta-analyses he surveyed. While such qualitative judgments about the various studies are of course necessary and important, the analyses must go further to become quantitative.

Hedges and Olkin go further than their predecessors in making quantitative sense out of a set of effect sizes for a set of studies. They ask questions such as whether the number of groups was two in each study; whether the sample sizes in the experimental and control groups in each study were the same; whether the variances of the experimental and control groups in each study were the same; and whether the studies can be considered homogeneous in some sense. We are offered a variety of suggestions as to how to combine effect sizes in a set of studies so as to be able to compute a confidence interval for mean effect size, and to test hypotheses of significance for each effect size, equality of effect sizes, and significance of effect size for the set of studies. While the Hedges and Olkin book appeared after these meta-analyses were carried out, sufficient literature had appeared in the last decade to apply some of these quantitative methods. Unfortunately, we are not told whether the evaluators of each of the meta-analyses actually carried out any tests of statistical meaningfulness on each of their data sets, which I think is crucial to a meta-analysis.

There were no standard errors for average effect sizes for the meta-analyses, nor were there any determinations of standard errors. Therefore, we cannot know whether the effect sizes were statistically significant at the usual significance levels. This is typical of many meta-analyses; only effect sizes are reported, although standard errors and complete distributions should be reported.

Despite the intentions of the sponsors, individual panel members ended up considering different subsets or supersets of the 19 studies deemed methodologically adequate. Thus, there was considerable room to obtain results in line with one's own thinking by selective inclusion of studies.

In his summary analysis, Cook reported mean effect sizes for reading and math in four meta-analyses, along with his own reanalysis of Wortman's meta-analysis. (See below.) He pointed out that results differ

	Armor	Miller	Stephan	Wortman	Cook's Analysis of Wortman
Reading	.06	.16	.15	.28	.26
Math	.01	.08	.00	.23	.08

principally because of differences in, first, the studies included for review; second, the way effect sizes were computed; and, third, a preference for some types of control groups over others within a few studies.

In general, results can differ among meta-analyses because of the type of method used for computing effect size. If an analysis of covariance were carried out to determine the effect of a treatment relative to a control, different results would be obtained if transformed variables (such as logs) were used instead of raw variables; if one set of covariates were used in one study and different sets of covariance were used in other studies; if multiple outcome variables were treated jointly; and if different statistical models were used for analysis.

Sample sizes of studies are not mentioned, as if standard deviation of the control effect (in the denominator of effect size) adjusts for differences completely. This is not true. Small sample sizes often make normality a less reasonable assumption; statistics assumed to be independent often become independent only in large samples (as in some stochastic regressions); tests, confidence intervals, and other inferences are affected.

A word is in order about the four frequency distributions of reading effect sizes for studies that four of the meta-analysts chose to use. A frequency distribution is meaningful only if the data points are independent and identically distributed. But these data points are obviously not—so what does it mean? It certainly *does not represent* an underlying density function. It does contain certain useful information, however. For example, it shows that for each of these four meta-analyses, the modal number of studies (anywhere from 5 to 8) found a "zero" effect size, or close to it. In each meta-analysis some studies found negative, and some positive, effect sizes. They are surely not all significant. Moreover, the studies were all different from one another, so the small differences found might be accounted for by other variables in the studies that were not held fixed.

The summary analysis contains many comparisons of means, medians, and modes of the different meta-analyses. Perhaps the effort at comparison is misplaced. We should be concerned with the ways in which the studies differed from one another, as well as with how homogeneous they were. Looking at effect sizes can be a dangerous and deceptive way to compare studies. We could ask about the backgrounds of the blacks and the whites in each of the studies. Were they all upper-middle-class whites and lower-class blacks, or were they lower-middle-class whites and lower-middle-class blacks, or what? What were the backgrounds of the teachers? In what type of neighborhood were the schools located? What were the grade levels of the desegregated children? How did the desegregation take place? By busing black kids in (and how far did they have to come)? Was desegregation voluntary or mandatory? And so on. Effect size alone does not capture what is happening in such a complex situation. The 19 studies used were surely not homogeneous in all of the variables just mentioned. Often this is where most of the action is, or ought to be, in a meta-analysis.

A meta-analysis should at minimum provide a table showing, for each study, the sample sizes of the experimental and control groups, the effect size of each study, and the value of each of the fundamental background variables of the study (such as, in the case of the school desegregation issue, large school district versus small, urban versus rural, socioeconomic backgrounds of the groups involved, etc.). If possible, standard errors in each treatment group in each study should be included as well.

Cook's final conclusion is worth repeating:

> The panel examined only 19 studies of desegregation, with most panelists rejecting at least two of them on methodological grounds. When the results for each study (or each comparison) are plotted for reading or mathematics, the distributions are based on so few observations that I could not accept the assumption that the obtained distributions closely approximate what the underlying population distributions are. Because of the small samples and apparently nonnormal distributions, little confidence should be placed in any of the mean results presented earlier. I have little confidence that we know much about how desegregation affects reading "on the average" and, across the few studies examined, I find the variability in effect sizes more striking and less well understood than any measure of central tendency.

Cook points out that "little confidence should be placed in any of the mean results present." I couldn't agree more. But this really means that we have learned very little from the meta-analyses about whether school desegregation has affected the academic achievement of black children.

8

On the Social Psychology
of Using Research Reviews

Harris M. Cooper

The objective of this research was to examine naturalistically how literature reviews are carried out and how they are evaluated by interested
readers. Obviously, the convening of NIE's panel on desegregation and
black achievement provided a rare opportunity for studying the process of
research synthesis. Six expert researchers were asked to draw conclusions
about a single hypothesis using a nearly common set of studies. Both the
Desegregation Studies Team and the panelists agreed to take part in my
research. It is the outcome of this research that will be reported in this
paper.

Because of the structure of the panel's assignment, certain aspects of
the reviewing process could be examined as part of the naturalistic study.
First, each panelist came to the assignment with extensive knowledge of
the topic. Nearly all panel members had previously written reviews of
desegregation research and had taken part in analysis of primary
desegregation data. Therefore, the sources of the experts' predispositions
toward the topic could be studied.

Note: The full-length version of this paper appears in Feldman (1986). The research was
supported by National Institute of Education grant no. NIE-G-82-0022, though the opinions
expressed do not necessarily reflect those of NIE. The author wishes to thank Richard Petty,
Lee Ross, and Lee Shulman for comments on an earlier draft, and Spencer Ward for help
throughout the research project.

Second, the assignment of the panel included a phase in which the quality of desegregation research was to be examined. This allowed for an assessment of the experts' beliefs concerning how a study's design affected its informational utility.

Third, it was possible to compare the panelists' prior beliefs about desegregation with their beliefs at the assignment's conclusion. An obvious question to ask was: Did the panel experience move the participants toward more positive or negative conclusions concerning the effects of desegregation? Also, did the panel experience enhance or diminish participants' confidence in their conclusions? And, perhaps most important, did the panel experience create greater consensus or dispersion among the opinions of participants?

Fourth, the written products of panel members could be examined. The six written reviews could be read by an interested audience and their reactions to the papers assessed.

Data Collection

Data collection for the first part of this study was accomplished through two telephone interviews with each panelist. The first interview occurred after the panelists met initially but before actual work on their papers began. This phone interview included closed-ended quantitative scale questions, open-ended questions, and nondirective requests for general observations.

Each participant was asked what his predisposition was concerning the research on desegregation—did it enhance, have no effect on, or diminish black achievement, or could no conclusion be drawn? Participants were also asked how confident they were that their interpretation was correct; and in the event that they believed there was a desegregation effect, participants described its magnitude on a scale from "very small" to "very large." The panelists next listed those variables that they felt might moderate the effect of desegregation. For instance, among the moderators offered were the child's age at desegregation, curriculum factors, and staff attitudes, to name a few.

In the final part of the structured interview, participants rank ordered six aspects of experimental design with regard to their impact on the "informational utility" of a desegregation study. The six aspects of experimental design included (1) the definition of desegregation employed in the study, (2) the adequacy of the control group, (3) the validity of the achievement measure, (4) the representativeness of the sample, (5) the representativeness of the environmental conditions surrounding the test, and (6) the statistical analysis. For instance, if a participant ranked the adequacy of the control group first, it meant that he felt this aspect of the research design had the greatest impact, either positive or negative, on the value of a study's results.

In the second telephone interview, the first three questions were repeated, thus allowing assessments of change in the panelists' conclusions, confidence in conclusions, and estimates of effect size magnitude. Participants were also asked about their general political beliefs and, in open-ended questions, about their reactions to the panel experience.

In the second phase of the study, the first drafts of the panelists' written papers were read by 14 post-master's graduate students in psychology and education. The graduate readers took part in interviews before and after reading the first drafts that paralleled the interviews with the participants. The readers also completed a separate questionnaire concerning each first draft on which they made judgments about the reviewer's positions and the quality of the paper.

Results: Reviewer Interviews

The first questions of interest involved the sources of the reviewers' predispositions. These impressions were gleaned primarily from the open-ended and nondirective responses of panelists during the phone interviews.

The most important source of predispositions for panelists was the outcome of their own primary research. Hands-on experience with primary desegregation data appeared to form a central set of expectations for the results of any research on the same topic. Seeing—or in this case collecting and analyzing data—is believing. Panelists with primary research experience in the area appeared to give greatest, and perhaps disproportionate, weight to the outcomes of their own studies.

Because the present study was naturalistic and the data on the panelists' initial dispositions were retrospective, the assertion that outcomes of personal primary research *caused* dispositions is clearly speculative. We must also entertain the notion that initial dispositions led panelists to structure their primary research designs and analyses in a manner that made supportive results highly likely. However, two of the panelists explicitly stated that their beliefs about desegregation effects changed in response to data collection. Probably the most defensible assertion is that both processes exist in nature (i.e., primary research influences beliefs and beliefs influence research design and analysis).

A second source of predisposition was the disciplinary affiliation of the reviewer. Disciplinary affiliations appeared to be most important with regard to the selection of mediators of the desegregation effect. Educators searched mainly for curriculum variables as mediators of the relation, psychologists offered mainly intervening variables associated with interpersonal interaction, and sociologists invoked mainly social structure mediators.

Finally, predispositions appeared to arise from the broader political and social belief systems of the panelists. While the present study could note only the consistency, but not causal interrelations, of general belief systems and specific interpretations of empirical data, cognitive consistency theories suggest that the pressures toward congruence will work to keep general and specific beliefs consonant with one another (Abelson et al. 1968).

The next set of questions dealt with the impact of research design on the utility of a study's results. Table 8.1 presents the panelists' rankings. The rankings revealed general agreement that design factors associated with internal validity most influence a study's utility.

The final set of reviewer data involves the changes in panelists' attitudes toward desegregation. Before the panel began, three participants expressed a belief that desegregation had positive effects and none changed his mind. Two of the three panelists who believed desegregation

Table 8.1   Rankings of Research Design Factors' Impact on the Utility of a Study's Results

	Panelists						
	A	B	C	D	E	F	$\bar{x}$
Experimental Manipulation (Definition of Desegregation)	1	1	3	2	1	2	1.6
Experimental Comparison (Adequacy of Control Group)	3	2	2	1	2	1	1.8
Outcome Measure (Measurement of Achievement)	2	6	1	3	4	6	3.6
Population Generality	5	5	4	4	5	5	4.6
Ecological Generality	5	3	5	6	3	4	4.3
Statistical Analysis	4	4	6	5	6	2	4.5

Note : Rank of 1 means factor was judged to have the most impact. The average correlation between rankings was $\bar{r} = +.47$, ranging from $r = -.29$ to $+.77$

sometimes had no effect and sometimes had positive effects experienced no general attitude change. One participant changed his opinion from this equivocal position to the position that no conclusion could be drawn, primarily because of an enhanced appreciation of the complexity of the issue.

With regard to panelists' confidence in their conclusions, three participants found that the experience enhanced confidence in their beliefs. For two participants, this change was dramatic. On a scale from zero (not confident at all) to 10 (totally confident), one moved from 2 to 6 and the other from 3 to 9. The third panelist showing enhanced confidence moved from 7 to 9. One participant lost a small, but perceptible, amount of confidence in his conclusion, moving from 9 to 7 on the scale. Two participants reported no change in confidence level, remaining at 7 and 8 on the scale.

Next, the panelists estimated the magnitude of the desegregation effect. Three panelists revised upward their estimates of magnitude, moving from "very small" to "small," from "small to moderate" to "moderate," and from "moderate" to "moderate to large." One panelist's estimate that the effect was "very small to small" did not change and two participants, who were reluctant to estimate an effect magnitude before the panel began, estimated the effect as between "very small" and "small" when their work was done. These results lead to a conclusion that there was some movement toward more positive impressions of the effect of desegregation. However, it is important to point out that a reading of the panelists' papers compared with their earlier writings generally gives the opposite impression—that is, desegregation seems to have less of an impact in the newer works. This assessment is supported by the review reader data to be discussed shortly.

The estimates of effect also give some clues about whether the panel experience created consensus or dispersion of opinion. Clearly, there was as much disagreement among participants when the panel concluded as when it began. After the experience, however, some panelists more firmly held their beliefs. Some mitigating circumstances may offer consolation. First, the issue of desegregation is an exceptionally emotional one involving moral and political stances as well as the scientific perspective. Other issues may prove more amenable to efforts at consensus-building through research synthesis and the panel format. Second, the members of the panel brought an unusually large degree of prior experience to their task. Their initial positions were well thought-out, complex integrations of knowledge acquired over years of study. Any expectation of dramatic attitude change would have been unrealistic and contrary to research that indicates prior knowledge and experience with an issue makes attitude change more difficult (e.g., Wood 1982).

Conclusion: Reviewer Interviews

In sum, hours of conversation with the panelists revealed that they probably hold disparate views on many social issues—in fact, they were chosen for participation based partly on their different perspectives. My impression was that the empirical data did create convergence in their thinking on the effects of desegregation though most of this occurred before the panel was convened, when the panelists' attitudes were more malleable. I think the panelists' positions would have been even more diverse had no data or prior synthesis activity taken place.

Finally, a potentially encouraging outcome of the panel concerns something that did *not* happen. Recent experimental evidence indicates that when people with conflicting beliefs are exposed to a set of studies containing conflicting results, attitudes can become even more polarized (Lord, Ross, and Lepper 1979). Other research indicates that further thought about an issue, even in the absence of new information, leads to polarization in the direction of one's initial tendency (Tesser 1978). There is little evidence that such attitude polarization occurred among the panelists.

Results: Reader Reactions

Measures of Change

The second phase of this study involved obtaining reader reactions to the six reviews. First, the 14 graduate student readers were interviewed before reading the reviews. Several questions concerned the readers' educational and topical background and general political beliefs. Four questions were identical to the repeated measurements obtained from the panelists and were meant to gauge the readers' beliefs about the effectiveness and moderators of desegregation and their confidence in these judgments. Also similar to the panelists', these four questions were readministered after all six reviews had been read. The change in responses to these questions will be examined first.

The graduate readers' general beliefs about desegregation's effectiveness changed little as a function of reading the papers. In contrast, their

Table 8.2   Graduate Reader Beliefs About Desegregation Before and After Reading the Reviews

Question	Before	After
What is the size of the desegregation effect?	4.41	2.58
	(2.57)	(1.38)
How confident are you that your belief is accurate?	6.00	7.00
	(1.92)	(1.36)
What variables or conditions mediate the effect? (number mentioned)	6.34	8.89
	(3.45)	(5.70)

Note: Standard deviations are in parentheses.

beliefs about desegregation as measured by three other indices changed significantly. Table 8.2 presents the readers' estimated effect size, confidence in beliefs, and number of suggested mediators of the effect.

In general, the readers' perception of the positive effect of desegregation dropped precipitously after reading the reviews ($t = -3.97$ on 12 degrees of freedom, $p < .004$). Before reading the reviews, the average effect size estimate was about "moderate," whereas afterward it was less than "small." Eight of 10 readers who estimated the effect size both times revised their estimates downward.

The graduate students' average level of confidence in their beliefs before reading the papers was identical to the reviewers' initial confidence levels (6.00). This would indicate that subjective confidence in beliefs about an empirical research area is not directly related (if at all) to objective expertise on the topic. However, after reading the papers, the students' confidence level tended to be higher, but the level did not jump as much as did the reviewers' confidence.

Finally, reading the reviews led graduate students to cite more moderators of the effect of desegregation than they initially proposed, though statistically the effect only approached significance ($t = -2.06$ on 13 degrees of freedom, $p < .07$). While about 6.5 moderators were mentioned on average before reading the papers, almost 9 were mentioned after reading the papers. Nine readers enhanced the complexity of their beliefs about desegregation's effect.

Table 8.3 lists the 11 broad categories into which mediators were placed for statistical analysis, reduced from 60 separate categories.

Table 8.4 presents an analysis of these categories. First, it should be noted that both before and after reading the reviews, the graduate students cited the attitudes of those involved in the desegregation effort as the most important influence on its effect.

Table 8.3   Coding Frame for Moderators of Desegregation Effects

Category	
1. Attitudes (support)	Of parents, white, black; of students, white, black; of teachers; of school administration; of politicians; of business; of clergy
2. Student Background	Parent education; family relations; family size; social class, blacks, whites; achievement/ability, blacks, whites; age; self concept/personality
3. Community Background	Area of country; urban vs. rural; size; historical conditions; media presentation
4. School Characteristics	Size; location; quality (curriculum)
5. Classroom Characteristics	Size (teacher/pupil ratio; number of teachers); seating (interaction) patterns; open vs. traditional
6. Teacher Characteristics	Ability; labeling (expectation) effects; training for desegregation; race
7. Achievement Definition	Measurement; subject matter; interpretation of measurement
8. Desegregation Definition	Voluntary vs. forced; community involvement in implementation; need (distance) for busing; black/white ratio; length of implementation; who gets bused
9. Money (expenditures)	Resources for teachers; other support services (personnel)
10. Change of School Problems (confusion)	Preparation of students
11. Other	

The two types of mediators that evidenced significant increases in citation after reading the reviews were the two categories involving how achievement was defined and how desegregation was accomplished.

The next analysis involved relating the readers' backgrounds to their beliefs about desegregation before and after reading the reviews. These results are displayed in Table 8.5, which contains nine variables. The variable "topic familiarity" is a composite of the graduate students' year in graduate school and their responses to the questions, How familiar are you with desegregation research? and How many scholarly articles related to desegregation have you read?

Table 8.4   Change in the Number of Moderators Mentioned by Readers in Eleven Categories

Category	Prior	Post	t-value	p-value
1. Attitudes	1.71	1.86		
2. Student Background	1.11	1.39		
3. Community Background	0.86	0.54		
4. School Characteristics	0.32	0.38		
5. Classroom Characteristics	0.11	0.25		
6. Teacher Characteristics	0.46	0.86		
7. Achievement Definition	0.14	0.79	3.23	.007
8. Desegregation Definition	0.96	1.75	2.27	.040
9. Money	0.46	0.25		
10. Change of School Problems	0.07	0.25	2.11	.060
11. Other	0.14	0.57		

The tests have very poor statistical power, and in some instances the correlations do not reach traditional levels of significance but are large enough to warrant attention in future studies.

The strongest relationships were between political beliefs and the size of the desegregation effect estimated after reading the papers. Specifically, the correlation of $r = .39$ indicates that more liberal readers estimated larger effects after reading the reviews. Before reading the reviews, the relation between political beliefs and effect size was near zero ($r = .01$). Although both of these figures are nonsignificant, the direction of change in the relation is revealing. Something like a polarization effect appears to have occurred, in that the readers' political beliefs may have guided their processing and interpretation of the data.

The research expertise of the readers was negatively related to their effect size estimates ($r = -.45$) and positively related to the number of mediators they cited ($r = +.54$) after reading the reviews. Thus, it appears that graduate students with more research experience came to see a more equivocal and complex situation as a function of the information input. This is probably what we would expect one of the implications of research expertise to be.

Finally, familiarity with the topic of desegregation was positively related to the graduate students' confidence in their beliefs both before ($r = .48$) and after ($r = .38$) reading the reviews, but the relation was somewhat stronger at the first measurement. Possibly, the mitigated effect is a function of those graduate students who were unfamiliar with the topic showing increased confidence in their beliefs after reading the six reviews. Topic familiarity was also negatively related to effect size estimates

Table 8.5 Relations Between Reader's Background and Prior and Post Beliefs About Desegregation

	Topic Familiarity	Research Expertise	Political Beliefs	Prior Effect Size	Prior Confidence	Prior Moderators	Post Effect Size	Post Confidence	Post Moderators
Topic Familiarity	—	-.04	-.02	-.47*	.48*	-.30	.35	.38*	-.24
Research Expertise		—	.05	-.01	-.06	.10	-.45*	.00	.54*
Political Beliefs			—	.01	.08	-.36	.39	-.35	.15
Prior Effect Size				—	.12	.51*	.01	-.53*	.07
Prior Confidence					—	.06	.48*	.09	-.38
Prior Moderators						—	-.12	-.19	.58*
Post Effect Size							—	-.22	-.38
Post Confidence								—	-.26
Post Moderators									—

Notes: All tests are based on between 9 and 13 degrees of freedom. More liberal beliefs were given higher numerical values. Effect sizes were coded as negative values if the reader thought desegregation had negative effects.

* .15 > p > .05

before reading the reviews ($r = -.47$). This indicates that those readers least familiar with desegregation research had the higher expectations for desegregation's effect.

Evaluations of Individual Reviews

The next set of analyses involved the graduate readers' evaluations of the individual reviews. The second set of questions asked the reader to make seven evaluative judgments about the review. Readers also gave an overall judgment of the review's quality and persuasiveness. Finally, readers were asked to make open-ended comments concerning their evaluation of the reviews.

The informal content analysis of the open-ended comments offered by readers at the bottom of each evaluation sheet showed that the readers most often mentioned that a paper was either well or poorly organized. Second most frequently mentioned was writing style, in particular the author's ability or inability to keep the interest of the reader. Third was how well or poorly focused the paper was on the topic of interest. Fourth was how well or poorly the reviewers used citations to substantiate any claims made in their papers. Next was attention or inattention to variable definitions and to mediating influences. Also mentioned were how well or poorly the reviewer described the methods of the individual desegregation studies and the methods of the review itself. Finally, the manuscript preparation, typically involving negative comments about typos or missing tables, was also mentioned by several of the readers.

To examine the responses to the closed-ended parts of the questionnaires, a factor analysis was first performed on five judgments concerning specific qualities of the reviews. The factor analyses were performed for each review separately. They revealed that a single quality factor probably underlaid all five judgments. Therefore, the composite measure of quality based on the five questions was used in all subsequent analyses rather than the single measure.

The final analysis entailed an examination of the covariation between readers' evaluations of the quality and persuasiveness of a review and their perceptions of the reviewers' beliefs. To carry out this analysis, the readers' responses to the closed-ended items on the individual review questionnaires were correlated with one another as well as with several of the reviewers' answers to questions given during the telephone interviews. These correlations were computed for each reader separately.

Of foremost interest are those perceptions of reviews that correlated with judgments of quality and persuasiveness. It was found that the quality of reviews was not related to the substantive position of the reviewer, as indicated by the perceived effect size or number of mediators offered. We must bear in mind, however, that the samples of both panelists and readers were all on the same side of the issue (i.e., no one felt that desegregation had negative effects). Had a wider range of beliefs been represented, a relation between judged quality and substantive position might have emerged. Instead, reviews judged to be of high quality were those in which the readers felt the most confidence, regardless of position ($\bar{z} = .42$, $p < .02$).

The persuasiveness of a review was positively correlated with its quality ($\bar{z} = 1.05$, $p < .0001$), with the reader's confidence in its interpretation ($\bar{z} = .66$, $p < .001$) and with the number of mediators the reader thought it mentioned ($\bar{z} = .32$, $p < .05$). This last relation, indicating that more persuasive reviews were those seen as mentioning more mediators, is of special interest because it indicates a relation between persuasiveness and complexity.

To summarize the results of the second phase of this study, the graduate readers showed greater flexibility in their attitudes than the reviewers, undoubtedly owing to differences in the two groups' initial states of knowledge. In general, readers' beliefs became more congruent with the reviewers' beliefs and more complex as a function of reading the papers. What was not examined, however, is whether under natural circumstances readers would choose to expose themselves to the variety of opinions contained in these papers or would seek out only papers that would confirm or bolster their initial positions.

The analysis of readers' backgrounds found little initial bias due to political beliefs but some indication that increased knowledge of the topic also led to increased congruence between general political beliefs and beliefs about desegregation.

Conclusions

The basic principles of attitude change appear to apply to the process of empirical knowledge synthesis. Rather than being an activity of a qualitatively different order, the attitude-relevant aspects of research reviewing, as exemplified by NIE's panel, are probably best understood by noting the special characteristics of the people and circumstances involved and by applying established principles to this unique situation.

First, the desegregation panelists began their synthesis task with a great deal of prior knowledge. This will lessen the possibility of change in basic beliefs because the synthesizer will encounter few arguments that are truly novel and will have a cognitive schema with which to integrate or counterargue information that is new.

Readers of research reviews who bring less tenacious beliefs to the topic area, such as the graduate students in this study, are more likely to experience attitude change and enhanced complexity of beliefs. The amount and direction of this change apparently will be a function not only of the reviewer's conclusions and treatment of the relevant material but also of the effectiveness of the reviewer's presentation, in particular the organization and style of the manuscript.

The empirical character of research syntheses is also critical to understanding related attitude change. The diversity of results often found in a set of empirical studies will inhibit attitude change in its consumers. If an initial opinion is minimally reasonable, an examiner of the related research will find some studies that confirm the initial belief.

Finally, even when a certain degree of consensus is reached on the objective outcome of a set of studies, in this case the size of the desegregation effect, the varying perspectives of reviewers and readers can still create discrepancies in the subjective utilities that are used to interpret the findings. Thus, while a great deal of agreement might be reached on the observation that an eight-ounce glass contains four ounces of water, there can still be much disagreement about whether the glass is half empty or half full.

In sum, the convening of NIE's panel on desegregation and black achievement proved to be an exciting natural laboratory for the study of knowledge synthesis. It would serve the purposes of both the social science community and the general public if efforts of this sort were continued in the future.

9

Moving Beyond Meta-Analysis

Harris M. Cooper

In this chapter I would like to expand the remarks I made in "On the Social Psychology of Using Research Reviews: The Case of Desegregation and Black Achievement" in three directions. To begin, I would like to examine the question of how quantitative estimates of effect size are given substantive meaning.

Giving Substantive Meaning to Effect Sizes

In Thomas Cook's summary (1984) of the meta-analyst's findings, he concluded that the estimates of the magnitude of the desegregation effect varied within a remarkably small range. His calculations revealed that all panelists agreed that desegregation did not cause a decrease in black achievement and that the mean gain in achievement ranged from 0 to .08 standard deviation units for math skills and from .06 to .16 for reading skills. Cook was led to comment, "Speaking personally, I am impressed by the degree of correspondence between the panelists when only the 19 core studies are considered."

In my study, I asked the panelists to estimate the magnitude of the desegregation effect on the more abstract and qualitative scale of largeness, ranging from "very small" to "very large." As might be expected, the results of this exercise revealed considerably less consensus than was found among the quantitative estimates. Three panelists interpreted the magnitude of the effect as being "very small to small," one saw it as "small," one as "moderate," one as "moderate to large."

Obviously, when the description of an effect moves away from being purely quantitative, there will be added opportunity for variance in characterization. Meta-analysts have been conscientious in attempting to ensure that our quantitative estimates of effect sizes are based on explicit and well-founded assumptions and are as mathematically precise as they can be. Remarkably little attention has been paid, however, to the next step: namely, placing the quantitative estimate in a meaningful context for substantive interpretation.

Jacob Cohen (1988) attempted to help with interpretation by proposing effect size values "to serve as operational definitions of the qualitative adjectives 'small,' 'medium,' and 'large.'" While Cohen was careful to stress that his conventions were to be used as a last resort, many meta-analysts have adopted his benchmarks without assessing their applicability to the particular circumstance.

Cohen recognized that judgments of "largeness" and "smallness" require a comparison between the item under consideration and some contrasting element. Therefore, in operationally defining these adjectives, he compared different magnitudes of effect "with a subjective average of effect sizes such as are encountered in the behavioral sciences" (p. 13). Thus, a small effect was defined as $d = .2$, which Cohen said was representative of personality, social, and clinical psychology research. Large effects of $d = .8$ were more likely to be found in sociology, economics, and experimental and physiological psychology.

As a social psychologist, then, I might interpret an effect size of $d = .3$ as small *compared to other behavioral sciences* but also as above average *compared to other social psychological effects*. At the time Cohen offered his guidelines, holding an effect size in a specialized topic area up against a criterion as broad as "all behavioral science" might have been the best contrasting element available. Estimates of average effect sizes for disciplines, subdisciplines, topic areas, or even single variables were difficult if not impossible to find. Today, thanks to meta-analysis, these calculations are plentiful. Therefore, it is inexcusable, or at best insufficient, to rely on an aid to interpretation as general as Cohen's.

Returning to the NIE panel, the interpretation of the desegregation effect is most meaningful when it is compared to other interventions which might, intentionally or as a side effect, enhance achievement. I suspect that a great amount of the variance in interpretation by panelists was a function of their having chosen different contrasting treatments for comparison. For instance, Walberg (1984) made his alternate treatment choices explicit. He spent the majority of his paper describing the results of dozens of meta-analyses involving various teaching strategies, class structures, and classroom and home interventions. He judged that many inexpensive and noncontroversial treatments revealed effect sizes above $d = .3$. Walberg concluded that, placed in this context, "desegregation does not appear to be promising in the size or consistency of its effect on learning of black students" (p. 187). While others may dispute Walberg's methods and/or his choice criteria, he did frame the question in a manner that allows meaningful debate.

In sum, meta-analysts can add precision and interpretability to their work by contrasting their obtained effect sizes with other magnitudes of effect that share similar conceptual or operational variables.

Consumers of meta-analyses should require that producers make multiple comparisons of average effects and that the nature and source of the contrasting data be explicitly described. Calling an effect size small or large without answering the question, "Compared to what?" is vacuous. Making a similar assessment based solely on Cohen's benchmarks places an effect size in such broad context that little gain in substantive interpretation is achieved.

Evaluating the Quality of Reviews

A second intriguing result of my study involved the readers' evaluations of the papers. In one set of analyses, open-ended comments offered by readers were subjected to an informal content analysis to discover what dimensions they employed when evaluating the quality of the reviews. These results indicated that a quality meta-analysis only begins with sound quantitative methodology. Now I want to call your attention to two efforts aimed at the complex question of how we can systematize the assessment of nonquantitative aspects of literature reviews.

Strike and Posner (1983) proposed that a good synthesis, whether the synthesis was of empirical research or of abstract ideas, required both intellectual quality and utility. First, according to Strike and Posner, a quality synthesis should clarify and resolve, rather than obscure, inconsistencies between the materials being synthesized. As we know, one of the benefits of meta-analysis is that its users are less likely to label a literature as inconsistent or in need of further replication (Cooper and Rosenthal 1980). Instead, the use of statistics permits reviewers to see patterns that are often obscured by traditional narrative synthesis procedures.

A second criterion is that the synthesis should result in a progressive problem shift, involving greater explanatory power, expanded scope of application, and increased capacity to pursue unsolved problems. Obviously, while meta-analysis may give a reviewer a leg up on pursuing these goals, creating a progressive problem shift primarily is a function of how the reviewer uses the results once they have been obtained.

Third, Strike and Posner said that a good synthesis demonstrates consistency, parsimony, and elegance. These criteria sound remarkably similar to those mentioned by the readers of the desegregation reviews. The readers also intuitively employed Strike and Posner's final quality assessment: utility. A useful synthesis is one that answers the question asked. It should leave readers with the sense that they got what they came for.

In sum then, the criteria for good literature reviewing range from the lofty pursuits of resolving conflict and stimulating progressive problem shifts to the more mundane concerns of presenting material effectively enough to get one's point across. Hard and fast rules for how these ideals can be accomplished will be difficult to come by. However, within the friendly confines of integrative research reviews, more progress toward applicable standards for quality judgments can be made. Establishing some of these standards is what I had in mind when I conceptualized the research review as a data gathering exercise (Cooper 1982, 1989). Table 9.1 displays this conceptualization. Similar to primary research, a research review involves problem formulation, data collection, data evaluation, analysis and interpretation, and public presentation. Each stage offers the reviewer choices concerning how to proceed. Different choices engender different potential threats to the validity of the outcome. Explicit and systematic guidelines for assessing many aspects of integrative research syntheses are possible and these rules can extend beyond the analysis phase of reviews.

Putting Integrative Research Reviews in a Broader Context

My first two points have asked that we expand our thinking concerning what research synthesizers can do in a systematic and explicit manner. Rather than concentrate strictly on more precise quantitative estimates of effect sizes, precision should also be added to the substantive interpretation of effects. Rather than focus only on analysis and interpretation in meta-analysis, we should pay equal, if not greater, attention to the other decision points in research reviewing. I would like to go yet a step further and suggest that we attend not only to integrative research reviews, but to other forms of literature integration as well.

Some of my recent efforts have centered on an attempt to construct a taxonomy for classifying reviews according to their major characteristics (Cooper 1988). Because the literature on literature reviewing hardly forms the basis for a review itself, the prior works on this topic were supplemented in two ways. First, in-depth, unstructured interviews were conducted with 14 scholars in diverse fields of education and psychology who were performing literature reviews. The interviews occurred at several points during the reviewing process and touched on all aspects of the task. Second, based on the interviews and on input from others involved in knowledge synthesis activities, a structured questionnaire was developed and completed by 68 scholars who had recently published reviews of research literatures (Cooper 1986).

The interviews and questionnaires led me to suggest six characteristics that distinguish integrative reviews from one another. These are listed in Table 9.2, and I will briefly define them here (see Cooper 1988 for details).

The *focus* of a review concerns the material that is of central interest to the reviewer. In practice, it is rare for a review to have only a single focus. *Goals* concern what the author hopes to accomplish. The most obvious goals involve some type of integration of the literature. The *perspective* a reviewer employs can range from an attempt to present the literature in a fashion that most accurately reflects the intent of the authors of the original works (or to be an "honest broker") to an attempt to muster the literature so that it supports an a priori set of contentions. *Coverage* concerns the extent to which the reviewer attempts to find and include relevant works in the paper. *Organization* involves how the material is arranged for presentation, and *audience* concerns the intended readership of the review.

Having defined the six characteristics of reviews, an obvious question to ask is: How often do different types of reviews appear in the literature? In order to get some data on this question, a survey was undertaken of recent literature review authors. The sample for the survey was generated by a computer search of ERIC and *PsychInfo* in which all documents assigned the descriptor "literature review" that had been published during 1984 and were online by December 4, 1984, were retrieved. Documents were excluded if the abstract indicated that they were primarily annotated bibliographies or project reports.

Questionnaires were then sent to a random selection of 130 authors, and 108 (77 percent) responded. The questionnaire described the taxonomy and asked the author to rank order within each characteristic those categories that applied to the review.

Table 9.1   Integrative Review Conceptualized as a Research Project

Stage Characteristics	Stage of Research	
	Problem Formulation	Data Collection
Research Question Asked	What evidence should be included in the review?	What procedures should be used to find relevant evidence?
Primary Function in Review	Constructing definitions that distinguish relevant from irrelevant studies.	Determining which sources of potentially relevant studies to examine.
Procedural Differences That Create Variation in Review Conclusions	1. Differences in included operational definitions. 2. Differences in operational detail.	Differences in the research contained in sources of information.
Sources of Potential Invalidity in Review Conclusions	1. Narrow concepts might make review conclusions less definitive and robust. 2. Superficial operational detail might obscure interacting variables.	1. Accessed studies might be qualitatively different from the target population of studies. 2. People sampled in accessible studies might be different from target population of people.

Source: Cooper (1982).

In general, the authors voiced little difficulty with placing their reviews into the categories. An "other" category that was supplied for authors who felt that the provided categories were inappropriate was used less than 6 percent of the time. Perhaps the best testimony for the taxonomy's robustness came from a group of ten reviews abstracted in ERIC that had appeared in a journal called *Analytic Chemistry.* It was not clear whether these papers should be included in the sample given their somewhat exotic topics, such as "dynamic electrochemistry" and "atomic absorption, atomic florescence, and flame emission spectronomy." The decision was made to include the papers and only one author returned the questionnaire saying his reply would be inappropriate. The other nine chemistry authors returned the completed questionnaire without comment.

Responses to the survey are presented in Table 9.2. The results revealed that about half of all reviews focused primarily on research outcomes,

	Stage of Research	
Data Evaluation	Analysis and Interpretation	Public Presentation
What retrieved evidence should be included in the review?	What procedures should be used to make inferences about the literature as a whole?	What information should be included in the review report?
Applying criteria to separate "valid" from "invalid" studies.	Synthesizing valid retrieved studies.	Applying editorial criteria to separate important from unimportant information.
1. Differences in quality criteria. 2. Differences in the influence of nonquality criteria.	Differences in rules of inference.	Differences in guidelines for editorial judgment.
1. Nonquality factors might cause improper weighing of study information. 2. Omissions in study reports might make conclusions unreliable.	1. Rules for distinguishing patterns from noise might be inappropriate. 2. Review-based evidence might be used to infer causality.	1. Omission of review procedures might make conclusions irreproducible. 2. Omission of review findings and study procedures might make conclusions obsolete

and three in four paid some attention to empirical results. One in five focused on practical application, and an equal number focused on theory. Only one in ten took as its primary focus attention to research methods.

The most frequent goal of a review was to critically analyze the literature, with two in five authors saying that this was their primary objective. About one in four cited formulating general statements and identifying central issues as a major aim and about one in ten cited resolving conflicts or bridging gaps between theories or ideas as a paramount interest.

The perspective category was dominated by authors who said that they took a neutral view of the literature and the organization of most reviews was conceptual. About two of every three reviewers said that they based their conclusions on all the relevant material and about half of these said that all the material was cited in their paper. About one reviewer in five said that he used a representative coverage strategy and one in ten, a central or pivotal strategy.

Table 9.2 Authors' Ranking of Various Categories to Describe Their Reviews

Characteristic	Categories	Primary	Secondary	Omitted
		Percentage of Authors Using as Descriptor		
Focus	Research outcomes	56%	12%	25%
	Research methods	9	17	47
	Theories	19	23	32
	Practices or applications	22	23	26
Goal	Integration			
	(a) Generalization	23	19	35
	(b) Conflict resolution	7	11	59
	(c) Linguistic bridge-building	8	6	68
	Criticism	42	16	24
	Identification of central issues	24	21	34
Perspective	Neutral representation	81	4	14
	Espousal of position	18	18	65
Coverage	Exhaustive	37	2	52
	Exhaustive with representative citation	21	4	70
	Exhaustive with central citation	14	7	75
	Representative	19	6	70
	Central or pivotal	7	6	78
Organization	Historical	7	9	77
	Conceptual	76	6	17
	Methodological	15	13	70
Audience	Specialized scholars	39	26	28
	General scholars	34	23	27
	Practitioners	31	18	28
	Policymakers	4	5	72
	General public	2	5	77

About a third of the papers were directed toward specialized scholars, a third toward general scholars, and a third toward practitioners. Policymakers and the general public were rarely the audience of reviews catalogued by the two abstracting services.

For this discussion, it would be informative to determine the percentage of reviews that might be considered candidates for meta-analysis. About one reviewer in six (17.6 percent) claimed that his or her paper primarily focused on research outcomes and had the goal of formulating general statements from multiple specific instances. These papers might be considered meta-analysis candidates. If we add the requirement that the author intended to be neutral in perspective and to base conclusions on exhaustive literature coverage, then the number of meta-analyses was one in eight (13 percent).

Through the use of such taxonomies, we can begin asking more explicit questions about the internal consistency and utility of literature reviews in general, not just meta-analyses. Obviously, these will still be highly subjective tasks. However, there would be progress simply in having a common, structured scheme for discussing these issues and in insisting that authors make their assumptions, aims, and procedures clear. Requiring this minimal standard of explicitness and systematization of all knowledge synthesizers at least allows ensuing debate to occur within a shared framework.

10

An Assessment from the Policy Perspective

David S. Cordray

Introduction

Although the statistical foundations for meta-analysis can be traced back at least 50 years, the idea of quantitatively combining the results of independent studies is relatively new within the social and behavioral sciences. Like many new ideas, it has been the focus of much debate. Shortly after Glass (1976) outlined the general tactics and conditions for summarizing evidence across studies, a series of critiques appeared in the literature. For some critics, meta-analysis was viewed as an unsatisfactory approach to understanding the cumulative effects of interventions; Eysenck (1978) went as far as characterizing it as an exercise in "megasilliness." Others have applauded Glass' work as one of the most significant contributions in recent times. After several rounds of claims and counterclaims, the research community appears to have moved from skepticism to cautious acceptance—in principle—of meta-analysis as a viable methodological strategy.

Given that the applicability of meta-analysis within a policy context has been less well explored, the Committee on National Statistics has initiated a systematic assessment of the strengths and weaknesses of current practices, with special attention directed at its relevance to policy questions. As part of this effort, I have been asked to comment on a recent meta-analysis sponsored by the National Institute of Education (NIE).

Note: The opinions expressed in this paper do not reflect official policy of the U.S. General Accounting Office.

This study focused on the effects of desegregation on the achievement of black students. In my comments, I have chosen to emphasize changes in practices that may be needed to enhance the policy relevance of meta-analysis.

This paper is divided into four sections. In the first section I describe the nature of the meta-analysis task, present a framework for judging the adequacy of practices, and propose a definition of relevance. With these issues in mind, in the second section I assess the NIE desegregation case study. In the third section I describe the current status of meta-analysis; and in the fourth section I discuss several factors that are likely to affect the future of meta-analysis.

Assessing Practices

In the policy context, determining the quality of the syntheses requires simultaneous consideration of two dimensions: technical adequacy and utility. Chelimsky (1983) identifies several factors associated with each dimension. For technical adequacy, the absence of gross analytical errors is essential. With regard to utility, the most important factors are timeliness and relevance of the evidence that is produced. Although these dimensions are not mutually exclusive and in practice trade-offs must be made, for clarity I will treat each separately.

Technical Adequacy

Meta-analysis, like other forms of research synthesis, is a collection of methods for summarizing the results of independent studies. In its most basic form it entails four sequential steps: (1) formulation of the question(s) to be addressed, (2) enumeration of relevant prior studies, (3) review and summarization of studies, and (4) synthesis of information. As is obvious, which studies are ultimately subjected to the quantitative methods of meta-analysis depends on practices associated with earlier steps. The ease with which studies can be located and summarized is dependent on the condition (i.e., quality) of the knowledge base.

If all primary studies were routinely available in the public domain, well-executed and adequately reported, meta-analysis would be largely a technical exercise of converting findings into a common metric (e.g., effect size), applying the appropriate aggregation rules, and testing for heterogeneity of results. In practice, the nature of the data we have to work with does not permit a mechanical application of meta-analytic tactics. Each application requires a certain amount of adaptation, problem solving and judgment calls. The question becomes, "On what grounds do we judge the adequacy of these practices?"

Several criteria come to mind. At the most abstract level, we could apply conventional standards of quality (e.g., the Evaluation Research Society, "Program Evaluation Standards," 1982). This seems justified by the fact that although some aspects of meta-analysis are unique (e.g., the standardization of results into a common metric), there is no compelling reason why meta-analytic practices should be judged on different grounds than other methods. Within this concept of quality, meta-analysts should aspire to produce results that are accurate, valid, and sufficiently documented so that others can replicate their procedures. Further, general standards prescribe that assumptions should be clearly identified, evidence should be presented in defense of critical methodological choices, and generalization of results should be appropriate. Judging whether a particular study meets these criteria invokes a second level of assessment, namely, an examination of the specific features of the meta-analytic task.

Given that meta-analysis is a cluster of methodologies, it is not surprising that practices bear a close resemblance to other research strategies (e.g., survey research). Inasmuch as the vulnerabilities of these other strategies have been systematically examined, it is useful to draw upon them as a means of structuring an assessment of meta-analysis practices. The approach I have taken is based on Kish's general model of total survey error (1965). In applying his concepts to synthesis practices, it becomes evident that several sources of systematic and variable (i.e., random) error are possible. Some of these have already been identified in the meta-analysis literature (see Rosenthal 1984); others have not. While the total survey error concept does not exactly correspond to issues in meta-analysis, it does provide a meaningful heuristic for organizing the issues that have and have not been examined. Given the interrelationships among practices and the influence of early errors on subsequent steps in the process, a development of a "total synthesis error" model seems warranted.

Variable Error

With regard to sources of random error, sampling error (in primary studies) is an obvious component which has been treated in detail by Hedges and Olkin (1985). Their formulation, one that decomposes systematic and nonsystematic sources of variability as part of the aggregation process, serves as the foundation for statistical significance testing and ascertaining the degree of heterogeneity within and across clusters of studies (Hedges 1984a).

Other forms of variable error arise from nonsampling sources. A somewhat trivial case is associated with routine data processing (e.g., errors in data entry). On the other hand, variable error due to unreliability of coding and transcription can be substantial. For example, in a reanalysis of a subset of the Smith, Glass, and Miller psychotherapy database, we found that, depending on the type of variable that was being recorded, interrater agreement ranged from 60 to 100 percent (see Orwin and Cordray 1985). Much of this was attributable to uncertainty arising from reporting deficiencies in the primary studies. Similar discrepancies have been noted across other meta-analyses of the same basic data by two independent sets of authors (see Cordray and Sonnefeld 1985). While the cumulative effect of these sources of variable error has not been investigated, it is clear that they can contribute to the overall precision of meta-analytic results.

Systematic Error

For survey research, Kish also identified several varieties of sampling and nonsampling bias that are relevant to features of meta-analysis. Technical developments in the field appear to have solved one of Kish's sampling biases and progress is being made on the other. Specifically, Hedges (1981) has provided a correction to estimates of effect sizes to eliminate bias caused by small sample sizes in primary studies. The second source, frame bias, is the consequence of using inappropriate selection procedures (e.g., duplication). Strube (1985) and Rosenthal and Rubin (1986) provide a means of integrating multiple results from a given study to avoid overweighting studies with multiple effects (a form of duplication in the sampling sense). Other selection issues, discussed in the next section, are also relevant.

On the nonsampling side, Kish identified four additional biases that are relevant to meta-analytic practices. Two refer to nonobservations (noncoverage and nonresponse), and two refer to biased observations (consistent processing errors and measurement problems). Here the survey research analogy breaks down somewhat. If we anthropomorphize a bit, the parallels can be made. That is, whereas survey research attempts to solicit information from individuals, meta-analysis gathers its evidence from studies. Because of reporting deficiencies, these studies are not always cooperative and trustworthy. As such, many of the same issues are encountered (e.g., hidden populations, missing data), and the same types of practices (e.g., imputation, sensitivity analyses) are needed to estimate the influence of these deviations from the ideal case.

With regard to nonobservation, the issues are fairly straightforward. Two types of nonobservation can occur. First, studies (or clusters of studies) can be excluded, that is, noncoverage. This issue is well recognized in the meta-analysis literature as the "file-drawer problem" (Orwin 1983; Rosenthal 1979). By making assumptions about the characteristics of studies that are excluded, a "fail-safe N" can be constructed. This index tells us how many unavailable studies it would take to overturn the reported aggregate results.

A less extreme form of nonobservation is nonresponse. Here the study fails to disclose important information on all or some variables of interest. At least two factors influence this type of nonresponse; the information is either missing or poorly reported. Methodological options for dealing with these problems include using estimates from other sources, imputing, establishing coding conventions, and recording the level of uncertainty associated with the particular information (Orwin and Cordray 1985). Each of these practices has strengths and weaknesses. In general, they probably introduce a systematic source of bias in the statistical results. For example, substituting the mean as a way of accommodating item-nonresponse systematically affects estimates of variability.

The final category in Kish's model pertains to systematic error associated with observations that are obtained. Two sources are possible—"field errors" and processing errors. These can occur at both the primary and meta levels of analysis. At the primary study level, field errors include measurement problems (e.g., reactivity) and other operational problems (e.g., inaccurate enumeration or classification). At the meta-analytic level, similar errors can be systematically interjected (e.g., coder bias). With regard to processing errors at the primary study level, inaccurate analyses, poor study designs, and other such practices can yield systematic distortions in the basic data for meta-analysis. Within the synthesis literature, considerable attention has been directed at accounting for differences in results due to characteristics of the studies. Nevertheless, processing errors are also possible. These range from consistent transcription errors (e.g., coding conventions) to more controversial issues such as the choice of standard deviations for calculating an effect size. (Here, the issue is not that one choice is right or wrong, but merely that a choice has been made which may influence the results systematically.)

As with variable errors, the cumulative influence of these potential sources of systematic error has not, to my knowledge, been assessed. It is clear, however, that each of these potential biases could influence the results or create uncertainty about the credibility of the synthesis. What is impressive about the meta-analysis literature is that so many of these issues have been acknowledged. Partial solutions to these problems, or at least diagnostic tests of their influence, have been developed for many of them. These come in a variety of forms, and sound meta-analytic practices appear to be associated with direct assessments of the influence of the methodological choices. While synthesis practices have not been fully explored as a means of examining practices within a "total synthesis error" model, the technical developments, to date, are promising.

Relevance and Timeliness

As indicated earlier, the quality of meta-analytic practices involves technical adequacy and utility. A key aspect of utility is the relevance of the information that is produced. The meta-analysis must also be completed in a timely fashion. In this section, both issues are discussed with specific reference to the policy context.

We all have an intuitive idea of what it means to be policy-relevant. Certainly, desegregation qualifies as an important social issue that is surrounded by considerable debate, making it a prime candidate for empirical research that could inform those discussions. Given that meta-analysis entails the quantitative integration of primary studies, it would appear that the policy relevance of meta-analysis is defensible if the primary studies are themselves policy-relevant. If life were this simple, we would not have the need for a conference on meta-analysis.

Simply shifting the burden of policy relevance to the primary studies does not get around the fundamental question of what we mean by the term "relevance." Further, we see that there are at least three aspects of relevance that need to be considered. First, studies that bear on the questions posed within a meta-analysis need to be available. However, in some situations the lack of relevant primary studies does not preclude performing the synthesis. As odd as this statement may seem, often the policy question revolves around the question of whether there is any evidence that could be brought to bear on a policy issue. While the quantitative side of synthesis (i.e., meta-analysis) may not be employed in this case, other features of the method are employed. This leads naturally to the second notion of relevance. That is, given that the questions initiating the synthesis are often specified by a congressional member or committee, the meta-analysis (synthesis) has to be responsive to the questions posed. Further, the nature of the policy context also invokes a third conception of relevance, namely, the extent to which the information needs of multiple constituencies are served.

As Tom Cook notes in his remarks about the NIE desegregation meta-analyses, one of the defining characteristics of a policy arena is the presence of multiple stakeholders, each with potentially different information needs. Whereas stakeholders with oversight responsibility may want to know if a program works, local administrators, classroom teachers, parents, and other important stakeholders are likely to have different agendas. As such, meta-analytic practices that are relevant to the concerns of some stakeholders may not yield the kind of evidence that other stakeholders desire. If meta-analysis is to be optimally useful in informing policy debates in this context (e.g., helping to resolve differences of opinion), practices must recognize this pluralism. In the NIE case example, the identification of researchers holding different value positions on the effects of desegregation is consistent with the issue of pluralism. In the policy context in which we have been working (principally, Congress), additional practices are employed.

Some of these practices associated with assuring relevance (and technical adequacy) have been incorporated into GAO's evaluation synthesis methodology. This methodology was specifically developed for use in a policy context (U.S. General Accounting Office 1983). While the four general steps depicted in Table 10.1 are similar to Jackson's general description of research synthesis (1980), the subtasks reflect the unique character of the policy context.

One main difference between normal meta-analyses and those done within the policy context is that the formulation of the questions to be addressed is determined collaboratively (i.e., the analyst has less freedom to choose the focus of the synthesis). Further, as we move from investigator-initiated applications of meta-analysis to policy-instigated questions, several changes in emphasis occur. As part of the formulation and question definition step, a deliberate effort is made to identify the salient policy concerns of key stakeholder groups (e.g., researchers, professional and public interest groups, agency officials). The logic here is simple. Rather than debating these issues at the end of the synthesis, "researchable" issues are identified as part of the front-end planning process. Then, methods, measures, and analyses are planned that could shed light on these positions and lend additional credibility and objectivity to the synthesis. This pluralism is carried forward into subsequent steps, as seen in Table 10.1. In particular, to ensure completeness, studies and other materials are solicited from stakeholders. To guarantee a balanced treatment of the issues, syntheses are routinely reviewed by experts representing varying positions.

Where policy relevance and practices converge rests within the notion of responsiveness. That is, information resulting from the meta-analysis

Table 10.1   Four Steps in the Evaluation Synthesis Methodology

Major Steps	Subtasks

A. Formulate and Define Questions	1. Identify issues
	2. Review literature and legislative history
	3. Conduct interviews
	   a. researchers
	   b. professionals and public interest groups
	   c. federal agency staff

B. Identify and Collect Relevant Studies	1. Conduct bibliographic searches
	2. Conduct interviews
	   a. researchers
	   b. professionals and public interest groups
	   c. federal agency staff

C. Assess Usefulness and Reliability of Studies	1. Classify by study questions
	2. Review studies
	   a. research design
	   b. methodology
	      (1) sampling
	      (2) data collection
	      (3) statistical analysis
	   c. findings
	3. Summarize

D. Synthesize Information	1. Assess studies and findings
	   a. strengths and weaknesses
	   b. similarities and trends
	   c. generalizability
	2. Relate findings to synthesis questions
	3. Summarize what is known
	4. Have experts review

(step D) has to be responsive to the questions raised in step A. Table 10.1 clearly shows that later steps of the process are dependent upon decisions made in earlier steps. For example, whether generalizability (part of step D) can be addressed depends on adequacy of practices in all of the earlier steps. Slippage can occur at numerous points along the way, with a corresponding loss of relevance.

In sum, whether meta-analysis is policy-relevant has to be viewed in relative terms. A study is not policy-relevant simply because it examines some aspect of a social problem. Rather, a study has to be responsive to the specific policy issues and clusters of questions. To be credible, it has to address these issues in a balanced fashion. The methodological strategies and choices should minimize the slippage between the initial questions and the final synthesis. Although serendipitous use of information is always welcomed, the evaluation synthesis methodology operates on the assumption that planning for relevance is likely to improve the chances of actual relevance and use. Of course, whether the results of a synthesis become part of the policy debates hinges critically on its timely execution.

Comments on the NIE Case Example

Overview of the NIE Case Example

To provide a common ground for discussing meta-analytic practices, the Committee has adopted a case study approach. The policy-related example that has been selected—NIE's desegregation meta-analysis—is unique in several ways. As such, using it as the sole touchstone from which to comment on the relevance of meta-analysis in the policy context is risky in at least two ways: (1) some pervasive problems in meta-analysis may go unnoticed because of its special features, and (2) issues noted in this particular case may be by-products of the unique processes that were imposed and not pertinent to "normal" meta-analytic practices. To gain a broader perspective on synthesis practices, other sources have been consulted in this paper.

In describing NIE's method of review, Uribe and Schneider (1983) noted that they used a modified meta-analysis strategy. Three departures from normal practice were undertaken. First, unlike a conventional study where a single researcher (or group) conducts a quantitative review of the literature, NIE deliberately selected six experts (David Armor, Robert Crain, Norman Miller, Walter Stephan, Herb Walberg, and Paul Wortman) who represented various positions (positive, neutral, and negative) on the issue of the effectiveness of desegregation on achievement; a seventh member of the panel (Tom Cook) served as a methodological specialist. Second, NIE asked each expert (two for each position) to independently meta-analyze a preselected set of "high quality" studies. The criteria for inclusion of a study were specified, and individual analysts determined which studies met these conditions. Third, unlike conventional meta-analysis practices, the NIE format involved an interactive synthesis of all results (Cooper 1986), providing an opportunity for participants to present, review, and interpret their individual findings as a collective. The final report contains their collective and individual analyses (National Institute of Education 1983).

Implications for Assessing Practices and Policy Relevance

As a basis for assessing practices, several points should be raised about this example. Specifically, the NIE study was as much a research project on the process of conducting meta-analysis as it was a true meta-analysis. This suggests the possibility that the six experts may have altered their practices in subtle ways. In some regards, practices exhibited within this case example exceeded those normally observed in meta-analysis. Micro-decisions (e.g., why a study was included or excluded) and procedures (e.g., standardization rules) were reported in substantial detail, making it clear what was done and why. In addition, given that the purpose of the meta-analysis was to resolve some of the discrepancies observed in prior meta-analyses, panel members performed numerous tests (e.g., sensitivity analyses) that are rarely reported in "conventional" meta-analyses.

In addition, the NIE format tried to induce a common ground across analysts by designating a core set of studies, thus resulting in the individual analyst's surrender of several important decision points. Without such constraints, the between-analyst variability in normal practice might have been considerably higher.

Finally, with respect to the technical adequacy of the practices that were employed, the panel members conducted their analyses during a period when new statistical procedures were being developed. As such, despite the fact that NIE initiated this work only four years ago, compared to current (1986) statistical standards, the procedures that were used are either incomplete, insensitive, or inaccurate.

Judging the NIE case example against the list of variable and systematic errors that were delineated in the previous section suggests that if these studies were reanalyzed today, the results would be different in three ways. First, adjusting effect sizes for small sample biases would probably reduce the aggregate effect size (sample sizes, per group, ranged from 10 to over 800). Second, weighting studies by their sample size would alter results. Short of recalculating the aggregate effects, the influence of this change is unpredictable. Third, using the heterogeneity test described (Hedges and Olkin 1985; Rosenthal and Rubin 1979) for the between-cluster comparisons (e.g., attempts to identify whether early exposure to desegregation resulted in the greatest effects) would be more sensitive than the conventional comparisons (with each study as the unit of observation) that were used (except for Miller). It is difficult to fault the statistical methods that were used, given the historical context within which this study was conducted.

If we assume that the imprecision and biases that may have been introduced were equal across panelists, other aspects of the synthesis process can be examined. Specifically, given that the panel members did not adhere to all aspects of the NIE plan, this case does provide a unique opportunity to examine the natural variation in many of the nonsampling/nonstatistical practices and their influence on the results and conclusions that are drawn. Moreover, NIE's deliberate selection of analysts with different a priori positions on the effectiveness of desegregation approximates some of the conditions that are likely to be encountered in a policy context. In this sense, the NIE example is instructive.

What Was Learned?

The NIE-sponsored meta-analysis is instructive in several ways. In this section, I will summarize the general lessons; each is discussed in more detail in the following sections. Concerning the strengths and weaknesses of practices, two general observations can be offered. First, this case shows quite clearly that the between-analyst variability in practices can be substantial. This has associated strengths and weaknesses. On the one hand, when results converge, the variability implies that the method is robust. Alternatively, when results are at odds, the first line of attack is the methodological decisions that were made.

Second, despite this considerable variability in the "nuts and bolts" of conducting the reviews, this case also reveals several kinds of narrowness in current practices. Again, this is both good and bad. On the positive side, the narrowness reflects the fact that meta-analysis entails a specifiable set of core practices that define it as distinct from other strategies. On the other hand, some of these practices have important but ritualized decisions, thus reducing their adaptiveness for answering important policy questions. To the extent that the narrowness is "out of step" with information needs, the utility of meta-analysis for policy purposes may be threatened. From our perspective, the apparent narrowness is of greatest concern. Consequently, a disproportionate amount of attention is devoted to discussing the latter observation in the following sections. Finally, whether the direct policy relevance of meta-analysis per se has been established by this case illustration is difficult to determine.

Variability in Practices

It appears that a key rationale for conducting this meta-analysis was to resolve the differences among several prior meta-analyses. The most obvious difference among them concerned the number and types of studies that had been included in the database (i.e., variability in practices associated with selection).

In reviewing the specific procedures used by the panelists, it is clear that practices did, indeed, differ. Even under the restrictive conditions set up by NIE, panelists analyzed different subsets of the core studies, differed in how they calculated effect sizes, and used different control groups as their basis for some comparisons. In most instances, these choices were defensible, and in the absence of any hard-and-fast rules about appropriateness, none could be considered right or wrong. Several panelists—especially Miller, Crain, and Wortman—devised tests to show the influence of their decisions. Treating methodological decisions as testable propositions is commendable and should be routinized in meta-analytic practices.

What is particularly encouraging about this study is the fact that despite countless differences in methodological details and predispositions of the analysts, the aggregate results are remarkably similar. Whether this "convergence" is a function of the way NIE structured the task, the relative "bluntness" of the meta-analytic procedures that were used, or the robustness of the meta-analysis process remains, however, difficult to tease apart.

Narrowness of Practices

The NIE case study provides a telescopic look at meta-analytic practices. For an assessment of practices associated with major steps in the process, this is not the most telling vantage point. If we step back from the microdecisions and associated practices and take a broad look at the types of policy questions that are being asked, it becomes clear that meta-analytic practices could be expanded. Some additional research and development will be necessary, however. In the next sections, I list some of the generic policy questions that are becoming more prevalent, examine how inclusion rules (e.g., what types of studies and information are to be included in the database) close off important avenues, and look at the influence of these inclusion rules on issues of generalization.

Types of Policy Questions

Meta-analysis was developed as a way of deriving an aggregate estimate of available evidence on the effects of interventions. While program effectiveness has been and continues to be an important policy question, other questions are being asked with increasing frequency. In particular, faced with a large (and persistent) national deficit, policymakers have begun to examine alternative actions. Many of these actions involve questions of how to maximize the federal investment in social and defense programs.

Although my list is not exhaustive (nor are the items mutually exclusive), I have tried to provide an array of the types of questions that have been or are being asked in the Congress and executive branch. From this list of concerns, it is possible to educe how meta-analysis practices might be broadened.

RELATIVE EFFECTIVENESS.   Justifying expenditures quite naturally leads to questions of whether we are getting the greatest return on our investment in programs. One simple extension of conventional meta-analysis is to compare the relative effectiveness of different program strategies for achieving the same policy objective. This is precisely the issue that Walberg raised in his paper for the NIE meta-analysis. Further, by conventional practices, this is not a radical alteration in procedures. In fact, such comparisons are frequently made (e.g., meta-analyses on the effectiveness of different modes of psychotherapy). When differences in program goals or methods of assessment (at the primary study level) are present, the validity of these comparisons can be hotly contested (Shapiro 1985). Moreover, given the rate at which ordinary meta-analyses are being conducted, it seems that the chances are good that comparisons will be made among meta-analyses that focus on different programs. It is probably better to confront these noncomparabilities systematically—performing methodological adjustments to make them more comparable—within a single meta-analysis than to simply allow them to be compared without recognition of such limitations. The possibility of abuse and misuse within policy debates seems quite likely.

COST-EFFECTIVENESS.   A more specific question on resource allocation would entail establishing the cost-effectiveness of interventions. While most cost-effectiveness analyses are conducted as primary studies, at least one example can be cited where meta-analysis has been merged with cost assessment. Specifically, Levin, Glass, and Meister (1984) examined the cost-effectiveness of four educational interventions. Their results are interesting and demonstrate nicely how refining estimates of relative effectiveness by estimates of cost can alter judgments about which strategy is superior. However, moving to a cost-effectiveness framework places additional technical burdens—beyond those already embedded in the meta-analysis process—on the analyst. The vulnerabilities in establishing cost estimates must be clearly recognized.

IDENTIFYING EXEMPLARY PROGRAMS.   In legislation, the Congress has exhibited a longstanding interest in the federal government's role in promoting effective programs. For example, the Educational Improvement and Consolidation Act specifically authorized expenditures for program improvement efforts. To this end, the Department of Education has developed several mechanisms with which to identify programs that seem to be particularly effective. There appears to be a natural place for meta-analysis in this process.

ANALYZING PROGRAM COMPONENTS.   In several of our evaluation syntheses, the requester has asked for an assessment of the relative contributions of various components of a total program. In the syntheses of the effects of the WIC program, congressional concern centered around whether health care, food, and educational counseling all contributed to the health status of participants. Although we concluded that the evaluation literature for the WIC program could not sustain this level of assessment, there are successful examples in the literature. For example, by using placebo conditions as the benchmark for comparing treatment effects, Prioleau, Murdock, and Brody (1983) attempted to assess the unique features of psychotherapy interventions.

The Need for Contextual Evidence

What meta-analysis could contribute to the policy discussions surrounding these types of questions is highly dependent upon the nature, scope, and quality of the knowledge base. Some theorists undoubtedly will argue that these questions are beyond the realm of meta-analysis. In his original description of meta-analysis, Glass (1976) delineated several conditions under which the results of independent studies could be quantitatively integrated. These are described by Uribe and Schneider (1983) as follows: "Meta-analysis can provide a meaningful summary of the collective results if the populations sampled, the treatment used, the time frame in which the evaluation was done, the measures of response, and the design under which data are gathered are essentially the same" (p. 4, fn. 2).

The NIE case example reiterates the difficulties and ambiguities associated with trying to determine why some studies yield large positive effects and others show negative effects. *Post hoc* probing for factors that account for the observed variability convincingly shows the limits of meta-analysis. Because of reporting problems, noncomparabilities among studies resulting from confoundings associated with differences in time, treatments, measures, populations, and so forth, make it very difficult (but not impossible) to answer the types of questions being raised by the policymakers. When evaluations of social programs are the focus of meta-analysis, it is difficult to argue that these conditions hold.

Although we could argue that these issues reinforce the point that meta-analytic tactics are too limited for synthesizing complex literature, it should be noted that meta-analyses are being conducted despite these noncomparabilities. The question is how can we improve practices to optimize their utility and accuracy.

Modeling Complex Systems

As with any observational data, one of the few ways we have of reducing uncertainty is to measure and model the factors that we believe contribute to the observed variability. Although more advanced statistical procedures are now available, little effort has been directed at the development of such models. One noteworthy exception is Finsterbusch's analysis of factors related to the impact of 52 AID projects (1984). For more complex social programs, it is possible to gain a better understanding of results by examining features of the program environment. Often this requires the analyst to look at literature beyond the studies selected for the synthesis. As shown in Table 10.1, the evaluation synthesis includes a review of legislative history.

For example, the Compensatory Education programs funded under the Elementary and Secondary Education Act of 1965 were routinely altered as part of the oversight process. In fact, these alterations resulted from evaluations—some of which could be included within a meta-analytic database. In this particular instance, a major study conducted by the NIE resulted in a respecification of eligibility rules for selection of participants. This was accompanied by a change in regulations that required a rank-ordering of the neediest students; those with the highest need were to be given highest priority. By examining the known changes that occurred within the program and mapping results onto this historical time frame, it is possible to gain a better understanding of when, how, and under what conditions the data were produced.

Inclusion Rules

One of the most striking features of current meta-analysis is the propensity to locate every study that was conducted (published or not) and then quickly separate the good from the bad studies. The synthesis effort is then directed at those studies that pass some test of "quality," and the others are excluded or not emphasized. For some applications, this decision rule is well justified (e.g., when the request is for an examination of only the best available evidence).

The NIE case study used a definition of quality that was not uniformly embraced by panel members. Crain went as far as stating that specifying a priori inclusion criteria was a fundamental mistake, and Wortman imposed a more stringent selection criteria. Studies were included as "high quality" if the study design was adequate and there was evidence of well-articulated desegregation "treatment." Implicit within this definition is a conjoint inclusion rule. Only those studies (and, in turn, programs or projects) that pass both tests are included. If we look at the other side—what has been excluded—we see that there are at least three other categories of studies that have been "lumped" together and by inference characterized as "poor quality" studies. These are depicted in the diagram shown here.

		Basis for Causal Attribution	
		WEAK	STRONG
Program	WEAK	A	B
Implementation	STRONG	C	D

Several points can be raised about the implications of these inclusion rules. First, labeling those studies classified within cell D as high in "methodological quality," as was done in the NIE meta-analysis, is misleading. Rather, what this particular decision rule has created is a cluster of studies that are more accurately characterized as a strong test of desegregation. Consequently, what is depicted is a set of studies that is not simply methodologically strong but also based on well-implemented programs.

Conjoint inclusion rules are not often used in meta-analysis, however. Normally, inclusion rules that focus on the strength of the designs (cells B and D) will combine programs that vary in level of implementation. Unless further stratification is initiated, effect sizes will be heterogeneous (assuming that a program is truly effective).

On the other hand, the conjoint inclusion rule, although providing a strong test of the intervention, ignores a substantial amount of potentially valuable qualitative information about the circumstances surrounding the program and the characteristics of the evaluation methods. For example, contrasting evidence from cell B and cell D provides a quasi-experimental comparison that is unique to meta-analysis. That is, additional probing of the differences between studies in each cell might reveal why program implementation is weak and corrective actions could be proposed.

Of course, attributes of programs (e.g., implementation fidelity and strength of the intervention) are in practice not dichotomous. This type of variation can be analyzed profitably in terms of a dose-response relationship (see Howard, Kopta, Krause, and Orlinsky 1986). Not only does this type of analysis exploit more of the available information, but it can provide guidance to policymakers and program managers about the added value of increasing the strength of an intervention. In our work for Senator Chafee, our analysis of the literature on programs for pregnant teenagers found no evidence that more comprehensive services were any more effective than less comprehensive services (U.S. General Accounting Office 1986).

Another form of information that is potentially overlooked by restrictive inclusion rules is evidence of operational problems. If one of the policy reasons for conducting the synthesis is to determine if programs should be expanded or to identify those that seem most promising, looking only at studies in cell D would not reveal evidence concerning the likely shortfalls or obstacles that could be encountered in other settings. Evidence from studies in cell B could yield information on problems associated with program implementation, and looking at studies within cell C could illuminate additional factors associated with method failures.

Influence of Inclusion Rules on Generalization

The issue concerning generalization of results has always been a problem in areas where the machinery of statistical sampling cannot be employed to derive a concise estimate of how far from the true value we are likely to be. Normally, meta-analysis circumvents this issue quite nicely by defining its population as "all available published and unpublished studies of X." In hopes of being able to conclude something about the population of studies, vigorous bibliographic searches are conducted to assure that all studies have been included. As a check that our conclusions are not affected by the "file-drawer" problem, procedures have been devised (e.g., fail-safe N) to assess how many unreported studies showing no effects might have to be tucked away in file drawers to overturn the reported results.

The issue of generalization is more complex within a policy context and is linked to the inclusion rules that are employed. Whereas the target of generalization within conventional meta-analysis focuses on the knowledge base (i.e., number of *studies* undertaken), the question of greater interest for policymakers with oversight responsibility is, "Does the program work?" To the extent that all projects have not been evaluated, it is obvious that the knowledge base will only partially reflect the true target

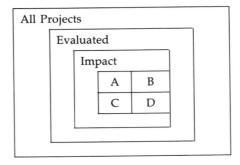

population. This point can be made concrete by considering the diagram shown here.

Obviously, the most restrictive inclusion rule (cell D) is not likely to represent the population of interest. More important, without additional information, it is impossible to speak to the issue of generalization. Crain did provide one analysis that highlights the importance of gathering and using information from other studies that are not included in the final synthesis. Specifically, he showed that based on the distribution of studies across all cells (A thru D), the selected core of studies used in the NIE meta-analysis differed in important ways that did not represent critical features of desegregation efforts.

From a sampling perspective, these inclusion rules result in the identification of convenience samples, and generalization is very limited. Crain's analysis is instructive in providing a basis for gaining a sense of what portion of the total population *might* be represented by the final selection of studies. These are the types of practices that will make meta-analysis more useful to relevant stakeholders.

Policy Relevance

Adopting the relativistic definition of relevance, it is possible to say that the NIE case example was policy-relevant *if* the policy question was simply, "Does desegregation affect the reading and math abilities of black students?" This was the question posed by NIE staff, and they seem to have obtained an answer, albeit some of the individual answers were more responsive to the question than others and many of the studies were conducted in the early 1970s. As Cook pointed out, however, how well the practices and results would be received by a more heterogeneous group of stakeholders is unknown.

The Current Status of Meta-Analysis

The nature of recent comments in the literature on meta-analysis suggests a shift from skepticism to cautious acceptance. Several factors have contributed to this shift in sentiment. First, while the viability of the method was being debated, a substantial research and development effort was under way. Work by statisticians (e.g., Hedges and Olkin 1985; Hunter, Schmidt, and Jackson 1982; Rosenthal and Rubin 1986; Strube 1985) has greatly contributed to our understanding of the statistical properties of the method. Further, the authors of several recent volumes on the synthesis process (e.g., Glass, McGaw, and Smith 1982; Light and Pillemer 1984; Rosenthal 1984; Wolf 1986) have organized these advances into a coherent set of practices. Others (e.g., Bullock and Svyantek 1985; Orwin and Cordray 1985) have investigated the effects of obstacles (e.g., deficient reporting in prior research) and proposed practical solutions to some of the problems identified by critics.

Second, as meta-analytic practices have matured, recognition of the epistemological footing of meta-analysis has grown. That is, given the observational character (in Cochran's sense) of meta-analysis as a strategy, it is basically descriptive. The discovery of firm explanations and broad generalizations are, for the most part, viewed as beyond its scope. However, experience also has shown that such descriptive knowledge can be highly useful in a policy context. Having realigned our expectations about what can be derived from meta-analysis, researchers have begun to ask different questions, some of which are more efficiently answered through meta-analysis than with new data collection (Light 1984).

Further, we have argued (see Cordray and Lipsey 1987) that research synthesis has come along at a propitious moment in the development of evaluation as a field. Reductions in federal funding for research and evaluation have forced attention to "summing up" what is known about the effects of interventions. These syntheses—if properly conducted—can not only reveal what is known about the effects of interventions, but also help to identify gaps in knowledge and serve as a rational basis for the development of subsequent programs and investigations. Despite its relatively short history, the meta-analytic perspective appears to have left a rather distinctive mark on basic and applied research.

The Future of Meta-Analysis

The long-term future of meta-analysis depends on two fundamental issues. First, it is critically linked to the continued production of primary research studies. Second, improvements in primary studies and continued development of the meta-analytic procedures are crucial to its future.

Expanding the Knowledge Base

As a form of inquiry, meta-analysis is useful to the extent that new studies are conducted. For policy purposes, this is critical. Changes in programs, in the political climate within which they operate, and in the composition of populations who are served means that the shelf life of prior research and evaluations is of limited value for many policy questions. However, as we have seen in numerous federal agencies, investments in research, evaluation, and statistics have declined considerably. As such, with limited resources, efforts have to be made to assure that funds are well spent *on high quality primary studies.* Meta-analytic procedures can be used to assist in this regard.

Improving Practices

As quantitative syntheses become more visible within the policy context, the value of investing in research should become more obvious. As already noted, commonly used inclusion rules overlook a substantial amount of potentially useful information that could be used in the planning of future studies, thereby improving the quality of primary research and evaluation. There are several ways that we could better understand the conditions under which high quality studies are produced. Returning to the diagram that partitions studies into four cells, it is possible to ascertain for cells A through C whether the null results are attributable to program implementation failures (cell B), method failures (cell C), or both (cell A). Synthesizing information from studies in these cells could reveal what types of alterations might be needed to assure that the next generation of programs and studies does not fall prey to the same errors. Several approaches to capitalizing on prior research for planning new studies appear in Cordray (1985).

The list of potential sources of systematic and variable errors that could enter into the synthesis process shows some of the methodological vulnerabilities of meta-analysis. The variety of procedures that NIE panelists used to test the influence of their decision rules appears to be the most hopeful solution to these types of problems, at least until reporting of primary studies improves.

In the past five years, the sophistication of meta-analytic practice has increased dramatically. Solutions for many of the problems identified in the first section have been developed. On the other hand, not all of the conceptual challenges have been solved. For example, if we look at what is considered the state of the art in evaluation research, it is obvious that simple pre-test versus post-test assessments are being replaced with structural models that emphasize mediational mechanisms, implementation issues, estimates of the influence of exogenous factors, and so on (see Cordray 1986). Despite the increased prominence of these models in the near future, little attention has been devoted to integrating the results of complex analyses. If meta-analysis is to continue to be useful in the future, it has to keep pace with the methodological developments in the primary literature.

PART IV

Vantage Points

11

An Evaluation
of Procedures and Results

Robert Rosenthal

In the years 1980, 1981, and 1982 alone, well over 300 papers were published on the topic of meta-analysis (Lamb and Whitla 1983). Does this represent a giant stride forward in the development of the behavioral and social sciences or does it signal a lemming-like flight to disaster? Judging from reactions to past meta-analytic enterprises, there are at least some who take the more pessimistic view. Some three dozen scholars were invited to respond to a meta-analysis of studies of interpersonal expectancy effects conducted by Don Rubin and me (Rosenthal and Rubin 1978). Although much of the commentary dealt with the substantive topic of interpersonal expectancy effects, a good deal of it dealt with methodological aspects of meta-analytic procedures and products. Some of the criticisms offered were accurately anticipated by Glass (1978), who had earlier received commentary on his meta-analytic work (Glass 1976) and that of his colleagues (Smith and Glass 1977; Glass, McGaw, and Smith 1981). In the present paper, the criticisms of our commentators are grouped into several conceptual categories, described, and discussed.

Note: This paper was prepared for the Committee on National Statistics; preparation of this chapter was supported in part by the National Science Foundation and by the John D. and Catherine T. MacArthur Foundation while the author was a Fellow at the Center for Advanced Study in the Behavioral Sciences.

Sampling Bias and the File-Drawer Problem

One criticism holds that there is a retrievability bias such that studies retrieved do not reflect the population of studies conducted. One version of this criticism is that the probability of publication is increased by the statistical significance of the results so that published studies may not be representative of the studies conducted. This is a well-taken criticism, though it applies equally to more traditional narrative reviews of the literature. Procedures that can be employed to address this problem have been described elsewhere (Rosenthal 1979a; 1984, Chapter 5).

Information Loss

Overemphasizing Single Values

The first of two criticisms relevant to information loss notes the danger of trying to summarize a research domain by a single value such as a mean effect size. This criticism holds that defining a relationship in nature by a single value leads to overlooking moderator variables. When meta-analysis is seen as including not only combining effect sizes (and significance levels) but also comparing effect sizes in both diffuse and, especially, focused fashion, the force of this criticism is removed (Rosenthal 1984, Chapter 4).

A special case of the criticism under discussion is that, by emphasizing average values, negative cases are overlooked. There are several ways in which negative cases can be defined: e.g., $p > .05$, $r = 0$, r negative, r significantly negative, and so on. However we may define negative cases, when we divide the sample of studies into negative and positive cases we have merely dichotomized an underlying continuum of effect sizes or significance levels, and accounting for negative cases is simply a special case of finding moderator variables.

Glossing Over Details

Although it is accurate to say that meta-analyses gloss over details, it is equally as accurate to say that traditional narrative reviews do so, and that data analysts do so in every study in which any statistics are computed. The act of summarizing requires us to gloss over details. If we describe a nearly normal distribution of scores by the mean and σ we have nearly described the distribution perfectly. If the distribution is quadrimodal, the mean and σ will not do a good job of summarizing the data. It is the data analyst's job in the individual study, and the meta-analyst's job in meta-analysis, to "gloss well." Providing the reader with all the raw data of all the studies summarized avoids this criticism but serves no useful review function. Providing the reader with a stem-and-leaf display of the effect sizes obtained, along with the results of the diffuse and focused comparisons of effect sizes, does some glossing but it does a lot of informing besides.

There is, of course, nothing to prevent the meta-analyst from reading each study as carefully and assessing it as creatively as might be done by a more traditional reviewer of a literature. Indeed, we have something of an operational check on reading articles carefully in the case of meta-analysis. If we do not read the results carefully, we cannot obtain effect sizes and significance levels. In traditional reviews, results may have been read carefully or not read at all, with the abstract or the discussion section providing "the results" to the more traditional reviewer.

Problems of Heterogeneity

Heterogeneity of Method

The first of two criticisms relevant to problems of heterogeneity notes that meta-analyses average over studies in which the independent variables, the dependent variables, and the sampling units are not uniform. How can we speak of interpersonal expectancy effects, meta-analytically, when some of the independent variables are operationalized by telling experimenters that tasks are easy versus hard or by telling experimenters that subjects are good versus poor task performers? How can we speak, meta-analytically, of these expectancy effects when sometimes the dependent variables are reaction times, sometimes IQ test scores, and sometimes responses to inkblots? How can we speak of these effects when sometimes the sampling units are rats, sometimes college sophomores, sometimes patients, sometimes pupils? Are these not all vastly different phenomena? How can they be pooled together in a single meta-analysis?

Glass (1978) has eloquently addressed this issue—the apples and oranges issue. They are good things to mix, he wrote, when we are trying to generalize to fruit. Indeed, if we are willing to generalize over subjects within studies, why should we not be willing to generalize over studies? If subjects behave very differently within studies we block on subject characteristics to help us understand why. If studies yield very different results from each other, we block on study characteristics to help us understand why. It is very useful to be able to make general statements about fruit. If, in addition, it is also useful to make general statements about apples, about oranges, and about the differences between them, there is nothing in meta-analytic procedures to prevent us from doing so.

Heterogeneity of Quality

One of the most frequent criticisms of meta-analyses is that "bad" studies are thrown in with good. This criticism must be broken down into two questions: What is a "bad" study? What shall we do about "bad" studies?

DEFINING "BAD" STUDIES.   Too often, deciding what is a "bad" study is a procedure richly susceptible to bias or to claims of bias (Fiske 1978). "Bad" studies are too often those whose results we don't like or, as Glass, McGaw, and Smith (1981) have put it, the studies of our "enemies." Therefore, when a reviewer of research tells us he has omitted the "bad" studies, we should satisfy ourselves that this has been done by criteria we find acceptable. A discussion of these criteria (and the computation of their reliability) can be found elsewhere (Rosenthal 1984, Chapter 3).

DEALING WITH "BAD" STUDIES.   The distribution of studies on a dimension of quality is, of course, not really dichotomous (good versus bad) but continuous, with all possible degrees of quality. The fundamental method of coping with "bad" studies or, more accurately, variations in the quality of research is by differential weighting of studies. Dropping studies is merely the special case of zero weighting.

The most important question to ask relevant to study quality is that asked by Glass (1976): Is there a relationship between quality of research and effect size obtained? If there is not, the inclusion of poorer-quality studies will have no effect on the estimate of the average effect size, though it will help to decrease the size of the confidence interval around that mean. If there *is* a relationship between the quality of research and effect size obtained, we can employ whatever weighting system we find reasonable (and that we can persuade our colleagues and critics also to find reasonable).

Problems of Independence

Responses Within Studies

The first of two criticisms relevant to problems of independence notes that several effect size estimates and several tests of significance may be generated by the same subjects within each study. This can be a very well-taken criticism under some conditions, and the problem has been dealt with elsewhere in some detail (Rosenthal 1984, Chapter 2; Rosenthal and Rubin 1986).

Studies Within Sets of Studies

Even when all studies yield only a single effect size estimate and level of significance, and even when all studies employ sampling units that do not also appear in other studies, there is a sense in which results may be nonindependent. That is, studies conducted in the same laboratory, or by the same research group, may be more similar to each other (in the sense of an intraclass correlation) than they are to studies conducted in other laboratories or by other research groups (Jung 1978; Rosenthal 1966, 1969, 1979b). The conceptual and statistical implications of this problem are not yet well worked out.

The Exaggeration of Significance Levels

Truncating Significance Levels

It has been suggested that all p levels less than .01 (Z values greater than 2.33) be reported as .01 (Z = 2.33) because p's less than .01 are likely to be in error (Elashoff 1978). This truncating of Z's cannot be recommended and will, in the long run, lead to serious errors of inference (Rosenthal and Rubin 1978). If there is reason to suspect that a given p level < .01 is in error it should, of course, be corrected before employing it in the meta-analysis. It should not, however, be changed to $p = .01$ simply because it is less than .01.

Too Many Studies

It has been noted as a criticism of meta-analyses that as the number of studies increases there is a greater and greater probability of rejecting the null hypothesis (Mayo 1978). When the null hypothesis is false and, therefore, ought to be rejected, it is indeed true that adding observations (either sampling units within studies or new studies) increases statistical power. However, it is hard to accept, as a legitimate criticism of a procedure, a characteristic that increases its accuracy and decreases its error rate—in this case, type II errors. When the null hypothesis is really true, of course, adding studies does *not* lead to increased probability of rejecting the null hypothesis. Adding studies, it should also be noted, does *not* increase the size of the estimated effect.

A related feature of meta-analysis appears to be that it may, in general, lead to a decrease in type II errors even when the number of studies is modest. Empirical support for this is provided in a study conducted by Cooper and Rosenthal (1980). Procedures requiring the research reviewer to be more systematic and to use more of the information in the data seem to be associated with increases in power, that is, decreases in type II errors.

The Practical Importance of the Estimated Effect Size

Mayo (1978) criticized Cohen (1977) for calling an effect size large ($d = .80$) when it accounted for "only" 14 percent of the variance. Similarly, Rimland (1979) felt that the Smith and Glass (1977) meta-analysis of psychotherapy outcome studies sounded the "death knell" for psychotherapy because the effect size was equivalent to an r of .32, accounting for "only" 10 percent of the variance.

The Binomial Effect Size Display (BESD)

Despite the growing awareness of the importance of estimating effect sizes, there is a problem in evaluating various effect size estimators from the point of view of practical usefulness (Cooper 1981). Rosenthal and Rubin (1979, 1982) found that neither experienced behavioral researchers nor experienced statisticians had a good intuitive feel for the practical meaning of such common effect size estimators as r^2, ω^2, ε^2, and similar estimates.

Accordingly, Rosenthal and Rubin introduced an intuitively appealing general purpose effect size display whose interpretation is perfectly transparent: *the binomial effect size display (BESD)*. There is no sense in which they claim to have resolved the differences and controversies surrounding the use of various effect size estimators but their display is useful because it is (1) easily understood by researchers, students, and lay persons; (2) applicable in a wide variety of contexts; and (3) conveniently computed.

The question addressed by BESD is: What is the effect on the success rate (e.g., survival rate, cure rate, improvement rate, selection rate) of the institution of a new treatment procedure, a new selection device, or a new predictor variable? It therefore displays the change in success rate (e.g., survival rate, cure rate, improvement rate, accuracy rate, selection rate) attributable to the new treatment procedure, new selection device, or new predictor variable. An example shows the appeal of the display. Suppose the estimated mean effect size were found to be an r of .32, approximately the size of the effects reported by Smith and Glass (1977) and by Rosenthal and Rubin (1978) for the effects of psychotherapy and of interpersonal expectancy effects, respectively.

Table 11.1 is the BESD corresponding to an r of .32 or an r^2 of .10. The table shows clearly that it is absurd to label as "modest" an effect size equivalent to increasing the success rate from 34 to 66 percent (e.g., reducing a death rate from 66 to 34 percent). Even so small an r as .20, accounting for "only" 4 percent of the variance, is associated with an increase in success rate from 40 to 60 percent (e.g., a decrease in death rate from 60 to 40 percent), hardly a trivial effect. It might be thought that the BESD can be employed only for dichotomous outcomes (e.g., alive versus dead) and not for continuous outcomes (e.g., scores on a Likert-type scale of improvement due to psychotherapy or gains in performance due to favorable interpersonal expectations). Fortunately, however, the BESD works well for both types of outcomes under a wide variety of conditions (Rosenthal and Rubin 1982).

A great convenience of the BESD is how easily we can convert it to r (or r^2) and how easily we can go from r (or r^2) to the display.

Table 11.2 shows systematically the increase in success rates associated with various values of r^2 and r. For example, an r of .30, accounting for "only" 9 percent of the variance, is associated with a reduction in death rate from 65 to 35 percent, or, more generally, with an increase in success rate from 35 to 65 percent. The last column of Table 11.2 shows that the difference in success rates is identical to r. Consequently, the experimental group success rate in the BESD is computed as $.50 + r/2$, whereas the control group success rate is computed as $.50 - r/2$.

Table 11.1   Binomial Effect Size Display (BESD) for an r of .32 that Accounts for "Only" 10 Percent of the Variance

	Treatment Result		
Condition	Alive	Dead	Σ
Treatment	66%	34%	100%
Control	34	66	100
Σ	100	100	200

Table 11.2   Changes in Success Rates (BESD) Corresponding to Various Values of r^2 and r

Effect Sizes		Equivalent to a Success Rate Increase		
r^2	r	From	To	Difference in Success Rates[a]
.00	.02	.49	.51	.02
.00	.04	.48	.52	.04
.00	.06	.47	.53	.06
.01	.08	.46	.54	.08
.01	.10	.45	.55	.10
.01	.12	.44	.56	.12
.03	.16	.42	.58	.16
.04	.20	.40	.60	.20
.06	.24	.38	.62	.24
.09	.30	.35	.65	.30
.16	.40	.30	.70	.40
.25	.50	.25	.75	.50
.36	.60	.20	.80	.60
.49	.70	.15	.85	.70
.64	.80	.10	.90	.80
.81	.90	.05	.95	.90
1.00	1.00	.00	1.00	1.00

[a]The difference in success rates in a BESD is identical to r.

The Propranolol Study and the BESD

On October 29, 1981, the National Heart, Lung, and Blood Institute officially discontinued its placebo-controlled study of propranolol because the results were so favorable to the treatment that it would be unethical to keep the placebo control patients from receiving the treatment (Kolata 1981). The two-year data for this study were based on 2,108 patients and χ^2 (1) was approximately 4.2. What, then, was the size of the effect that led the institute to break off its study? Was the use of propranolol accounting for 90 percent of the variance in death rates? Was it 50 percent or 10 percent, the overly modest effect size that should prompt us to give up psychotherapy? We find the proportion-of-variance-accounted-for (r^2) as follows:

$$r^2 = \frac{\chi^2}{N} = \frac{4.2}{2,108} = .002$$

Thus, the propranolol study was discontinued for an effect accounting for one-fifth of 1 percent of the variance! To display this result as a BESD we take the square root of r^2 to obtain the r we use for the BESD. That r is about .04, which displays as shown in Table 11.3.

As behavioral researchers we are not accustomed to thinking of r's of .04 as reflecting effect sizes of practical importance. If we were among the 4 per 100 who moved from one outcome to the other, we might well revise our view of the practical import of small effects!

A Concluding Note on Interpreting Effect Sizes

Rosenthal and Rubin (1982) proposed that the reporting of effect sizes could be made more intuitive and more informative by using the BESD. It was their belief that the use of the BESD to display the increase in success rate due to treatment would more clearly convey the real world importance of treatment effects than would the commonly used descriptions of effect size, especially those based on the proportion of variance accounted for.

One effect of the routine employment of a display procedure such as the BESD to index the practical meaning of our research results would be to give us more useful and realistic assessments of how well we are doing as researchers in applied social and behavioral science and in the social and behavioral sciences more generally. Employment of the BESD has, in fact, shown that we are doing considerably better in our "softer" sciences than we thought we were.

Some Benefits of Meta-Analysis

Our focus so far has been on the criticisms of meta-analysis and on the evaluation of the practical significance of the effect sizes obtained in meta-analytic work. This paper concludes with a brief consideration of some of the better-known and some of the lesser-known benefits of meta-analysis.

Table 11.3 Binomial Effect Size Display for the Discontinued Propranolol Study

Condition	Treatment Result		Σ
	Alive	Dead	
Propranolol	52%	48%	100%
Placebo	48	52	100
Σ	100	100	200

Most Obvious Benefits

COMPLETENESS. Meta-analytic consideration of a research domain is more complete and exhaustive, though this does *not* mean that all studies found are weighted equally. Indeed, every study should be weighted from zero to any desired number. These weights, of course, must be defensible. (It will not do to weight all my results $+1.00$ and all my enemies' results 0.00.)

EXPLICITNESS. The quantitative nature of the process of obtaining effect sizes, standard normal deviates, and weights forces explicitness on the analyst. Vague terms like "no relationship," "some relationship," a "strong relationship," and "very significant" are replaced by numerical values.

POWER. Empirical work has shown that meta-analytic procedures increase power and decrease type II errors (Cooper and Rosenthal 1980).

Less Obvious Benefits

MODERATOR VARIABLES. These are more easily spotted and evaluated in a context of a quantitative research summary. This aids theory development and increases empirical richness.

CUMULATION PROBLEMS. Meta-analytic procedures address, in part, the chronic complaint that social sciences cumulate poorly compared to the physical sciences.

Least Obvious Benefits

"THE NEW INTIMACY." This new intimacy is between the reviewer and the data. We cannot do a meta-analysis by reading abstracts and discussion sections. We are forced to look at the numbers and, very often, compute the correct ones ourselves. Meta-analysis requires us to cumulate *data*, not *conclusions*. "Reading" a paper is quite a different matter when we need to compute an effect size and a fairly precise significance level—often from a results section that never heard of effect sizes or precise significance levels (or the APA publication manual)!

THE DEMISE OF THE DICHOTOMOUS SIGNIFICANCE TESTING DECISION. Because meta-analytic procedures faithfully record p levels and effect sizes, there is no need for the continued indefensible practice of claiming a .05 result as evidence against a null and a .06 result as evidence for a null. Two .06 results are much stronger evidence against the null than one .05; and 10 p's of .10 are stronger evidence against the null than 5 p's of .05.

THE OVERTHROW OF THE OMNIBUS TEST.   Meta-analytic questions are basically contrast questions. Any F test with $df > 1$ in the numerator, any χ^2 with $df > 1$, any multivariate analysis of variance, any canonical analysis provides answers to questions that are vague and diffuse to begin with; they are useless in meta-analytic work. (Except for exploratory work they are *nearly* useless in most other work as well.)

THE APPLICABILITY OF META-ANALYTIC PROCEDURES BEYOND META-ANALYSES.   Many of the techniques of contrast analyses among effect sizes, for example, can be used within a single study (Rosenthal and Rosnow 1985). Computing a single effect size from correlated dependent variables or comparing treatment effects on two or more dependent variables serve as illustrations (Rosenthal and Rubin 1986).

THE DECREASE IN THE SPLENDID DETACHMENT OF THE FULL PROFESSOR.   Meta-analytic work requires careful reading of research and moderate data analytic skills. We cannot send an undergraduate research assistant to the library with a stack of 5×8 cards to bring us back "the results." With narrative reviews, that seems often to have been done. With meta-analysis, the reviewer must get involved with the actual data and that is all to the good.

12

A Survey Perspective

Norman M. Bradburn

At this workshop, doing a meta-analysis has been compared to conducting empirical research in which one wants to treat the data quantitatively. I believe that it is similar to designing a survey except that the units of analysis are studies rather than individuals. The same decisions required in designing a good survey are required in designing a meta-analysis.

My definition of a meta-analysis is a study that summarizes the literature of a particular subject area in a quantitative way. In order to do this, one must devise a metric that can be applied across all units and achieve comparability among the various studies. Much of the discussion at the workshop has dealt with problems in finding the right measures to apply in an analysis. Obviously, there does not need to be a single metric; several could be applied. This problem is similar to that in analyzing a survey, in which one might define a variable in terms of a single question asked of an individual, or multiple questions, the responses to which are combined into a single variable.

One of the most important problems under discussion is that of constructing the sampling frame. Everyone seems to be dissatisfied with the present state of computer searches of literature to yield the sampling frame: By looking at titles, we do not identify everything that is relevant. Computer searches that use a key-word-in-context approach often miss studies because their titles or descriptions are different from the words being used in the search. For example, Sudman and I did a meta-analysis of response effects in surveys a number of years ago; because we did not call it a meta-analysis, it does not turn up on lists of meta-analyses we have seen.

An important and difficult problem concerns the questions that are asked about the studies; that is, what types of coding categories should be used to classify studies and the type of "effect" that is calculated. Once a set of coding categories has been defined, are these categories applied uniformly across all studies, or are they applied differently to various studies, and do different coders interpret them differently? The problem of coder reliability has been mentioned and at least one study has systematically looked at the problem of coding reliability in abstracting the data from studies.

A particularly intractable problem with meta-analyses concerns the different quality of studies that go into the sample. (This theme was mentioned by many speakers at the workshop, but there is no consensus about how to deal with this problem.) A minimum criterion for inclusion would seem to be that there be sufficient information in the study to be able to arrive at a calculation of the "effect" that one is interested in studying. In our meta-analysis, Sudman and I found a much larger number of studies than we could use because many studies did not provide sufficient data to enable us to calculate a response effect.

In general, the tendency is to treat all studies as though they are equal in quality. One strategy is to weight differentially studies of differing quality. I think most people feel uncomfortable with not making any qualitative differentiation, but, on the other hand, many people, including myself, are uncomfortable about giving a weight of zero to studies that are of questionable quality but still could contribute toward understanding the problem.

Another possible solution is to code studies for their quality and then do analyses with successive elimination of studies in different quality categories or in conjunction with quality as a covariate. If the fundamental conclusions are not affected by eliminating the lower or higher quality studies, then one would have more confidence that the particular effects found are real. If, on the other hand, conclusions are extremely sensitive to the inclusion or limitation of certain studies, one might worry about what is really going on.

I was puzzled in one way by the desegregation study. I am not sure that this study should really be called a meta-analysis. Instead, it looks as if it were five replications of a meta-analysis because each individual selected his own set of studies and performed his own meta-analysis. Perhaps this study might be thought of as a meta-meta-analysis. In any case, it is an unusual sort of meta-analysis and is perhaps not a very good example of the sorts of things that are being done today.

In closing, I would like to take issue with one point made by several participants that meta-analyses are cheap to do. While it is true that they may be less expensive than some studies in which primary data are collected, they are not all that cheap. The study that Sudman and I did took three years and required the help of a number of research assistants and a long time just to find the sampling frame for the population. Getting all the studies together so that they can be worked on is a tedious job. Unlike sample surveys of individuals, there are no organizations that specialize in sampling and data collection for meta-analyses. People who undertake them typically work with research assistance or, in some instances, work alone. I have the impression from some of the things said here today that people who embarked on a meta-analysis have discovered that it was much more complicated than they thought and might be reluctant to undertake another one. I do not think that the method should be sold to people as something that can be done quickly and cheaply.

13

Methodological Observations on Bias

Fredric M. Wolf

There have been increasing advances in the application of quantitative methods to literature reviewing. All innovations in method or application hold both promise and problems, and meta-analysis is no different in this regard. The advancement of knowledge is a historical, cumulative process. Trial-and-error and serendipity, as well as planfulness, have played roles in the evolution of the scientific method in advancing knowledge. Indeed, the "self-correcting" nature of science was recognized from the onset as one of its principal advantages over what Charles Peirce (1968 [1877]) considered the other three ways of knowing (tenacity, authority, and intuition).

Tenacity, authority, intuition, and science all have played a role in both the development and the criticisms of meta-analysis. With regard to the pioneering psychotherapy outcome meta-analysis, Glass has asserted that his critics have misunderstood (or rejected) the rationale for the choice of object field, taxonomy, and methodology in this study: that his purpose of inquiry was "to determine how and in what ways the judgments, decisions, and inclinations of persons (scholars, citizens, officials, administrators, policymakers) ought to be influenced by the literature of empirical research on the benefits of psychotherapy," and not the "construction of big theory about changing behavior," which is the purpose of inquiry of

Note: Preparation of this paper was supported in part by NIH grant R01 LM 04885 from the National Library of Medicine.

the primary studies included in the meta-analysis (Glass and Kliegl 1983, p. 35). "Meta-analysis takes methodologies as part of its object field. Meta-analysis tests and casts doubt on unwarranted methodological principles" (p. 36) and treats "methodological rules as empirical generalizations whose value must be verified rather than as a priori dogma" (p. 28).

The assertion that meta-analysis is atheoretical and evaluative rather than explanatory appears not to be well understood by some, and disputed by others. Glass asserts that its role is to accurately summarize research as it is reported, while other meta-analysts use it to develop and test theory—for example, to obtain a more accurate estimate of the true population treatment effect size (e.g., Hedges and Olkin 1985; Hunter and Schmidt 1982; Rosenthal 1984). It has been pointed out that the identification of moderator variables and studies whose results are outliers in the batch of results synthesized can be helpful in generating new hypotheses, which can help advance theory (e.g., Light and Pillemer 1984; Rosenthal 1984; Wolf 1986). Additionally, there are hypotheses that can be tested in meta-analyses that cannot be tested in single, well-designed primary research studies (e.g., design effects, interaction/moderator effects in true experimental designs). The implications for meta-analysis of this philosophic distinction are just beginning to be explored (e.g., Bangert-Drowns 1986). There is need for increased understanding and discussion of how this difference in philosophy affects both the choice and application of various statistical procedures and the interpretation of results derived from the procedures.

However unfortunate, science typically "does not begin with a tidy question. Nor does it end with a tidy answer" (Tukey 1980). Science has not been able to provide answers to all questions because the uncertainties involved are not always amenable to statistical evaluation. And those that can be evaluated statistically are subject to potential biases which may distort the design, execution, analysis, and interpretation of research. Given all the "real world" problems that may arise:

> We should: Measure what is needed for policy guidance, even if it can only be measured poorly. Recognize change as often more important than level. Face the inadequacies of standardization for broad groups, making further corrections. Use more flexible and diversified adjustments. . . . If the price is first a preliminary value and then a revision, let us pay it. (Tukey 1979, p. 786)

The methodological problems and needs of meta-analysis are analogous to those confronting primary analysis in individual research studies.

The central difference is, of course, that whereas the unit of analysis in primary research typically is the result for an individual subject or person, the unit of analysis in meta-analysis is the result from an individual study. Given this central difference, many of the issues are similar. Methods for conducting a quantitative literature review, like those in primary research, are not perfect, nor agreed upon, nor free of criticism, abuse, or misuse. The fact that there are disagreements and unresolved issues, however, ultimately serves to stimulate further work that in turn helps to advance the state of knowledge.

Defining Bias

Bias can be defined in various ways—for example, as "something other than the experimental [intervention] that causes a difference between the treatment groups" (Ingelfinger, Mosteller, Thibodeau, and Ware 1983, p. 224) or as "a process at any stage of inference tending to produce results that differ systematically from the true values" (Murphy 1976, p. 239). Bias can occur potentially at any stage of the research process (Murphy 1975; Sackett 1979):

1. In specifying the research question.
2. In the study design, particularly in specifying and selecting the study sample.
3. In implementing the experimental procedure.
4. In estimation.
5. In analyzing the data.
6. In interpreting the results.
7. In reporting or publishing the results.

There are many sources of bias, some of which are not known. Sackett (1979) has cataloged over 50 different biases that can occur in analytic research in the various stages of a single study (i.e., primary analysis). The following discussion briefly outlines some of the biases or problems that may occur in a meta-analysis in each of the above stages of the process.

Bias in Specifying the Research Question

There has been considerable controversy in meta-analysis regarding what has been called the "apples and oranges" problem. Different scientists define and operationalize their taxonomy of constructs in varying ways, often to the chagrin of other scientists working on similar questions. What may appear to be the confounding of two constructs to one scientist may not seem so to another, and the debate that ensues hopefully sharpens the articulation of the various points of view, even if the disagreement is not resolved. This issue can affect the choice of both the independent and dependent variables. Broadly defined independent variables can be examined in one analysis and stratified into separate categories for further individual analyses and comparisons; for example, the results of all types of psychotherapy were examined in one meta-analysis and then examined individually in a set of additional meta-analyses by Glass and his colleagues. This can be done for dependent variables as well, although there still appear to be considerable differences among meta-analysts in their willingness to do so. Selecting more than one study result for inclusion in the same meta-analysis raises problems of nonindependence in the data that need to be addressed in the analysis.

Bias in the Study Design: Sampling

Different taxonomies developed by scientists for similar object fields (events to be explained, predicted, or understood) define the population of studies to be included in a meta-analysis. Once this population is identified, studies must be selected for inclusion in the analysis. There is considerable disagreement over whether or not all identified studies should be included. As stated earlier, Glass considers the empirical examination of methodology, such as study design (degree of randomization, type of controls, etc.) to be part of his object field of study in a meta-analysis. He has been steadfast in advocating the inclusion of all studies and the coding of their features for empirical examination. This allows both well- and ill-designed studies into the sample for comparative purposes. Since his stated purpose is description of the research literature, this presents no problem for him. However, scientists wishing to perform a meta-analysis in order to obtain a more accurate estimate of the population treatment effect size than can be obtained from individual studies find it problematic to allow weakly designed studies to be included and possibly bias this estimate. They seek only the most methodologically pure studies available. Obviously the results of meta-analyses of the same research domain by different investigators can vary. It is imperative that the inclusionary and exclusionary criteria for studies be explicitly stated so that efforts to understand differences can be enhanced.

Related to this issue is that of model specification. Hedges has developed random- and fixed-effects models for effect sizes, analogous to those in analysis of variance (see Hedges and Olkin 1985). In the simplest case, the fixed-effects model assumes that individual studies are random samples from a population with a single, fixed-effect size. The random-effects model assumes the population effect size is randomly distributed with its own mean and variance. In the first case, variability in sample effect sizes reflects sampling error, while in the random-effects model, variability reflects both sampling error and population variability. Rarely if ever are samples of studies in a meta-analysis true random samples from the population. There is a need to understand the implications of this discrepancy and how it influences the interpretation of meta-analytic results. How do we know whether a particular collection of studies really constitutes an adequate sample of a particular domain? "The 'data' in meta-analysis typically represent a nonrandom, biased sample of studies, each of which addresses a common conceptual hypothesis" (Strube et al. 1985, p. 66). This can lead to nonrepresentative estimates of effects.

Additionally, Hunter, Schmidt, and Jackson (1982) have proposed correcting the variance of a collection of effect sizes and adjusting the correlations between study characteristics and effect sizes for sampling error, but it is not widely done in practice. The implications of doing this warrant further examination. Sampling decisions clearly influence estimates of effect size.

Bias in Implementing the Experimental Procedure

"Meta-analysis itself is an observational study with strengths and weaknesses associated with that design. Unlike the investigator in a prospective, primary study, the meta-analyst has no control, except through selection of papers, over what 'treatments' have been applied or how 'subjects' are assigned to them" (Louis, Fineberg, and Mosteller 1985). Once explicit criteria for study selection, coding, and inclusion have been established, it is imperative that the locating of study results, the calculating and recording of study statistics (e.g., p-values, effect size estimates), and the coding of study characteristics be done in a consistent and reliable fashion. Controls for recording errors are typically established and the level of interrater agreement is assessed and improved if necessary. The implications of these types of error for the internal validity of a meta-analysis are just beginning to be understood.

Several studies have examined empirically the effects of deficiencies in reliability on meta-analytic results. For example, results of a study by Orwin and Cordray (1985) raise the issue of whether reliability corrections should be incorporated into meta-analyses. Their findings indicated that correcting for coding reliabilty affected both the size of R^2 and the relative importance of predictors in a regression analysis performed on a subset of the Smith, Glass, and Miller psychotherapy data set. The pervasiveness of this problem is not known.

Bias in Estimation

Each meta-analyst must make judgments concerning the methods of estimation of individual test statistics and effect size measures for the study results to be included in the synthesis. These judgments can affect the magnitude of the estimates obtained. Some of these judgments include (1) selecting a measure of variability for calculation of effect sizes, (2) deciding whether or not to calculate unbiased (weighted) estimates of effect size, (3) deciding whether or not to adjust for measurement error and restricted range (Hunter et al. 1982) and (4) selecting procedures for reconstructing test statistics and effect sizes when full information is not provided in primary research reports.

   1. *Selecting a measure of variability for calculation of effect sizes.* Several different formulas can be used to calculate the standardized mean difference in outcomes between groups (typically a treatment versus a control) when it is used as an effect size indicator. These variations result from using (1) an estimate of either the pooled within-standard deviation or the control group standard deviation and (2) either N (the sample size) or N − 1 to calculate the estimate of the population standard deviation. The difference between using N and N − 1 is obviously greater for small samples; the difference diminishes as N approaches infinity. As a practical matter the pooled estimate is more stable than the control-group-only estimate; however, use of the pooled estimate ignores the problem created by the effect of the treatment on the experimental group standard deviation. Recently Kulik and Kulik (1986) noted that operative and interpretable effect sizes are identical only for the post-test-only, independent-group design. They criticized the wide use in meta-analysis of operative effect sizes (which are used in power analysis; see Cohen 1977) instead of interpretable effect sizes. Because *operative* effect sizes reflect differences in experimental design, such as blocking, covariance, or matching, Kulik and Kulik (in press) state that they are inappropriate to use in meta-analysis without first converting them to *interpretable* effect sizes. They believe that operative effect sizes typically result in overestimates and provide an example of a published effect of 2.04 that was mistakenly (they assert) calculated as an operative effect size when the true interpretable effect size was 0.44.

2. *Deciding whether or not to calculate unbiased (weighted) estimates of effect size.* Hedges has developed the sampling distribution for the standardized mean difference effect size and has shown that effect size estimates are slightly biased when using the procedures above. Hedges and Rosenthal and Rubin have presented methods for obtaining unbiased estimates (see Hedges and Olkin 1985, Rosenthal 1984, or Wolf 1986 for detailed explanations and references). It has been noted that this correction factor is very near unity when the number of study effects to be aggregated is greater than ten. While more theoretically and technically correct, this adjustment has not been shown to have practical import. It is common practice to report both corrected and uncorrected effect sizes.

3. *Deciding whether or not to adjust for measurement error and restricted range.* Hunter et al. (1982) recommend adjusting each study effect size for both the unreliability of the independent and dependent variables (correcting for attenuation) and restriction of range. There is still much disagreement among meta-analysts concerning whether this should be done. Some believe these procedures to be too burdensome and overly restrictive and suggest looking for correlates (mediators) of effect size in lieu of them (e.g., Rosenthal 1984). Hunter et al. (1982) believe that corrections for these artifacts (and for sampling error among the set of results aggregated) are necessary *before* examining correlates of study outcome in order to reduce the likelihood that mediating variables would account for error variance in effect size. They reported that 72 percent of the variability in a set of 152 effect sizes in their employment test validity study was accounted for by measurement error, range restriction, and sampling error. While some meta-analysts do make these adjustments, it is not common practice. The amount of variability accounted for by these artifacts in most meta-analyses is unknown, as is the degree to which they influence the presence or strength of mediating effects. While the recommendation to *always* report uncorrected effect sizes (e.g., Rosenthal 1984) is well taken, there is still debate regarding the practicality and importance of calculating and reporting corrected effect sizes.

4. *Selecting procedures for reconstructing test statistics and effect sizes when full information is not provided.* Sometimes the meta-analyst must try to reconstruct effect sizes and test statistics when information reported in a primary research study is incomplete. For example, Wortman (1984) discussed the situation where information in the primary report does not include the value of the test statistic nor the precise significance level. If convention is followed and only $p < .05$ and $p < .01$ are reported for significant results, statistical tables can be consulted to translate these imprecise p-values into their analogous test statistics (e.g., t-values). Effect sizes can then be calculated from these test statistics. These indirect esti-

mates will tend to be conservative and underestimate the true effect sizes. Since p-values are not customarily provided for nonsignificant results, the expected mean p-value of the distribution of nonsignificant effects (i.e., .50) can be used following the suggestion of Cooper. These estimates are always somewhat imprecise and make conclusions drawn from a meta-analysis less reliable. There have been increasing calls for researchers and journals to provide more complete information and precise p-values. The latter practice would necessitate a major change in the customary approach to significance testing and reporting. Indeed, a major impact of meta-analysis may be its effect on the conduct and reporting of primary research.

Bias in Analyzing the Data

There are many potential ways in which the analysis of data in a meta-analysis can lead to biased results. Two of the major issues relate to statistical assumptions and independence of data.

Statistical Assumptions

A logical starting point is to use graphical methods such as stem-and-leaf displays and other exploratory data analysis procedures to see what the distribution of effect sizes looks like. An important question to consider is whether or not the data are normally distributed enough to warrant the calculation (in a parametric context) of an average effect size for the collection of study findings. Seldom is this discussed in published meta-analyses. While nonparametric meta-analytic methods have been proposed (e.g., Kraemer and Andrews 1982; Hedges and Olkin 1985), rarely have they been used in practice. Their largest drawback is the necessity to have access to the raw data for each study. Rarely are these effect sizes themselves, or the information necessary to reconstruct them, reported in the primary research studies. Major changes in both research reporting and direct access to data from primary analyses would be necessary for nonparametrics to play a major role in meta-analysis. Even when nonparametric effect sizes can be estimated, it is not clear how potential mediating effects could be tested (additional analyses by subgroups might be one possibility).

Some of the questions that need to be addressed: How tenable are the assumptions underlying the statistical models that have been used and what are the implications of departure from these assumptions? What does it mean if the study effects are heterogeneous? How can tests of homogeneity of effects be made more useful? Does violation of the assumption of homogeneity lead to misleading results and conclusions, or is it to be expected and ignored? Should outliers be excluded or clustered into separate categories for analysis? Murphy (1975) has argued that outlier exclusion may be unjustified and could lead to what he calls "tidying up bias." Careful examination of outliers can provide important understandings and generate new hypotheses that might otherwise be missed.

What statistical adjustments should be made (e.g., weighting, corrections for measurement or sampling error)? Kulik and Kulik (1986) have pointed out that rarely are sampling error estimates or tests of homogeneity adjusted when information concerning pretests or covariates is available.

Nonindependence of Data

Nonindependence of data has been one of the most controversial issues in meta-analysis. The issue arises when the study finding, and not the study itself, is considered the unit of analysis. The problem occurs when there is more than one finding in a study. Depending on how the multiple nonindependent findings from a study are treated in the analysis, the degrees of freedom and thus statistical power may be inflated and increase the likelihood of a Type I error, and a study may have more opportunties to influence the overall estimate of effect in the synthesis than a study with only one finding.

There are many types of possible nonindependence of data used in a meta-analysis. Landman and Dawes (1982) identified five types of nonindependence in the psychotherapy data set used by Smith and Glass in their meta-analysis: (1) multiple outcome measures (dependent variables) obtained from the same subjects within single studies; (2) measures taken at multiple points in time from the same subjects; (3) nonindependence of scores within a single outcome measure—for example, using both a global total score and a more specific subscale (independent variables); (4) nonindependence of studies within a single article; and (5) nonindependent samples across articles.

Nonindependent findings have been treated in a variety of ways, including (1) treating them as if they were independent, (2) using the average of the findings for each study, (3) selecting the "best" one finding from each study, (4) delimiting the number of findings (e.g., two) from each study, and (5) performing separate meta-analyses for each type of outcome measure.

Strube (1985) and Rosenthal and Rubin (1986) have developed promising statistical techniques for handling the multiple outcome situation when certain information (e.g., intercorrelations among variables) is available or can be reliably estimated. Glass et al. (1982) have discussed Tukey's jackknife procedure and an intrastudy correlation coefficient (similar to the intraclass correlation). The practical utility of these approaches has not been fully explored and warrants further examination.

Bias in Interpreting the Results

Meta-analysis "depends most heavily on the assumption that the average bias is zero with respect to threats to internal, external, construct, statistical conclusion, or any other type of validity" (Cook 1984, p. 39). This, of course, may not be true and is an empirical question that each meta-analyst can examine. It is important to consider the adequacy of the statistical procedures and adjustments.

O'Grady (1982) discussed three major factors that influence the magnitude and interpretation of measures of effect: psychometric, methodological, and theoretical. Psychometric factors include measurement error. Strube et al. (1985) have asserted that unreliability in the independent and dependent variables limits the upper bounds for estimates of effect and the power of statistical tests. To the degree that variations in reliability within and between studies produce variations in effects, interpretative problems arise. This raises the question of whether the variation among effect sizes due to mediating variables is real or the result of measurement or sampling error.

Some of the methodological factors that could affect interpretabilty include the intentions of the researcher (e.g., understanding versus prediction), the population sampled (e.g., criteria for study inclusion, heterogeneity), and the design of the meta-analysis (e.g., coding decisions, selection of potential mediating features).

Theoretical factors in scientists' selection and delimitation of an object field of study and taxonomy of definitions (and the degree of isomorphism) can influence the magnitude and interpretation of effect sizes. These decisions can contribute to a failure to "exhaust the hypothesis space" (Murphy 1975). How these three factors come into play can be seen clearly in the different results obtained from independent meta-analyses of the school desegregation literature, where Cook (1984) noted the tendency for the effect sizes to vary according to the meta-analysts' prior professional commitments regarding the issue.

Bias in Reporting the Results

Bias in reporting the results is a problem at the primary research level, which has implications for meta-analysis. A meta-analysis will likely reflect any publication biases that exist, as discussed in Chapter 2 (pp. 19–20). Procedures for calculating "fail-safe N's" for both combined tests and effect sizes provide an estimate of the stability of the effect obtained by suggesting the number of studies averaging zero effect that would be needed to reverse the conclusion that an effect exists. They provide no help, however, when the goal of the meta-analysis is to estimate as precisely as possible the true effect size. New approaches to addressing this issue are needed.

Summary and Conclusions

The use of meta-analysis to quantify the effects of research pertaining to a common research question has advanced the process of literature reviewing considerably. The results of a meta-analysis, however, are influenced by decisions regarding the general philosophic aim of the meta-anaylsis, the choice of the object field of study, the definitions of the taxonomic constructs, and the methodological plan. Bias can occur at any stage in the research process: in specifying the research question, in designing the study, in implementing the experimental procedure, in making estimations, in analyzing data, in interpreting results, and in the reporting or publishing of results of primary research that a meta-analyst must rely upon. Many of these problems are not unique to meta-analysis and must be confronted in any review, whether it is a traditional literary review or a quantitative meta-analytic review. Both a meta-analysis and a literary review typically represent a nonrandom, biased sample of the research domain to be synthesized. When interpreting results, it is important not to lose sight of the assumptions that have been made.

Currently existing statistical adjustments that can be made need to be reexamined closely regarding their impact and appropriateness. New approaches need to be developed and experimented with in order to reduce as much as possible potential biasing influences. Some of the important issues and adjustments to be considered include homogeneity/heterogeneity of effects, sampling error, mediating variables, coding unreliability, measurement error, restriction of range, bias in estimation, nonindependence, and formulae for effect size. Many of the current advances in meta-analysis have had direct applications in primary research as well—for example, the increasing use of measures of effect size in primary research reports. It can be anticipated that future advances in meta-analytic methods will have a similar positive impact on the conduct and reporting of primary research.

Some of the problems need to be remedied at the primary research level. Multiplicity and nonindependence of data, incomplete reporting of results, and so on, are problems at the primary research level. One of the major contributions of meta-analysis may be as a stimulus for change in this area. While there are some indications that primary research quality may be improving (e.g., Hall, Ward, and Comer 1986), there is still much to be done. Journal editors can assist immeasurably by devoting the space necessary for the inclusion of the descriptive information in primary studies that is needed in a meta-analysis. More precise information needs to be provided for nonsignificant findings, and the mystical adherence to the .05 significance level needs to be reevaluated. Fisher, who was the first person to formally mention $p = .05$ as a criterion for statistical significance, considered it to be a matter of convenience and preference (Cowles and Davis 1982). It may no longer be as convenient and preferred today as a result of advances made since the 1920s. Rosenthal and others have argued that two findings, each of which is $p < .06$, are stronger support for a hypothesis than is one finding at $p < .05$. This is another issue in the philosophy of science and would necessitate changes in professional attitudes and publication practices.

Changes in the reporting and publishing of primary research, however, would not completely solve the problem of inadequacy of information. There are not enough journal pages, nor are publication priorities high enough, for all studies failing to reject the null hypothesis to be published. How to make these results accessible to the scientific community remains a problem. Publication of abstracts is one possibility, but this would necessitate some mechanism for making more information, or the data, available to meta-analysts. If nonparametrics are to play a larger role in the quantitative synthesis of research, then access to data from primary research would be needed in many instances. The complicated issues surrounding the sharing of data are beginning to be discussed more seriously at a national level (e.g., Fienberg, Martin, and Straf 1985).

The issue of whether or not there should be technical standards for the conduct of a meta-analysis is being raised more and more often. While guidelines for conducting a meta-analysis have appeared (e.g., Cooper 1984; Wolf 1986), they have no endorsement of authority and represent privately held views based on individual readings of the "state-of-the-art." While ensuring that each meta-analysis attains a minimum and sufficient level of quality is certainly desirable, the imposition of standards is fraught with problems, not the least of which would be to put a damper on the development of new approaches.

> In meta-analysis, varying the assumptions underlying an analysis is desirable because it makes heterogeneous those facets of research where no "right" answer is available and fallible human judgment is required. To attempt to legislate a single "right" way either to compute effect size or to sample studies would be counterproductive so long as none of the analysts is clearly wrong. (Cook 1984, p. 9)

There is a need for more reviews (meta-analytic or otherwise) of the meta-analyses that have already been conducted in order to better understand the implications of the varying philosophical, methodological, and statistical practices that have been used. For example, Glass et al. (1981) reviewed the relationship between findings in a group of meta-analyses and source of publication, research quality, and date of publication, respectively, and Kulik and Kulik (in press) have reviewed results of meta-analyses in education. Taking a Monte Carlo approach, Tracz and Elmore (1985) examined the effects of violation of the assumption of independence on meta-analyses using correlational effect sizes, while Spector and Levine (1987) examined the susceptibility of meta-analysis to Type I and Type II errors. The challenge is great and the work is just beginning, but the prospect for future advances promises to be exciting.

PART V

Where Do We Go From Here?

14

A New Perspective

Donald B. Rubin

Introduction

These comments are designed to be provocative and thereby stimulate new directions for research in meta-analysis. Often, the right way to add provocative stimuli is to claim that everything everybody is doing is wrong. Even when this isn't true (and it certainly can't be in this context), it is often useful to take such an attitude and see how far it can be pushed. So I begin by claiming that everything everybody's been doing statistically for meta-analysis, including the things that Bob Rosenthal and I have done and do, are irrelevant and have missed the point. We all should really be doing something else.

Of course, I don't necessarily believe that we're all entirely off course, but I want to see how far I can push the position that certain things that have been repeated lots of times and seem to be accepted in the meta-analysis literature are in fact misguided. For example, consider the idea that sampling and representativeness of the studies in a meta-analysis are important. I will claim that this is nonsense—we don't have to worry about representing a population but rather about other far more important things. Here is how my argument goes.

Meta-Analysis as Literature Review Versus Understanding Science

There are basically two kinds of meta-analyses: those for literature synthesis and those for understanding the underlying science. I think that the current view, which I'm going to rebel against, is really one of literature synthesis and seems to be clearly reflected in the writing and comments of Glass, Bradburn, Hedges, and others, and in the statistical analysis techniques of Hedges and Olkin, Rosenthal and Rubin, and others. Consequently, the current view is concerned with survey sampling the finite population of studies in the world—the population out there of studies that have been done, which is a little fuzzy because it's not exactly clear what constitutes a study. In any case, our objective under this view is to summarize all existing studies by their average population effect. Of course, the average population effect that is desired might not be the gross average in the whole population of all studies. Individual studies might be weighted by "quality of study" or something like that, and they might be summarized within some strata or some domains of the population as defined by certain characteristics. But under this view, there's a conceptualization that a population of studies exists that we're after.

If we accept this perspective, some key issues concern the representativeness of the studies that we have in a meta-analysis, and their independence, because all the inferences back to the finite population (or even a conceptually infinite population) of studies depend upon certain assumptions about random sampling or randomness and independence of the units of study. I believe that this view of meta-analysis is commonly accepted. Certainly Norm Bradburn makes the point very clearly in his comments, when he draws his analogy about the issues that arise in sampling finite populations of people and studies. He is clearly thinking about the finite population of studies and that's why representativeness is important. In Larry Hedges' comments there is a clear statement of that perspective—very sharp and very clear. At the Hedgesville conference, Fred Mosteller raised a question about whether this analogy was really appropriate. My response is that it depends on whether one accepts the perspective of literature synthesis.

A contrasting view is, I believe, more enlightening. I will call it "building and extrapolating a response surface," and that is what I'm going to present. It is different from Wolf's theoretical perspective, because I think Wolf's view is a philosophical perspective without a prescription for analytic techniques. I'm going to propose a specific conceptual framework with associated analytic techniques. In this conceptual framework, none of the techniques we now use in meta-analysis will be truly appropriate. Not all of statistics are changing obviously—we're still playing the statistics game, drawing inferences from data to populations. But none of the specific analytic techniques will be the same. That's the sense in which everything everyone is now doing is wrong.

Meta-Analysis Conceptualized as Building and Extrapolating Response Surfaces

So what is going on that makes all previous work wrong? There are two key points. The first one is that we really don't care about the population of imperfect studies per se. Out there is a world of studies which vary from being very carefully done to very uncarefully done. For example, I can think of an especially uncareful study: I had a dream last night, and I dreamt I did a study and I randomized some people, and I wrote down the results this morning. Do you want that study summarized in your meta-analysis? I doubt it. But it is a study in some sense. There is a whole gradation of studies from good to bad. Should we really care about summarizing this population of studies that vary so much in quality? They are all imperfect. They all have problems. My answer is "no." We really do not care about the population per se. But then what should we care about?

My answer, which is the second key point, is that what we want to do is estimate "true" effects of treatments (defined shortly) and their interactions with scientifically important moderator variables. That is what I mean—I think we all mean—by a scientific inquiry: understanding what's really going on. Although we may need to use existing studies to address the scientific question, the studies themselves are not really of interest.

Now for a critical point: I define "true effects" as results that would be obtained in an infinitely large, perfectly designed study or sequence of such studies. Under this view, we really do not care *scientifically* about summarizing this finite population. We really care about the underlying scientific process—the underlying process that is generating these outcomes that we happen to see—that we, as fallible researchers, are trying to glimpse through the opaque window of imperfect empirical studies.

Why specifically does this view of meta-analysis imply that current techniques are inadequate? Here is some notation—rough conceptual notation, rather than notation for any particular model. First, Y denotes a bunch of outcome variables, usually assumed for simplicity to be a single variable. Second, there are treatments that may affect Y; say that there are only two treatments: experimental (E) versus control (C). The estimand is the effect of E versus C on Y. In fact, there could be many treatments and E versus C could really be a linear contrast, but in this context the estimand has to be defined to have only one degree of freedom, so that the estimand has a direction to it. I do not like omnibus estimands any more than anyone else. Finally, there are factors (X, Z) describing studies that might be used to estimate the effect of E versus C on Y.

There are two kinds of factors, and it is important to distinguish between these two types. The first, X, consists of scientific factors: the gender of the subjects, the age of the subjects, classroom sizes, and all those other things that we care about, that have scientific interest. The second, the Z's, are scientifically uninteresting design variables: the sample sizes of the study; the kind of controls being used; indicators for whether it was randomized, a paired comparison, nonrandomized but carefully matched, even the size of standard errors of the study; an indicator for which lab the study was done in; maybe even the date of the study if time trends are suspected. There should also be study indicators to handle studies with multiple outcomes. Thus Z consists of variables that are purely descriptive of study design and are not themselves of intrinsic scientific interest. Of course, this dichotomy between X and Z is vague. There are certain factors that sometimes would be design factors and other times would be more usefully thought of as factors of scientific interest. Nevertheless, let us accept for now that we can usefully make this dichotomy.

How Does One Build
and Extrapolate a Response Surface?

Having established this notation, let us turn to defining and extrapolating the response surface of interest. The response surface of interest is the effect of treatment E versus C on Y as a function of the two kinds of factors, X and Z. It is a whole function in a multidimensional space. It is a whole surface. The relationship between effect and (X,Z) is approximate in the sense that there is some residual noise: the effect of E versus C on Y cannot be perfectly predicted by X and Z. But the attempt is to build a model that expresses the typical treatment effect as a function of scientific factors and design factors such as we conceptualize them.

What is to be extrapolated? That gets back to the idea of the ideal study. I want to extrapolate the responses, the estimated treatment effects, into the region of ideal studies. I do not care about the responses in the region where I get to observe them, because that is not the region of primary scientific interest. The estimated effect of E versus C in fallible studies is not the scientific issue. I want the effect of E versus C on Y when Z is Z_0, where Z_0 indicates values of the design variables for a perfect study—I want to fix Z at the ideal study: when the sample sizes are infinite from a perfectly controlled randomized study. That is where I want to get the treatment effects. But all I have are fallible studies floating around in journals, file drawers, wastebaskets, and gray matter. I really want the answer that is out there in the platonic ideal world. I think that is what we mean by the "true" effect size—the answer we would get if we had done an infinitely large, perfect study. This ideal answer is a whole function of values of scientific interest, because it gives the effect size as a function of the scientific factors, with design factors fixed at perfect studies.

I believe that this extrapolated response surface is the objective of meta-analysis and how one should conceptualize the grand flow of data analysis.

Standard statistical tools can be used to build and extrapolate this treatment-effect response surface, although in some novel ways perhaps. One first builds a response surface for the treatment effects as a function of scientific factors X and design factors Z, which is estimated by regressing (in a general sort of sense, not necessarily least squares) the observed effect sizes on the X and Z descriptors of all the studies and outcomes. Standard techniques assume that there is exchangeability given X and Z. Because X and Z incorporate everything one knows about the studies, exchangeability is just a valid statement of ignorance about any other descriptors. So, the independence comes automatically for those who like de Finetti's Theorem. For those who don't like de Finetti's Theorem, there is nothing else one can do anyway, so the ignorance of the factors just implies independence. It is a very conditional type of independence, however, and very different from the kind of independence that we all commonly talk about in meta-analysis (independence of studies, independence of different outcomes within the same study). Because all of the indicators for the different studies are incorporated in (X,Z), the kind of independence that has to be bought to build response surfaces is conditional on (X,Z), and, moreover, there is nothing in the data to contradict it.

Nevertheless, when doing this kind of modeling, one has to be very sensitive to certain observable features in the data. First of all, the sampling variance of the observed estimated effect sizes will depend upon (X,Z), so one cannot perform the usual regression where there is constant residual variance common at all values of the predictor variables. The smaller studies will have more variability in estimated effect sizes, and the bigger studies will have less variability. Also, studies with larger standard errors and worse control will have more variability in their estimated effect sizes. Consequently, the conditional variance, the residual variance off this regression plane (the response surface), will depend upon the Z factors explicitly. Curvilinearity is very important; obviously we have to be sensitive to curvilinearity when doing extrapolation of any kind. In some cases, we can get around curvilinearity with proper parameterization; for example, the size of the study makes more sense in terms of $1/N$ than N. We also have to be sensitive to interactions, product terms in (X,Z). Finally, we will have to be aware of estimation issues of smoothing because the estimation of a response surface in (X,Z) will involve a large number of factors and therefore a large number of parameters—thus we can't go around estimating these very high dimensional response surfaces using standard methodologies such as simple least squares and simple hypothesis testing. We have to be very careful about smoothing all of these extra parameters. But I'm not going to say anything here about how that is done, and just assume access to modern statistical techniques that address this problem.

Extrapolating the Response Surface to $Z = Z_0$

After having built and estimated a model for the response surface from the observed studies, how do we extrapolate it to an ideal study? An ideal study is defined by some particular values of the design variables, for example, randomized, infinitely large, with many very carefully controlled blocks. To extrapolate the response surface, mathematically one sets $Z = Z_0$. In practice, instead of one dimension to Z there may be 30 dimensions to Z, but in any case, the objective is the same. In this conceptual picture, we extend the studies to where they are perfect. The response surface is flattening out, asymptotically approaching a value, and that value is what we mean by the true effect size. It is the answer we would get if we did the perfect study. Now, this extrapolated response surface may have large standard errors associated with it. But I think that that is the honest state of the world: whenever we do extrapolation, we have an extra component of variability. If we found out from data, for example, that the estimated effect sizes do not change as the quality of the studies improves, then there would be little sensitivity to that extrapolation and the standard errors would be relatively small. But if we found evidence that as the studies improved, the estimated effects changed systematically, then we would have to admit that there is uncertainty as to what the effect would be in the ideal study.

The extrapolated response surface is still a function of X, so the true effect size generally depends upon X factors, thereby reflecting the possible existence of interactions of treatments and X. The response surface at the ideal study may still be a complicated function with many interactions, but then that would be the scientific summary of the situation.

Conditional Answers Versus Average Answers

It is important to see that, in this perspective I am proposing, answers are conditional on those factors that describe the science, X, and an ideal study $Z = Z_0$. That is where we are making inferences. In contrast, the current view (the Glass view, or the view in most of the comments here) pursues averages of this response surface, average answers over the values of the scientific factors and the designs that current investigators have, for some reason, chosen to use. Another way to describe the distinction is that the response surface, this function, is science: that is what God has done. Now, current investigators have taken various choices of X that they happen to want to look at—different ages of kids, different sex ratios, different races, different size schools, either for convenience or for matters of real interest. These investigators have also confronted design considerations; some have been careful, others not so careful. But the current choices of (X,Z) among investigators define the current collection of studies that we have. And the current view is that this collection of X and Z values, which reflects psychological choices that study designers have made, is the right population to use in averaging the response function. I believe there is no reason for that choice of averaging at all, for that mix of psychology and science. The science is the response surface, and the psychology is why current researchers happen to choose the X's and Z's that they have over the past 20 years, and the resulting collection defines a pretty strange average of designs. Why is that the right average to take? I do not want to say that it might not be of interest to take averages over some population, but the current collection of fallible studies is a strange population for a scientist to be interested in— something that is idiosyncratic to the current collection of researchers and the current laboratories who happen to do work on the problem.

What to Do If Population Averages Are Desired

A target population is defined by the distribution of X that we happen to like; Z does not affect this scientific population since it is fixed at Z_0, the ideal study. For example, one might say, "I want an average over a distribution of ages that is like the ages in the United States, and equally weights males and females." Defining the population is equivalent to defining a distribution over the scientific factors X—it has nothing to do with design or with idiosyncratic choices of designs that people have made. Having defined a target population by a distribution of X, we can obtain an average effect for that population by taking the extrapolated response surface, $F(X,Z = Z_0)$ and averaging it over the chosen X distribution. Note that this average to be estimated has scientific interest that is not tied to any peculiar collection of studies that we happen to have seen. Of course, estimates of this estimand, or any function of the response surface more generally, will depend on the current collection of studies from which data are available.

More Work But Commensurate Payoffs

Certainly more work is needed to build and extrapolate response surface models rather than to use the current collection of meta-analytic techniques for literature synthesis. I envision that massive model building efforts may be involved. Such a plan has potential payoffs, however, and here is a list of reasons for my liking it.

1.   There's a conceptual clarity in my perspective regarding the objective of meta-analyses that is entirely absent from the current view of literature summarization. There is a clear statement of what we want to estimate, the estimand of scientific interest. It is obvious that we may not be getting decent estimates of that estimand using the current collection of meta-analytic techniques. We may, by fortune, get decent estimates because estimated effects from small randomized experiments may not change as the studies get bigger and better. But that's an empirical question, not one that we can decide before trying some response-surface modeling.

2.   Also there is conceptual clarity to realizing that the current population of studies and its definition are entirely irrelevant to defining estimands. I do not care what the current population of studies is. Studies that I happen to be able to get are only useful for helping me build my model, not for defining estimands. It is the conditional distribution of the effect size given the X's and Z's that is of interest, not the average over the existing population of X's and Z's. Therefore I do not care about describing or representing the population of studies that has been done so far.

3.   Consequently, in my view of meta-analysis, the sampling representativeness of the studies included is a minor issue because the representativeness at issue is really given X and Z—for characteristics X and Z, do I have a representative sample? Have I distorted the sample in some way at fixed (X,Z) values? It is a much more minor issue than having a simple random sample overall. So my answer to Fred Mosteller's question, mentioned earlier in these comments, is that the concern with representativeness and random sampling is overblown for meta-analyses aimed at scientific understanding.

4.   It follows that on the issue of which studies to include, I would include all the studies, no matter how bad they are, because there is an automatic down-weighting of the poorer studies when we extrapolate toward the ideal study. That is, poorer studies are in a part of the factor space, a part of the Z space, that is basically irrelevant. Any sort of proper response surface model building will down-weight them—allow them to provide only a little bit of information concerning the surface at $Z = Z_0$, the ideal study. What we are interested in is the shape of this function in the ideal study world, which is beyond the data, and these poorer studies are very far from that. They will have a small effect on the estimation, but not nearly as much as the better studies. As the studies get better and better, there will be an automatic increased weighting of their effect on the extrapolated response surface. We do not have to worry about which studies to include and which studies to exclude.

5.   The concern with independence of studies and results is clarified and simplified in this perspective. We must simply include variables in (X,Z) indicating studies, laboratories, and so on. When building the response surface, the only issue of independence is one of conditional independence given (X,Z). That is, are two outcomes with the same values of (X,Z) a priori exchangeable? Without data to dispute the exchangeability, they may be modeled as i.i.d. given (X,Z), and thus the conceptual issue of independence reduces to which (X,Z) variables to include in the response surface construction. It may be hard practically to decide which indicators are important to include, but it is not a deep conceptual issue. The fuzziness in the ideas surrounding independence is gone in this perspective. The issues involve the usual model building efforts, such as in standard regression problems. Since we will have more descriptors (X,Z) than we know how to build easily into a prediction equation, we will have to do the estimation using modern statistical tools and ideas.

6.   Missing values will certainly occur, since some studies have more complete information than others, but they can be handled. There is a whole technology that now exists for handling missing values (cf. Little and Rubin 1987). It is not necessarily easy or trivial, but there is a way to handle them, and all studies do not have to have measured the same X's and Z's. The ones that omit X's and Z's provide less information about what the response surface looks like conditionally given complete X and Z. That can be taken care of automatically by suitable procedures.

7.   A final payoff to this perspective on meta-analysis relates to the choice of new studies: Which new studies should we do? In this perspective the choice of new studies relies on ideas of experimental design, not on survey sampling. We want to choose studies, that is, values of X and Z, that are cost-effective for learning about the response surface at the ideal

study. The design question concerns how we best gather information about the estimands, the quantities of interest, which are summarized by the extrapolated response surface. The old design question concerns how we represent the current population of studies better, how to estimate the average effect in the current finite population better. I think our game is clearly to learn about the science of the situation, not about the idiosyncratic population of studies that people have done. Our objective in designing new studies is to gain maximum information for minimum cost about this response surface at the ideal study.

Remaining Problems

Obviously, some problems do not go away just by reconceptualizing meta-analysis. For example, the confounding in X, the fact that the scientific predictors are confounded across many observed studies, remains. The fact that the observed studies do not constitute any nice balanced design is a problem that doesn't go away. Nevertheless, the problem of the confounding in Z does go away, because Z is just a subspace of noise, which we're extrapolating to $Z = Z_0$. All I want to do is get an adjusted estimate for some subspace $Z = Z_0$. I don't care how correlated the individual components of Z are. It doesn't make any difference in terms of the precision of the estimand—the treatment effect as a function of X at $Z = Z_0$. Certainly, study sample size and standard errors are going to be highly correlated, but such confounding of Z factors is irrelevant. The confounding on X is still relevant and still poses a hard problem for how we should do the modeling.

The problem of precisely defining the estimand—what is the effect size parameter—certainly doesn't go away either. And here I echo Fred Wolf's point about the need to have clearly defined estimands of interest—clearly defined effect sizes—so we understand what we're estimating. This response surface idea would be really weak if the final estimand at the ideal study were not interpretable. I envision a very simple estimand like the binomial effect size display (BESD) of Rosenthal and Rubin (1982) as a function of X, something clean and easy that we all understand. There may be a big statistical machine churning away, a big modeling effort going on underneath in order to get the extrapolated response surface for effect size as a function of scientific factors X, but the final answer will be clear and interpretable if the effect size definition is clear and interpretable.

Conclusions

How seriously do I believe this structure I have erected saying we have all been doing it wrong? In designing the arguments presented here I have come to like it very much—and maybe even to believe in it fully. I'd like to try an analysis from this perspective to see how it really works. At the first pass at least, there is a significant conceptual clarity that comes from accepting it. Of course, I would have to modify my views if I tried to apply the framework in a situation in which it should be able to succeed, and it was a failure. But at present, I feel that there is some real potential payoff from trying it, not only with respect to increased conceptual clarity but also with respect to consequent analyses that might lead to answers that are worthwhile improvements over current answers.

15

Concepts Under Scrutiny: Discussion

This chapter presents transcripts of four of the discussions that took place at the workshop in West Virginia. The topics covered are (1) completeness of search, (2) main effects, (3) the desegregation studies, and (4) Rubin's response surface model. The transcripts have been edited, but were left close to their original form in order to convey some of the excitement at the meeting.

Completeness of Search

MOSTELLER: The point I'd like to make deals with the question we've all talked about here. Should we be trying for completeness? Why are we trying to get all these data? Why shouldn't we have some statistical device that tells us when we've got enough? Or tells us that we've got the core of it, which is important. Or tells us how much each section of a paper is worth. I'm not trying to settle that. For a while we talked as if we have to get everything. Maybe that's right, but maybe you don't have to be so inclusive. It might not be worthwhile.

COOPER: This morning, the lack of reporting means and standard deviations was mentioned. As bad as this is, in most literature reviews reporting is even worse with regard to information retrieval techniques. It is a step forward just to require literature reviewers to describe what processes were employed to gather the information that's in the report. Just *that* is a step forward, because the audience can evaluate the conclusions against their own standards. Personally, I think it is incumbent upon someone doing a literature review to have all of the information. If they then employ some selective procedure for determining what to include, that's fine as well, as long as they are explicit about the procedures used. With regard to the aphasia group and how exhaustively they should have looked for the literature, I would say look in every nook and cranny. Every place they could look, they should look. As to whether or not they have to address every one of those master's theses and term papers in their write-up, that's another question. If they're explicit about their criteria, then we're still better off.

Question: Why Do We Have to Do a Comprehensive Search?

COOPER: Because when you're going to make a statement that says, "I've seen this literature, I can describe it, and I can summarize it for you," I think it ought to be assumed that the person doing this is at least aware of everything that's gone on.

WOLF: Do you limit the parameters of your search? By saying, "Within this time frame"—why is that not a legitimate way to go? "Within these two years, this is what the literature says about this."

COOPER: There are always practical constraints.

BRADBURN: I don't think that the time frame is the thing that one worries about. My answer to why one looks at everything is that there may be some systematic omission because of a bias in the way we look.

LAIRD: But if you describe what you did very carefully, then your biases should be up front.

WOLF: But the problem is you don't know what the universe is.

LAIRD: I think the problem is that the population you're sampling from is vague. And so you can't say what it means to have a representative sample from that population, because you don't normally know what it is.

BRADBURN: If it turns out that the way people describe their work is systematically related to something else that's important in the substantive areas, we'll miss that. And you probably don't know what you didn't do.

LAIRD: That's why you can't do what Harris wants. You can't get it all, if you don't know how you're missing it.

BRADBURN: I am urging people to be creative about it. It's being aware of what other ways you could raise a question or describe a study in order to look for other work in the area. And if we could do all that and say, "Having thought of this, we're going to omit them," that would be all right. It's the not knowing that you have missed these studies that bothers me.

FIENBERG: I'm troubled by that response. It reminds me of discussions that we've engaged in in other arenas where we are interested in making inferences from samples to something, and whether or not we should use the probability structure of the sample or whether you go out and create a model. And the question is, What do we want to make inferences about? It seems to me that in meta-analysis settings, the issue is whether or not you've got the *important* set of studies. It may well be that there's a whole bunch of studies out there, and it doesn't really matter if you don't have one, for a variety of reasons. I agree that you have to worry a little about that issue, about why you don't have them. But in the end, it seems to me you have to come back and ask, "What have I missed? Is it going to be important for the enterprise that I'm engaging in?" It seems to me that the answer is that you don't have to strive systematically for this completeness. This is especially true as you move away from the more quantitative approaches to the broader notion of literature, a literature review on a given topic. If there's an important paper or idea and it has enormous influence, anything you do will trip that paper and those ideas in some form. To continue to search forever to find that elusive paper with the important ideas seems to me rather misguided. What you end up searching for is the peripheral parts of the literature, not the central parts.

COOPER: Nobody's out there searching forever. If they are, they're certainly not the folks who are here. They're still at the library and have never published. But I think it's incumbent on us to have a strong ethic for comprehensiveness, and I believe it is also important to be incredibly explicit about how you went about finding the literature, and what criteria you used in determining what to cite.

FIENBERG: I don't disagree with the latter.

COMMENT: Both of those, I believe, are enormous steps forward, steps that have been highlighted by meta-analysis.

OLKIN: I think at some point we would like to be able to sample. But right at this moment, as Harris noted, people get their references from ERIC, from abstracts, and from key researchers. So it's very difficult to feel that you know what populations you're sampling. But, I think, one of the recommendations we might make is that there should be better titles of articles, and better key words and phrases. Because that's the way we're going to be searching in 1990. If we have that, then we won't miss these various sources. And we will know how we're sampling. And I think that's a critical point. If some important researchers are omitted, that could lead to an important bias. It's essential that you don't do that. I think that at some point in our technology we really will be able to sample in a reasonable way from various constituencies, because we will know the constituencies. But right now, I don't think we do know them.

COOPER: I don't think the problem is quite as black and white as that. Terminology changes all the time. It is impossible for us today to know how to describe our paper in a manner that will identify it meaningfully five years from now. An example in that regard is the term "teacher burnout." There's an enormous literature on "teacher burnout" that is not called "teacher burnout." And it's not because the authors were remiss in not using the term, but they did their studies of "teacher burnout" before the term "teacher burnout" existed.

GREENHOUSE: I would like to comment on the question, Why do we feel this compelling need to completely search the literature? An analogous situation is that of censoring in "time to response" studies. The concern is that if we ignore the censoring and the censoring is informative, then the inferences that we will make about the parameters are going to be biased. If we are not going to invest the time and the effort into considering ways of modeling the bias due to incomplete retrieval of the literature, then I think we feel more comfortable about the effect of the bias on our inferences if we have retrieved all of the possible literature.

WACHTER: [See Introduction.] Davida gave us a very good illustration of this process. Whether or not to try to find all the possible literature is an empirical question. Usually, researchers get the papers in a sequence, and it's possible, after you have the whole set, to look back and see whether the last 20 you got added anything more than a larger sample size to the first 80 you collected. This seems to me a research program that could be well incorporated into the work of people who do meta-analysis. I gathered, from the description Davida gave, that the last set she got was a significant contribution, something new and important. It sounded as if her case was a case in defense of being as exhaustive as possible. Is that a fair interpretation?

FROMM: Yes, until the final stages. I went through and looked at the quality of the last set of studies identified and what they offered. There was really only one study that had the kind of measures that we needed and had decent designs and information. The rest suffered from some combination of obscure treatment methods, poor reporting, or poor designs. Actually, at the end the search was not very productive.

WACHTER: Has anyone seen a published meta-analysis where the rank order of when the study came into the sample was used as a stratifying variable?

COMMENT: If we analyze the survey research, that would be clear.

WACHTER: Exactly, well this might be something that we could profitably take over from survey research in the practice of meta-analysis.

HEDGES: I can actually think of a couple of examples in which that has been done, in fact, as a quantitative predictor of study results. There were studies of various sorts of sex differences, for example, showing a decline over time.

WACHTER: I don't mean over time, I mean the time when a study was found. I'm referring to the accessibility of the study.

STRAF: I don't think researchers want to admit that they overlook, even for a month, a very important study. And I found Davida's paper unique in a sense that she laid out all the difficulties that all of us have when we're compiling literature. There's always a big gap, but we strive for completeness because we were taught to. And the journals encourage us to have these views. Bibliographies can make our papers sound more important.

WACHTER: Especially references to the referee who reads it! [Laughter.]

RUBIN: I think one of the issues is that there are two kinds of meta-analyses. The first kind is really literature synthesis, which we've talked about. But there's another kind, which I don't think is really conceptualized properly. For that kind of meta-analysis we must really understand the underlying science. I don't think, for this second type, you really do care about the literature being complete. This type is harder to do, but it's more concise, and we don't need completeness for that.

FIENBERG: That's what I was referring to also.

MOSTELLER: A little terrifying fact illustrates the difficulties of setting limits on a search. Three of the latest texts in the same medical field have very few common references.

OLKIN: Do you think that's intrinsic to medicine? Or do you think that might be a general phenomenon?

FIENBERG: No. There are multiple directions for activities emanating from the same research ideas, and the same research findings. You could create what, on the surface, looks like a really great bibliography. Fred could go and do the same thing: tell you about exactly the same science, or almost the same science. But he may be approaching it from a slightly different perspective. The two bibliographies may have no papers in common. Yet the cumulative knowledge that you get from those bibliographies may be similar. The fact that the reference lists don't overlap doesn't mean that the scientific knowledge is not similar.

Main Effects

WACHTER: I think we're really now moving into the period of general discussion of the future of meta-analysis.

MOSTELLER: One piece of information might be of use. Kenneth Warren, a former vice-president of the Rockefeller Foundation, is very interested in citation. He is motivated, in part, by the issue of the size of the library required by a small country. How many of the hundred thousand medical journals are really needed in your hospital, for example? And so he has done an enormous study of schistosomiasis, the literature of schistosomiasis, attacking it from a great number of different directions. How do you tell what articles are important? He gets articles and citations, and he has perhaps a hundred or so journals concerned with the topic. He gets them all rated on how many of the good articles are cited. He finds that some journals do very poorly, even though their names might suggest that they would be first class for their field. He uses experts, and he has several different approaches. Someone interested in that area would want to read Warren's working paper from the Rockefeller Foundation on the schistosomiasis literature. He's done other work on coping with the literature, and that's of some interest to us too. I think that this work parallels our interest in citation.

The other point I thought I'd mention: I once gave a talk, and when it was over Deming came up to me and said, "Now Fred, there's just one thing I want you to remember all your life, and that is, there's no true value." I have remembered it all my life and I've found it more impressive as I've aged. It is very helpful to think that there *might* be a true value. And it certainly helps organize our discussions. But it does seem important to recall that there is no true value. You might then think, "Well, we can look at *differences*, anyway." But you have to remember what Joseph Berkson said, "Who says that if you have two wrong numbers their difference is correct?" So this true value area is one that we need to look at with care.

RUBIN: I want to say a couple more things about that true value idea, because I certainly don't believe in a true value either. And I think people who believe least may be survey type people who understand that everything is changing—the finite population they're going after is always changing. On the other hand, almost any scientist who does work has a model inside his mind of what he's trying to learn. And I think it would be sort of antiscientific to say that he shouldn't act as if there were true values out there, which are parameters in the models being used.

WACHTER: I'd like to raise a rather different issue that has begun to trouble me, in thinking back over the conference and the course it's taken and what has been said relative to what some of us anticipated or forecast might be said. I'd like to throw out the possibility that the community or the people here are engaged in a process of killing off meta-analysis and doing it to death with kindness. It seems to me a lot of the emphasis on what's going to happen in the future of meta-analysis in this meeting has been to say that we're going to look for more and more complicated pictures of the world. In an extreme case, in Don Rubin's picture, we're going to go to plotting out whole response surfaces. We're going to work with more covariates, we're going to use more complicated sample size adjustments and all kinds of things. And we're going away from saying "yes or no" on some simple issue to saying "what works in what circumstances under what conditions," and so forth.

Now the only dissenting voice to that I've really heard was Bob Rosenthal, when he reminded us that main effects are sometimes important, and it seems to me that the initial appeal of meta-analysis was to try to cut through all the complexity of research literature. With enough studies and a big enough enterprise, all the details of the design of experiments and the details of what contacts you had here and there and elsewhere would fade into background detail. Certain broad generalizations would finally come out into the foreground. With individual studies we may not get a main effect out there, with enough studies we can.

And it seems to me that because all of us can only hold rather little information in mind at one time, especially when ranging over broad fields (in my own case, I have only a very tangential interest in desegregation effects in twentieth century America because there is always thirteenth century England and lots of China and other things), I think I'm certainly not going to be able to remember the ins and outs of whether starting in kindergarten in 1960 was better than starting a mandatory program in seventh grade for math somewhere else. But there is some knowledge that is of general appeal and that we can act on and want to have. And an answer that says that desegregation does have a positive effect on black achievement scores but not very much is something I think we can carry away. I suspect that as much as program administrators would like to know the details, what many people in Congress and many of their constituents would like to have is more of a generalization at that level. The original Glass psychotherapy studies, the appeal of the aphasia study—I think the appeal of most meta-analysis studies—is that we get back to some kind of simple world, recognizing there is a complex world behind it. But we have something we can go and store and hang onto.

I was particularly struck by this when we started this endeavor and we had only one copy of the desegregation studies. I left this one copy with the department secretary to make a few more copies. These are people who get hundreds of things to copy every week, and this one didn't get copied, and I tried to find out why it didn't get copied, and it turned out everyone in the office was reading that set of studies. It caught on. There were a couple of thousand things that had come over their desks and this was the first document that they really found worth going into. And it seems to be the evidence of Harris Cooper's work and my own experience that one comes away persuaded of something with the best meta-analysis, for all its faults and all its crudity.

So I would suggest that maybe we're pushing this subject in entirely the wrong direction, with too much response surface work, too many covariates, too much sophistication in the propounding of models, the kinds of things Larry Hedges was mapping out for us as a direction. Maybe that's just going to wipe the subject out. And perhaps what we should be thinking of instead are ways to rescue the simplicity, to treat those things that are a challenge to getting simple, believable generalizations.

ROSENTHAL: I don't think so. I think paradise has been lost, and we've been kicked out of the Garden of Eden. I think people still are interested in gross main effects. Psychotherapy does work; people are going to become increasingly dissatisfied with knowing *that*; they're going to want to know the moderators. I don't know if they're going to want to know all that Don Rubin or Larry Hedges want to tell us, but probably eventually they will. So I'm not disturbed by it. People are still going to want to know if psychotherapy works, and that may be the main result you want to tell them. But after you've done that, they're going to ask, "Is it better if it's two hours a week or one?" That's the time to go into the details of the meta-analysis, if you have all the data ready. We'll want the moderator variables.

HEDGES: I think it's a mistake to think that just because you've moved toward more complicated and therefore more realistic modeling procedures, that you necessarily lose the possibility of some simple conclusions. And I think, moreover, that what conclusions you do derive from the analysis are likely to be much more credible if the modeling takes into account what anybody who knows anything about those sorts of studies would be aware of. An anecdote comes to mind: A sociologist from the University of Manchester who was visiting Chicago about two years ago sat in on a seminar I gave about meta-analysis. She didn't know anything about the subject, but had been a researcher in a field that had to do with sex differences in education. The thing she came away with after the exposure to meta-analysis was that she found the meta-analyses that she read most credible when she knew the least about the subject matter. And with the subject matters she knew the most about, she found the meta-analyses she read the *least* credible because she knew too many things that were glossed over in the analyses. Now admittedly she was looking at first generation meta-analyses. But I think the point is probably well taken that the general public might be impressed with a meta-analysis that looks at a main effect and nothing else, but researchers who know about the complexities of the research domain are going to demand that those complexities in some way be addressed, at least some of them.

WACHTER: To argue the other side, what is the original appeal of randomization at all? The original appeal of randomization is to cut through a lot of details. If you really went out and measured everything about the soil of all the plots at Rothamsted, then randomization would be inappropriate. Randomization was a technique which said, "Forget about needing to know all kinds of things about the experimental context." [*Audible disagreement here.*] And it seems to me—well, people are shaking their heads, but let me finish—meta-analysis as it has caught on and is being done in practice out there is a technique that gains its power from hoping that a lot of things will cancel out. And if one has to go into all the real detail of complicated studies, when every little subtlety may ultimately be part of the picture, then I don't think that kind of research summary is going to catch on. We're going to be thrown back to those terrible summaries that just look at the conclusion page. If you make things too complicated, I don't see how you can make the technique serve a purpose.

ROSENTHAL: I think that as a way of getting close to the true value that doesn't exist, some complicated procedure could be very useful, like what Don Rubin may be developing. Once you've got that, there may be relatively simple ways to simulate it—so you take three times the weight of the top level studies plus one time the weight of the second. This is so that the practitioner in the field doesn't need these fancy computer programs to get Don's number, but Don or Ingram Olkin or Larry Hedges will produce a simple algorithm by which he or any person in the field can do it himself. So I see it as a as kind of criterion value against which you can calibrate the rough and ready procedures.

RUBIN: On randomization, I think the analogies are very good and the reasoning for it is very good. Randomization caught on at Rothamsted because of it's internal validity—the experiment provided its own estimate of error. So historically it's not that randomization cuts out detail, but that it provides an internal estimate of error.

Which direction should meta-analysis take? Audiences involved in the work really want to know what is going on, I think. Policy people and congressmen need gross summaries. But if we're the scientists who are producing gross summaries, we certainly should be confident that in the gross summaries one would find the truth. And if all you do is calculate the gross summaries and never look at the interactions or complexities, you'll never know whether your gross summary effects (as in psychotherapy) work as a result of averaging over different sizes of positive effects or from averaging some big negative effects with some even bigger positive effects, or whether the study samples are strange. And I think before we produce those gross summaries for a more policy-oriented audience, we should be confident that they are the *right* summaries. And so I think we have to do more complicated things.

WACHTER: If you want to know something about aphasia, you may plan to do a really complicated interaction meta-analysis with lots of variables in there, lots of codings and recodings and things of that sort. Does it make more sense to work from the 100 studies with their crude reporting or does it make more sense to invest your time and money in a new primary study that will have as much as possible under your control? That's the trade-off. I'm not arguing against looking at a few salient contrasts. I oppose the general picture of making these analyses more and more complex and adding more and more interaction. It seems to me then that the choice between doing the meta-analysis and doing a new study with control over the experimental designs and treatments has shifted toward the doing of another primary study, compared with the use of the previous literature.

RUBIN: But how are you going to decide what new primary study to do, what it should look like? I would think you would want, if it's a very expensive and all-encompassing study, to make sure that the design factors really *are* chosen with the greatest care, based on the other studies which you already have.

COOPER: And since the design factors can be intercorrelated with one another in the meta-analysis, in the new primary research the object would be to unconfound the variables.

RUBIN: If I'm going to do a $2 million study, I would probably look at what's around already.

STRAF: I don't think Ken Wachter is saying you can't use meta-analysis in a complicated sense to help design the next experiment or take the next observation, but that's not the primary purpose of conducting the meta-analysis.

COOPER: Ken Wachter posed the question as, How should I spend my time? Should I do this meta-analysis or should I do the next study? What Don Rubin is saying is that the question is wrong. First you do the meta-analysis and *then* you do the next study.

OLKIN: But even then you can't always *do* the next study. Astrophysicists know k has to be −1, 0, or +1 [a reference to the curvature parameter in the General Relativity Theory Friedmann model for the universe mentioned in Singer's presentation]. Why aren't *they* doing the next study and saying, "Ah, it's $k = 1$, we know that." Why aren't they doing that?

WACHTER: They are *mainly* doing it.

COMMENT: But they can't do it. The problem is that in the kinds of studies they do, it takes years to get a picture of the universe, because they seldom follow the track. If you get a picture, you get a picture.

OLKIN: And then something happens where the picture is slightly incomplete and they have to do another main study. If you're talking about desegregation, it's the same kind of problem that the astrophysicist has.

HEDGES: I think there is another point that Ken Wachter is making implicitly and nobody has yet challenged, and that is that there is a point of diminishing returns in increasing the complexity of the models. Diminishing returns in the sense that you begin to see that you don't get anything for it. And so people won't go on adding epicycles forever because, at least in most of the data sets I've looked at, there's a point beyond which there is no variability left to explain. You're not going to say, "Gosh, I'm going to add 15 more variables," because it just doesn't seem like it will get you anywhere. So I think there is a sort of natural control that will keep people from elaborating the complexity of their analyses endlessly.

WACHTER: Empirically this seems to be true, since very few people have pursued the complexity even to the first stage that we're all for. But I would argue in the other direction that the more you get into this, the more the extreme detail you will present in the reporting of particular studies. There are a lot of ways in which studies differ, and if you're willing to build sufficiently complex models, you will have the problem that, in the end, you're arguing that one particular study is better than all the others. If you delve too much into this, and take it too seriously, and begin to weigh all the factors that are reported in all the texts of all the papers, it seems to me you come quickly back to where many scientists are: you end up making choices that bring you down to individual studies again.

COOPER: I think that what Larry Hedges and Bob Rosenthal and the rest of the statisticians here are talking about is making available flexible meta-analytic models that can use data sets of different complexities. What people will bring to that may be sets x and y, and in some instances these sets will have one variable in them and in other instances they will have more. Obviously in meta-analysis, or at least in the desegregation study, you could come up with 60 or 100. In other areas you don't find nearly that degree of complexity of conceptualization. So there are really two processes going on: one is building meta-analytic models that are flexible enough to contain complex conceptualizations of reality, and the other is what researchers know about the process that is to be plugged in. And *that* will always be less than the technology of the moment is capable of handling. I hope we don't get to the point, and I know it happens quite frequently, with both primary and meta-analysis, where we do it just because the technology is there, where we do complex models not because they make sense, but because the technology allows us to. I think that would be a very bad reaction for practicing meta-analysts. But we should have those models available so that we can accommodate different levels of conceptual complexity.

MOSTELLER: There just isn't any natural number of variables to adjust for. I recall a study that had 161 variables. Some thought that there were too many variables to control. What I was impressed by, reading the paper and listening to the author, was that physicians want to be concerned about every one of those variables. I'm very much on the Ken Wachter end of the scale. That is to say, physicians know too many things. Physicians know too many things that aren't true. They want to be sure to do something about *all* the variables, and we tend to exaggerate the importance of variables that *are* available. We have the difficulty that we can't stratify on all the variables.

I'm always tempered a little by the fact we can't control or defend against the future of science. It is easy (and this is why the physicians have to control all of these variables) for the biologist to give an example of a study in which knowing one variable is crucial. Once that variable is known, everything works. Since we can't promise that examples like that won't happen, we're stuck with that possibility of failure in the future. And we're also stuck with the fact that we can't randomize in the selection of studies.

So, where are we? We're stuck with the observational study kind of situation and we can try to get main effects. It's weak-kneed methodology. There's nothing wrong with Don's idea [see Chapter 14] except that it isn't ready. We don't know how to do it in meta-analysis. Nobody has any examples of it and whether it will work or not, I don't know. We are, of course, used to dosage response curves, but we have not developed the variables Rubin requests.

RUBIN: There are two attitudes toward meta-analysis: looking at those problems that current technology can give good answers to versus pushing the technology to handle the complexity. I was proposing something we don't know how to do, which raises all kinds of statistical issues, but it seems to be a better conceptualization of what the real scientific problem is. It is also more attentive to what people think might be important. As part of the outcome of a technology like this, we would put in all these variables and people could find out they don't matter at all. I guess I take the attitude "Let's see what the scientific possibility is in all its glory," and then try to push the statistical technology to handle that to see how close we can come to the ideal kind of analysis. The more practical solution in the short term is to pull our sights in a lot and get answers to those problems that current technology can handle well. That's the big reason for what we all do now. We all know it's wrong in some sense, but the technology works really easily and we don't have to put much into it, and we get simple answers and feedback. But when the questions become more complicated . . . .

The Desegregation Studies

HEDGES: I'd like to make a comment on the desegregation studies because I've also looked at them, and have in fact carried out a sort of short analysis of some of the studies which are part of the larger database Bob Crain [the author of one of the busing studies in the meta-analysis] looked at. I found interesting results which might be worth sharing, since there have been some comments about how variable these effect sizes were.

The database I looked at was Crain's 93 studies less those studies that created synthetic standard deviations for standardization purposes, that is, studies that used norms from a test manual, not real sample standard deviations. I excluded 20 or so studies that synthesized the standard deviation artificially. I carried out an analysis that essentially examined the variability of effect sizes within three categories of methodological adequacy. The first group of studies was a small group of experiments in which the treatment and control were randomized. My second group had somewhat poor control, from my point of view. These were studies that involved national, prospective matching, matching individual students on an achievement test score, and that sort of control. And a third set of studies used an even less adequate control, from my point of view. The experimental and control groups were matched on some broad cohort sorts of characteristics, for example, socioeconomic status. There might not be agreement with that particular set of types, but there is a clear progression in the amount of control, I think, from cohort matching, to those that matched on explicit pretests, to randomized experiments.

What is interesting is that one finds the same pattern of results across all three types of studies. The basic tendency seems to be that studies that analyze early desegregation (in kindergarten or first grade) show larger effects than studies that analyze later desegregation—these studies show essentially zero effect. But what is interesting is that within the two groups of studies which had better control, the randomized experiments and the experiments that used explicit matching, the effect sizes were really not as variable as you might think. That is, if you were to ask what is a decent point estimate of the variability in the underlying parameters represented by those studies (taking the grade effect out), the results are very consistent. Essentially, there was not a substantial amount of variability beyond what was caused by the small sample sizes.

In regard to sample size and adequacy of study design, the randomized returns were all very small, but on the other hand, the results were very consistent given the fact that the data weren't very good. The same thing was true of the cohort studies. If you wanted to estimate an underlying variance design, you would come up with an estimate of zero, beyond the grade effect. There was a great deal of variability in the studies, which is not surprising. Studies that had lousy control to begin with showed a great deal of variability in their effect. So I just wanted to make that comment because I had looked at the variability and it is surprising there is not more variability given the diffuse nature of the treatment. It is astonishing in some ways that randomized experiments or cohort studies don't show greater variability.

Question: What Was the Relationship Between Average Effect Size and Study Quality

HEDGES: If you ran the analyses in the three control categories in parallel and looked at the results, there was a tendency for the effects to be bigger for studies that desegregated earlier. The finding was most pronounced in the randomized experiments, and the differences were smaller in the cohort studies. If you were asked, "Is the pattern the same?" I think any reasonable person would say, "Yes, the pattern is the same in all three types of studies." The difference was that the variability of effects was 50 times greater among the studies with cohort controls than among the randomized experiments.

ROSENTHAL: A plot of the effect sizes versus a quality-of-study score within each of the types of control group would be useful. Such a plot often shows the most pronounced effect size differences within the randomized studies.

WOLF: That's an interesting finding in another regard. Often you hear the criticism that controlled studies overestimate the effect size. What you found was that the better controlled studies actually showed smaller effects.

ROSENTHAL: Even though poor studies often get large effect size estimates, they also have large standard errors, so that the resulting standardized effect size estimate is comparable to that of a good quality study.

WACHTER: I'd like to introduce a bit of controversy if possible by challenging some of the suggestions that David Cordray was making that these studies would look very different today, and that we're on an upward grade toward better and better studies. It seems to me the desegregation studies illustrated dramatically two generic problems of meta-analysis for policy purposes.

The first problem is that we have a set of techniques whose background rationale depends on having a fairly big sample of studies. If there are many dozens or hundreds of studies, one has some faith that all the specific biases and heterogeneities, to a certain extent, will balance out. But when you come down to doing the meta-analysis and trying to select the sample of studies that you can do anything at all fancy with, and justifying putting in high expertise people on it, you end up restricting yourself to a tiny portion of the total literature. So you end up doing detailed analysis on some 18 studies out of 90 or 200 or something like that. And it doesn't seem to me that that is a problem that is going to go away by changing the primary studies. The fact is, most research out there is terrible and it is not going to change overnight. I don't see at the moment that we have a good way of facing that problem, of either bringing in this larger universe or using the small sample size. So it seems to me this is a good illustration of why meta-analysis seems to founder on policy issues. We tried to find the best example for this conference that we could, and this is it.

The second generic problem that the NIE studies seem to illustrate is that, although these new techniques have been presented clearly and well systematized and discussed in the journals, what turned out was that very little of the more detailed statistical approaches got used. And this is a bunch of clever people and these are careful analyses. I think Jim Press has pointed out there was very little done with weighting schemes, very little with standard deviations and sample sizes. But if you read the studies, I have little faith that doing more of that would have changed what came out. What turned out was that the action seems to have been at the point of sample inclusion and choice of controls, and what made the small differences you can see were the nonstatistical issues. These meta-analyses may be interesting reading, I suppose, for people who want the details of these cases and who want to know these incidents from the interior of the studies. But I think the second generic problem being illustrated here is that when you land with your small group of studies that you can do anything at all with, statistical techniques cease to explain much of the variance in the final outcome and cease to be where the action is, and one is thrown back on the nonstatistical side. And I don't see that in 1986, compared to 1982, we have any more solutions to that. There doesn't seem to be a big role in this kind of work for much intelligent statistics, as opposed to much wise thought.

CORDRAY: I would probably come down on the same side. A one-in-seven usable study rate out of 153 is not very promising. The same thing happens when you look at the medical reviews; few studies are found to be useful and high in quality. I think there are a couple of issues here: the first is that identifying systematically that the studies cannot be used in this format flags that we need to do something. Meta-analysis can *do* something; it can identify those kinds of studies, separate the good from the bad and try to do what it can with the good ones. My point is that the procedures that were used by the six individuals were not sensitive enough; they used conventional applications of statistical procedures. They did things which run contrary to current thinking and did not take into account sample size and variability.

So I would take issue with the wisdom of the folks who did this to begin with. They didn't use the kinds of statistical procedures (with the exception of Miller, who did use many procedures) that are currently being used. Even with the small set of studies, it would be possible to disentangle some of the problems and come to a sharper agreement about the amount of heterogeneity and whether or not there were different clusters. You *have* to look at that. My first reading of this meta-analysis was there is really no point in commenting on it, that it is historically out of step with what is currently going on. And more than that, if it was used as a basis for determining the policy relevance of this stuff, it would be a serious mistake because it is out of step with the advances that have occurred recently.

STRAF: I spoke with Paul Wortman [the author of one of the busing studies in the meta-analysis], and he agrees that in terms of the statistics and methods, today would have been different.

SCHNEIDER: One of the problems was that the [busing meta-analysis authors] knew what every one of those studies said before they ever chose the criteria for inclusion. They knew that literature inside and out and every time they made a methodological decision, they knew exactly which study to use. It always seemed to me like an interesting event, but as far as I was concerned the whole thing was over with when they sat down at the table and made those decisions. After that, it was just a matter of the reporting process. I don't know how you get around that. How do you bring together somebody, or a group of people, who know the literature, know the outcomes of what all the research says, and then use selective criteria to judge it. It's a toughie, it's a very hard thing, and we never got around it.

Rubin's Response Surface Model

RUBIN: I have a feeling there is some payoff here, not only in the concept but also in the analysis, and in getting answers that might be worthwhile.

STRAF: I've some questions about Don's assumptions. First of all the conditional independence seems to be crucial, and I'm not sure if we have that in practice. We've seen where studies generate others and so I question that. The most important problem I have—I love the conceptualization, it does get away from lots of problems—is that as you're extrapolating, you have this smooth line, but in fact you might be going from observational studies to experimental ones, and there is no smooth line. It's more like dropping off a cliff or climbing up a mountain.

RUBIN: I don't know. The observational studies vary greatly by standard of control, how much matching is done, and how the covariates are used. Randomized studies, moreover, vary in how close they are to being true randomized studies. People drop out along the way. Has anybody ever known a randomized study where no one has ever dropped out?

STRAF: The path of this extrapolation may be rockier than a smooth line. You also mentioned that poorer studies are downweighted. That may be true in terms of effects, but maybe not in terms of the contributions they make to the estimates of standard error, especially when you look at extrapolated effects.

RUBIN: I would think that, again, the region for the poorer studies probably has a lot of variability, and so I've got a conditional variance that grows with poorer studies. The poorer the study, the bigger the variability. If that's *not* true, that's an interesting empirical fact.

STRAF: That's where I wonder if the dependence comes into play, somehow holding the variance down. But the major point I have is, I wonder if our goal is not to extrapolate to an idealized experiment but is, if I can borrow another term from Box, "evolutionary operation." We're looking for the best therapy for aphasia, and it may differ from the one we have articulated. So we don't want to go in the direction of finding the effect of the ideal experiment for *that* therapy, but we want to head in the direction of something that works better. Maybe looking at the response surface a little differently and just seeing what directions are optimal for effects, one step at a time, would be a goal.

16

Summing Up

Frederick Mosteller

I enjoyed the workshop that led to this volume, because the ideas have been well thought out. The two case studies, although they do not appear in my summing up, played an outstanding role in the development of the ideas.

In summing up, I have not always tried to mention who was responsible for an idea—often authors are multiply responsible. I organized my summary by tasks that the Committee on National Statistics (CNSTAT) and others promoting the future of meta-analysis might want to take up.

To sum up the summary: first, we need to provide guidelines for carrying out meta-analyses. Among the topics are "how to search," "how to report," and "how to be persuasive." "How to report" falls more on the statistical or academic side, "how to be persuasive" falls more on Harris Cooper's line of attack. Perhaps CNSTAT could produce a pamphlet on this subject. Considerable homework would be required, especially by studying many meta-analyses before writing the pamphlet.

Second, we need guidelines for quantitative papers, as distinct now from meta-analyses. The first point dealt with meta-analyses, but a major thought brought out again and again (especially by Cooper) is that distinctions are usefully made between studies prepared as primary studies, review studies, and meta-analyses. We need guidelines for quantitative papers and primary papers; that is, studies that report original data and their analysis. We do not have such guidelines yet; again, a pamphlet could be useful.

Third, when we started the workshop that lies behind this volume, we were told that it was about three things. The first dealt with using meta-analysis for policy, the second with limitations and weaknesses, and the third with the future of meta-analysis. We saw possible policy uses for both case studies. Cordray's paper emphasized the use of quantitative research, possibly meta-analyses, for policy. He also gave guidelines which would make a paper more useful for the policymaker. One of his key points was that we need to handle the political nature of a political problem. Any policy problem by its name already says, "I am a political animal." The idea that authors could use various devices to pay attention to that issue was nicely brought out. This is not an idea widely known to statisticians, and so it ought to be stressed. The tendency and training of statisticians leads them to avoid the political aspect of the problem rather than to address it. I have discussed this more extensively in Mosteller (1988).

Another idea that was presented in several different forms was the possibility of finding out that the information is inadequate to answer the question. Establishing that finding firmly is success, not failure. But it also poses a question for the policymaker: Would you like to get some information, and if so, do you have money to spend for it?

That's a major question, and it addresses another concern: to promote primary studies. Once it has been established that the data are not available, it means that the policymaker may be making policy in a vacuum, and may have the obligation to acquire more information in the future. A major problem in many areas—policy, social sciences, and medicine—is that experts often hold strong beliefs that have no evidential foundation. We need some ideas about the ethics of belief. A key problem about the ethics of belief is that people may believe strongly in something they know little about and have little evidence for.

We have few studies of cost-effectiveness. In the policy area, we do need more studies of cost-effectiveness because it is relevant to every field of policy. Policymakers also worry about policy comparisons—not the cost as much as the effectiveness and the acceptability of the policy. Various program components sometimes bring out important ideas for policy.

Many authors of this volume urge us to work with journal editors to improve the primary literature. The proposal to study the guidelines of *statistical* journals is especially relevant, prior to seeking liaison with other groups (see, e.g., Bailar and Mosteller 1988). For example, Olkin suggested seminars for editors. Depending on the topic, this work could be done by different groups. Although these editorial activities are not directed at meta-analysis, they would contribute to meta-analysis insofar as they influenced the primary literature.

The next set of activities arises from technical or methodological problems. For example, how deep should a meta-analytic search be? Does this depend on the purpose of the study? The present volume scarcely settles this issue. Some authors suggest that we must find every article, but it would be a hopeless task to search through tens of thousands of research articles. If we *must* have all the articles, the next one may overturn everything—we have occasional revolutionary breakthroughs. However, if the next one were *not* a breakthrough and we already have many studies, why is it so important? If I want to know the current state of reporting on quantitative matters in surgery, I could just look at a year's worth of papers in a few journals as an index to performance (Emerson et al. 1984). We need a more systematic treatment of the search needs required for different kinds of problems.

How shall we handle the quality of studies? Frequently people talk about weights and some have spoken of "bias adjustment." In this volume, this issue arises in two different contexts. One is in the context of Rubin's formulation where the investigator wants to know the outcome in a particular portion of the space of the variables that give the properties of the study. Others write of bias adjustment as well as weights, but I don't think that the idea of bias adjustment is abroad in the land. We all do use the idea of weights though we may not know how to choose them. Statisticians and other social scientists often talk about bias, but they usually do not plan to do more than complain about it. Cochran's book on the design and analysis of observational studies (1983) emphasizes that it is not enough to talk about bias; we should measure it and do something about it. In only a few places do statisticians routinely do something about bias. For one attempt see Colditz et al. (1988). Another occurs in sample surveys, where researchers sometimes measure changes in response as successive waves of later and later questionnaires come in; they then extrapolate and use that information to reduce bias from nonresponse. Some methods of imputation probably secretly do something about bias, but for the most part statisticians do not have systematic treatments for bias adjustment. The Census Bureau held a conference on nonsampling errors, and some of those papers offer adjustments for biases. But both generally speaking and in meta-analysis in particular, I have not seen many constructive suggestions for bias adjustment. The study of omissions (because of search failure or nonpublication) has been mentioned by several people, but I don't know what to do about that in meta-analysis. Begg and Berlin (1988) propose some solutions.

Some other important ideas have emerged—it's amazing how many good ideas at this conference have little to do with meta-analysis. One is that we need to promote primary studies, since meta-analyses must depend on them. Unfortunately, we have few ideas about *how* to promote them. We have views about how to improve the quality of primary studies but not how to increase their number.

Although the need for a clearinghouse of meta-analyses was discussed at the workshop, I don't recall anybody's pursuing it. I don't know how practical it is. The Institute of Medicine (IOM), through its Council on Health Care Technology, is about to work on a clearinghouse for technology assessment, and we might watch how that develops. They hope to get information on assessments of technology, put it in a data bank, and have it available for the whole industry that cares about the results of the assessments. In 1989, they were just hoping to go on line. If we would like to see a clearinghouse for the meta-analysis area, we might wait to see how that develops for the IOM. Many of the studies social scientists care about would fit in. The aphasia studies could be regarded as a form of technology assessment rather than just as a meta-analysis. The total number of meta-analyses is trivial compared to the amount of technology assessment the IOM council must deal with.

A new idea for me, brought out in several chapters, uses meta-analysis to sharpen questions. Or, alternatively, a way to do better meta-analyses takes questions, breaks them down into sharper questions, and then deals with those sharper questions. This approach tends to break up the primary studies into smaller groups and generate several meta-analyses instead of one. I don't know whether that's in opposition to the Wachter proposal that we should deal only with main effects, or whether it's in support of it. Sharpening offers a special way of going about meta-analysis. Carried to an extreme, though, one will be left with single studies and no meta-analysis.

Laird's point about not being too ambitious in meta-analyses is, as in any research, wise advice. I labored under a terrible strain in a study that I designed where I feared there would be too many primary papers for us to handle in timely fashion. It was arranged so that we could drop out quarters at random as appropriate. But something went awry and to avoid biases, we had to do all the papers instead of about 50 percent. I've never seen anybody write down Laird's point, but this example shows that I vibrate to it.

Although I feel some surprise, I have an impression of disagreement about measures of effect size. Some people think that some measures are good, while others disagree. Although I have my own prejudices, I think this shows that we do not have good agreement about how to measure outcomes. Clearly this matter needs some systematic attention.

We have new developments represented in these pages, like Don Rubin's formulation. Along with mathematical material, I hope Rubin will in future work include some concrete examples of the kind of approach being introduced.

Similarly, the problems Burt Singer raised at the workshop on assembling information either from several surveys or from disparate sources sounds like a new approach for meta-analysis. People do mention it from time to time. For instance, Chalmers tried to study the cost and effectiveness of treatment—he had some hundreds of studies available, but he had only about four studies in which both cost and effectiveness were measured simultaneously. Singer's discussion suggests that we might measure cost in one place and measure effectiveness in another place. Perhaps we can carry information from one kind of study to another, and thus put items together that were not connected originally. Executing such a maneuver may be challenging, and convincing others of its validity even harder. For example, when I served on a committee (Institute of Medicine 1981) to find out the benefit of reducing health hazards for the population, about 55 statistical series were identified by the National Center for Health Statistics. Of those 55, only 4 had a connection between the hazard and the outcome. Although many series measured the hazard and many measured the outcome, only 4 connected the two. These 4 were all geographic measures—that is, a district was measured and the series reported on the district. No series was based on joint exposure and outcome of individuals. This situation exemplified the need for the approach Singer discussed, but offers no guarantee of its validity.

Wachter asked, "When should we stick to main effects?" That's a good question, and one that needs even more careful discussion and scrutiny.

Considering the views represented in this volume, can we set out an agenda of action for the future? Groups, like the Committee on National Statistics, that wish to contribute to this area, might consider ways to improve primary studies, which are the basis for meta-analyses, and ways to improve the methods of meta-analyses.

1. Ways to improve primary studies:
   a. Analyze the presentation of primary studies in statistical journals and create guidelines.
   b. Work with groups, such as the Institute of Medicine's Council for Health Care Technology, the Council of Biology Editors, and other journal editors to improve the quality of primary studies. Seminars are a suggested mode.
   c. Develop guidelines for publishing quantitative research papers that are primary studies.

    d. Develop guidelines on how to compare the effectiveness of policies or programs and on how to find exemplary programs.

    e. Develop some empirical studies of the uses by policymakers of policy analyses that employ quantitative methods and use the results to help improve policy analysis and the statistical system.

    f. Develop guidelines for research on adjustment for bias.

2. Ways to improve methods of meta-analyses:

    a. Develop guidelines on how to search for studies for meta-analyses.

    b. Develop guidelines on how to report studies in meta-analyses.

    c. Develop guidelines on how to be persuasive in meta-analyses.

    d. Develop a clearinghouse for meta-analyses, such as the Institute of Medicine is doing in the area of technology assessment.

    e. Encourage the sharpening of both policy and technological problems into more pointed questions that can be addressed more easily in meta-analyses.

    f. Suggest to researchers who do meta-analyses that they not be too ambitious.

    g. Develop some standards and criteria for judging measures of the size of effects in meta-analyses.

Let me reemphasize the summary aspects of those remarks. Many additional ideas that stimulated the group at the workshop are articulated in the chapters of this volume, and I am bound to have omitted important topics and failed to attribute suggestions to their originators. But we have certainly reviewed the state of meta-analysis and have come up with a variety of tasks to be pursued by CNSTAT and the whole community of meta-analysts.

References

Abelson, R. P.; E. Aronson; W. J. McGuire; T. M. Newcomb; M. J. Rosenberg; and P. H. Tannenbaum, eds.
  1968   *Theories of Cognitive Consistency: A Source Book.* Chicago: Rand McNally.

Armor, D.
  1972   The evidence on busing. *Public Interest* 28:90–126.
  1973   The double double standard: A reply. *Public Interest* 30 (Winter):119–131.

Bailar, J. C., III, and F. Mosteller
  1988   Guidelines for statistical reporting in articles for medical journals. *Annals of Internal Medicine* 108:266–273.

Bakan, D.
  1966   The test of significance in psychological research. *Psychological Bulletin* 66:423–437.

Bangert-Drowns, R. L.
  1986   Review of developments in meta-analytic method. *Psychological Bulletin* 99 (3):388–399.

Bayarri, M. J. and M. DeGroot
  1987   Bayesian analysis of selection models. *The Statistician* 36:137–146.

Becker, B. J.
  1986   Influence again: An examination of reviews and studies of gender differences in social influence. pp. 178–209. In J. S. Hyde and M. C. Linn, eds., *The Psychology of Gender: Advances Through Meta-Analysis.* Baltimore: Johns Hopkins University Press.

Begg, C.
  1985   A measure to aid in the interpretation of published clinical trials. *Statistics in Medicine* 4:1–9.

————, and J. A. Berlin
1988   Publication bias: A problem in interpreting medical data (with discussion). *Journal of the Royal Statistical Society,* Series A, 151, pt. 3.

Berger, J.
1985   *Statistical Decision Theory and Bayesian Analysis,* 2nd ed. New York: Springer-Verlag.

Bozarth, H. D., and R. R. Roberts, Jr.
1972   Signifying significant significance. *American Psychologist* 27:774–775.

Bracht, G., and G. V. Glass
1968   The external validity of experiments. *American Educational Research Journal* 5:437–474.

Bradburn, N., and S. Sudman
1974   *Response Effects in Surveys: A Review and Synthesis.* Chicago: Aldine.

Bradley, L., and G. Bradley
1977   The academic achievement of black students in desegregated schools. *Review of Educational Research* 47 (3):399–450.

Bridge, G.; C. M. Judd; and P. Moock
1979   *The Determinants of Education Outcomes: The Effects of Families, Peers, Teachers, and Schools.* New York: Teachers College Press.

Brown, R.
1986   The issue of independence of effect sizes in meta-analyses. Paper presented at the annual meeting of the American Educational Research Association, San Francisco, April 16–20.

Bryant, F. B., and P. M. Wortman
1984   Methodological issues in the meta-analysis of quasi-experiments. In W. H. Yeaton and P. M. Wortman, "Issues in Data Synthesis," *New Directions for Program Evaluation,* no. 24. San Francisco: Jossey-Bass.

Bullock, R. J., and D. J. Svyantek
1985   Analyzing meta-analysis: potential problems, an unsuccessful replication, and evaluation criteria. *Journal of Applied Psychology* 70 (1):108–115.

Bunker, J. P.; B. A. Barnes; and F. Mosteller, eds.
1977   *Costs, Risks, and Benefits of Surgery.* New York: Oxford University Press.

Chelimsky, E.
1983   The definition and measurement of evaluation quality as a management tool. *New Directions for Program Evaluation,* no. 18. San Francisco: Jossey-Bass.

Cochran, W. G.
1983   *Planning and Analysis of Observational Studies.* New York: Wiley.

Cohen, J.
1988   *Statistical Power Analysis for the Behavioral Sciences,* 2nd ed. Hillsdale, NJ: Erlbaum.

Colditz, G.; J. Miller; and F. Mosteller
1988   The effect of study design on gain in evaluation of new treatments in medicine and surgery. *Drug Information Journal*, 22:343–352.

Coleman, J. S.; E. Q. Campbell; C. J. Hobson; J. McPartland; A. M. Mood; F. D. Weinfeld; and R. L. York
1966   *Equality of Educational Opportunity*. Publication no. 38001. Washington, DC: U. S. Department of Health, Education, and Welfare.

Cook, T. D.
1984   What have black children gained academically from school integration?: Examination of the meta-analytic evidence. In T. Cook, D. Armor, R. Crain, N. Miller, W. Stephan, H. Walberg, and P. Wortman, eds., *School Desegregation and Black Achievement*. Unpublished report. Washington, DC: National Institute of Education. ERIC no. ED 241 671.

————, and D. T. Campbell
1979   *Quasi-experimentation*. Chicago: Rand McNally.

Cooper, H. M.
1981   On the significance of effects and the effects of significance. *Journal of Personality and Social Psychology* 41 (5):1013–1018.
1982   Scientific guidelines for conducting integrative research reviews. *Review of Educational Research* 52 (2):291–302.
1986   Literature searching strategies of integrative research reviewers: A first survey. *Knowledge: Creation, Diffusion, Utilization* 8 (2):372–383.
1986   On the social psychology of using research reviews: The case of desegregation and black achievement. pp. 341–363. In R. Feldman, ed., *The Social Psychology of Education*. Cambridge, England: Cambridge University Press.
1988   Organizing knowledge synthesis: A taxonomy of literature reviews. *Knowledge In Society* 1:104–126.
1989   *Integrating Research: A Guide for Literature Reviews*, 2nd ed. Newbury Park, CA: Sage.

Cooper, H. M., and R. Rosenthal
1980   Statistical versus traditional procedures for summarizing research findings. *Psychological Bulletin* 87(3):442–449.

Cordray, D. S., ed.
1985   Utilizing prior research in evaluation planning. *New Directions for Program Evaluation*, no. 27. San Francisco: Jossey-Bass.
1986   Quasi-experimental analysis: A mixture of methods and judgment. *New Directions for Program Evaluation*, no. 31:9–27.

Cordray, D. S., and M. W. Lipsey, eds.
1987   *Evaluation Studies Review Annual*, vol. 11. Beverly Hills, CA: Sage.

Cordray, D. S., and L. J. Sonnefeld
1985   Quantitative synthesis: An actuarial base for planning impact evaluations. *New Directions for Program Evaluation*, no. 27:29–47.

Cowles, M., and C. Davis
1982   On the origins of the .05 level of statistical significance. *American Psychologist* 37(5):553–558.

Crain, R., and R. Mahard
1978   Desegregation and black achievement: A review of the research. *Law and Contemporary Problems* 42 (3):17–56.
1981   Some policy implications of the desegregation-minority achievement literature. pp. 172–209. In W. D. Hawley ed., *Assessment of Current Knowledge About the Effectiveness of Desegregation Strategies*, vol. 5. Nashville, TN: Vanderbilt University, Center for Education and Human Development Policy, Institute for Public Policy Studies.
1982   *Desegregation Plans That Raise Black Achievement: A Review of the Research*. Santa Monica, CA: Rand Corporation (N-1844–NIE).
1983   The effect of research methodology on desegregation-achievement studies: A meta-analysis. *American Journal of Sociology* 88:839–854.

Cronbach, L. J.
1980   *Toward Reform of Program Evaluation: Aims, Methods and Institutional Arrangements*. San Francisco: Jossey-Bass.

Dempster, A. P.; N. Laird; and D. B. Rubin
1977   Maximum likelihood estimation from incomplete data via the EM algorithm. *Journal of the Royal Statistical Society*, Series B, 39:1–38.

Dempster, A. P.; D. B. Rubin; and R. K. Tsutakawa
1981   Estimation in covariance component models. *Journal of the American Statistical Society* 76:341–353.

DerSimonian, R., and N. Laird
1983   Evaluating the effectiveness of coaching for SAT exams: A meta-analysis. *Harvard Educational Review* 53(1):1–15.

Eagly, A. H., and M. Crowley
1986   Gender and helping behavior: A meta-analytic review of the social psychological literature. *Psychological Bulletin* 100(3):283–308.

Elashoff, J. D.
1978   Box scores are for baseball. *The Behavioral and Brain Sciences*, 3:392.

Emerson, J. D.; B. McPeek; and F. Mosteller
1984   Reporting clinical trials in general surgical journals. *Surgery* 95:572–579.

Evaluation Research Society
1982   ERS program evaluation standards. *New Directions for Program Evaluation*, no. 5:7–21.

Eysenck, H. J.
1978   An exercise in mega-silliness [Comment]. *American Psychologist* 33:517.

Fienberg, S. E.; M. E. Martin; and M. L. Straf, eds.
1985   *Sharing Research Data.* Washington, DC: National Academy Press.

Finsterbusch, K.
1984   *Statistical Summary of 52 AID Projects: Lessons on Project Effectiveness.* College Park: University of Maryland.

Fiske, D. W.
1978   The several kinds of generalization. *The Behavioral and Brain Sciences* 3:393–394.

Giaconia, R. M., and L. V. Hedges
1982   Identifying features of effective open education. *Review of Educational Research* 52:579–602.

Glass, G. V.
1976   Primary, secondary, and meta-analysis of research. *Educational Researcher* 5:3–8.
1977   Integrating findings: The meta-analysis of research. *Review of Research in Education* 5:351–379.
1978   In defense of generalization. *The Behavioral and Brain Sciences* 3:394–395.

————, and R. M. Kliegl
1983   An apology for research integration in the study of psychotherapy. *Journal of Consulting and Clinical Psychology* 51(1):28–41.

Glass, G. V.; B. McGaw; and M. L. Smith
1981   *Meta-Analysis in Social Research.* Beverly Hills, CA: Sage.

Glass, G. V, and M. L. Smith
1979   Meta-analysis of the relationship between class size and achievement. *Educational Evaluation and Policy Analysis* 1:2–16.

Greenwald, A. G.
1975   Consequences of prejudice against the null hypothesis. *Psychological Bulletin* 82(1):1–20.

Hall, B. W.; A. W. Ward; and C. B. Comer
1986   Published educational research: An empirical study of its quality. Paper presented at the annual meeting of the American Educational Research Association, San Francisco, April 16–20.

Hedges, L. V.
1981   Distribution theory for Glass's estimator of effect size and related estimators. *Journal of Educational Statistics* 6:107–128.
1982a   Estimating effect size from a series of independent experiments. *Psychological Bulletin* 92:490–499.
1982b   Fitting categorical models to effect sizes from a series of experiments. *Journal of Educational Statistics* 7:119–137.
1984a   Advances in statistical analysis. *New Directions for Program Evaluation,* no. 24:25–42.

1984b   Estimation of effect size under nonrandom sampling: The effects of censoring studies yielding statistically insignificant mean differences. *Journal of Educational Statistics* 9:61–85.

1988   Improving statistical procedures for validity generalization. pp. 191–212. In H. Braun and H. Warner, eds., *Test Validity for the 1990's and Beyond.* Hillsdale, NJ: Erlbaum.

————, and I. Olkin

1980   Vote counting methods in research synthesis. *Psychological Bulletin* 88(2):359–369.

1985   *Statistical Methods for Meta-Analysis.* New York: Academic Press.

Henderson, R. D.; M. von Euler; and J. M. Schneider

1981   Remedies for segregation: Some lessons from research. *Educational Evaluation and Policy Analysis* 3(4):67–76.

Himel, H. N.; A. Liberati; R. D. Gelber; and T. C. Chalmers

1986   Adjuvant chemotherapy for breast cancer: A pooled estimate based on published randomized control trials. *Journal of the American Medical Association* 256:1148–159.

Hine, L. K.; N. Laird; and T. C. Chalmers

1986   Meta-analysis of randomized control trials of routine antiarrhythmic therapy of post acute myocardial infarction patients indicates urgent need for more trials. Unpublished abstract.

Howard, K. I.; S. M. Kopta; M. S. Krause; and D. E. Orlinsky

1986   The dose-response relationship in psychotherapy. *American Psychologist* 41 (2):159–164.

Hunter, J. E.; F. L. Schmidt; and G. B. Jackson

1982   *Meta-Analysis: Cumulating Research Findings Across Studies.* Beverly Hills, CA: Sage.

Ingelfinger, J. A.; F. Mosteller; L. A. Thibodeau; and J. H. Ware

1983   *Biostatistics in Clinical Medicine.* New York: Macmillan.

Institute of Medicine

1981   *Costs of Environment-related Health Effects: A Plan for Continuing Study.* Washington, DC: National Academy Press.

Iyengar, S., and J. Greenhouse

1988   Selection models and the file-drawer problem (with discussion). *Statistical Science* 3:109–135.

Jackson, G. B.

1980   Methods of integrative reviews. *Review of Educational Research* 50:438–460.

Jung, J.

1978   Self-negating functions of self-fulfilling prophecies. *The Behavioral and Brain Sciences* 3:397–398.

Katz, B. M.; L. A. Marascuilo; and M. McSweeney
1985   Nonparametric alternatives for testing main effects hypotheses: A model for combining data across independent studies. *Psychological Bulletin* 98:200–208.

Kish, L.
1965   *Survey Sampling.* New York: Wiley.

Kolata, G. B.
1981   Drug found to help heart attack survivors. *Science* 214:774–775.

Kraemer, H. C.
1983   Theory of estimation and testing of effect sizes: Use in meta-analysis. *Journal of Educational Statistics* 8:93–101.

————, and G. Andrews
1982   A nonparametric technique for meta-analysis effect size calculation. *Psychological Bulletin* 91:404–412.

Krol, R. A.
1978   A meta-analysis of comparative research on the effects of desegregation on academic achievement. Unpublished doctoral dissertation, Western Michigan University.
1980   Meta-analysis on the effects of desegregation on academic achievement. *Urban Review* 3:12.

Kulik, J. A., and C-L. C. Kulik
1986   Operative and interpretable effect sizes in meta-analysis. Paper presented at the annual meeting of the American Educational Research Association, San Francisco, April 16–20. ERIC, no. ED 275 758.
1989   Meta-analysis in education. *International Journal of Educational Research* 13, no. 3.:221–340.

Laird, N. M.
1978   Nonparametric maximum likelihood estimation of a mixing distribution. *Journal of the American Statistical Association* 73:805–811.
1982   Empirical Bayes estimate using the nonparametric maximum likelihood estimate of the prior. *Journal of Statistical Computation and Simulation* 1:211–220.

————, and T. M. Louis
1987   Empirical Bayes estimate based on bootstrap samples. *Journal of the American Statistical Association* 82:739–750.

Lamb, W. K., and D. K. Whitla
1983   *Meta-analysis and the integration of research findings: A trend analysis and bibliography prior to 1983.* Unpublished manuscript, Harvard University, Cambridge.

Landman, J. T., and R. M. Dawes
1982   Psychotherapy outcome: Smith and Glass' conclusions stand up under scrutiny. *American Psychologist* 37(5):504–516.

Lane, D. M., and W. P. Dunlap
1978   Estimating effect sizes: Bias resulting from the significance criterion in editorial decisions. *British Journal of Mathematical and Statistical Psychology* 31:107–112.

Levin, H. M.; G. V. Glass; and G. R. Meister
1984   *Cost-Effectiveness of Four Educational Interventions.* Stanford, CA: Institute for Research on Educational Finance and Governance, School of Education, Stanford University.

Light, R. J.
1984   Six evaluation issues that synthesis can resolve better than single studies. *New Directions for Program Evaluation*, no. 24:57–73.

———, and D. B. Pillemer
1984   *Summing Up: The Science of Reviewing Research.* Cambridge, MA: Harvard University Press.

Linn, M. C., and A. C. Peterson
1985   Emergence and characterization of sex differences in spatial ability. *Child Development* 56:1479–498.

Little, R. J., and D. B. Rubin
1986   *Statistical Analysis with Missing Data.* New York: Wiley.

Lord, C.; L. Ross; and M. Lepper
1979   Biased assimilation and attitude polarization: The effects of prior theories on subsequently considered evidence. *Journal of Personality and Social Psychology* 37:2098–109.

Louis, T.A.; Fineberg, H.V.; and Mosteller, F.
1985   Findings for public health from meta-analyses. *Annual Review of Public Health* 6:1–20.

Madow, W. G.; H. Nisselson; and I. Olkin
1983   *Report and Case Studies.* Incomplete Data in Sample Surveys, vol. 1. New York: Academic Press.

Madow, W. G., and I. Olkin
1983   *Proceedings and the Symposium.* Incomplete Data in Sample Surveys, vol. 3. New York: Academic Press.

———, and D. B. Rubin
1983   *Theory and Bibliographies.* Incomplete Data in Sample Surveys, vol. 2. New York: Academic Press.

Mayo, R. J.
1978   Statistical considerations in analyzing the results of a collection of experiments. *The Behavioral and Brain Sciences* 3:400–401.

Melton, A. W.
1962   Editorial. *Journal of Experimental Psychology* 64(6):553–557.

Mosteller, F.
   1988   Broadening the scope of statistics and statistical education. *American Statistician* 42:93–99.

Murphy, E.A.
   1976   *The Logic of Medicine.* Baltimore: Johns Hopkins University Press.

National Institute of Education
   1984   School desegregation and black achievement. Unpublished report. Washington, DC: U.S. Department of Education, NIE. ERIC, no. ED 241 671.

O'Grady, Kevin E.
   1982   Measures of explained variance: Cautions and limitations. *Psychological Bulletin* 92(3):766–777.

Orwin, R.
   1983   A fail-safe N for effect size in meta-analysis. *Journal of Educational Statistics* 8:157–159.

———, and D. S. Cordray
   1985   Effects of deficient reporting on meta-analysis: A conceptual framework and reanalysis. *Psychological Bulletin* 97(1):134–147.

Peirce, C.
   1968   [1877]   Approaches to philosophy. *Popular Science Monthly.* pp. 31–42. In J. A. Gould, ed., *Classical Philosophical Questions,* 2nd ed. Columbus, OH: Merrill.

Pettigrew, T. F.
   1973   Busing: A review of the evidence. *Public Interest* 30:88–118 (Winter).

Porch, B.
   1967   *Porch Index of Communicative Ability.* Palo Alto, CA: Consulting Psychologists.

Prioleau, L.; M. Murdock; and N. Brody
   1983   An analysis of psychotherapy vs. placebo studies. *The Behavioral and Brain Sciences* 6, no. 2:275–285.

Raudenbush, S. W., and A. S. Bryk
   1985   Empirical Bayes meta-analysis. *Journal of Educational Statistics* 10:75–98.

Rimland, B.
   1979   Death knell for psychotherapy? *American Psychologist* 34:192.

Rosenthal, R.
   1966   *Experimenter Effects in Behavioral Research.* New York: Appleton-Century-Crofts.
   1969   Interpersonal expectations. pp. 181–277. In R. Rosenthal and R. L. Rosnow, eds., *Artifact in Behavioral Research.* New York: Academic Press.
   1979a   The "file-drawer problem" and tolerance for null results. *Psychological Bulletin* 86(3):638–641.

1979b   Replications and their relative utilities. *Replications in Social Psychology* 1 (1):15–23.

1984   *Meta-Analytic Procedures for Social Research.* Beverly Hills, CA: Sage.

———, and R. L. Rosnow

1985   *Contrast Analysis: Focused Comparisons in the Analysis of Variance.* New York: Cambridge University Press.

Rosenthal, R., and D. B. Rubin

1978   Interpersonal expectancy effects: The first 345 studies. *The Behavioral and Brain Sciences* 3:377–415.

1979   A note on percent variance explained as a measure of the importance of effects. *Journal of Applied Social Psychology* 9:395–396.

1982a   A simple, general purpose display of magnitude of experimental effect. *Journal of Educational Psychology* 74:166–169.

1982b   Comparing effect sizes of independent studies. *Psychological Bulletin* 92:500–504.

1986   Meta-analytic procedures for combining studies with multiple effect sizes. *Psychological Bulletin* 99(3):400–406.

Rubin, D. B.

1980   Using empirical Bayes techniques in the law school validity studies. *Journal of the American Statistical Association* 75:801–816.

1981   Estimation in parallel randomized experiments. *Journal of Educational Statistics* 6(4):377–401.

1987   *Multiple Imputation for Nonresponse in Surveys.* New York: Wiley.

Sackett, D. L.

1979   Bias in analytic research. *Journal of Chronic Diseases* 32:51–63.

St. John, N. H.

1975   *School Desegregation: Outcomes for Children.* New York: Wiley.

Shapiro, D. A.

1985   Recent applications of meta-analysis in clinical research. *Clinical Psychology Review* 5(1):13–34.

Slavin, R. E.

1984   Meta-analysis in education: How has it been used? *Educational Researcher* 13:6–15.

Smith, M. L.

1980   Publication bias in meta-analysis. *Evaluation in Education: An International Review Series* 4:22–24.

———, and G. V. Glass

1977   Meta-analysis of psychotherapy outcome studies. *American Psychologist* 32:752–760.

Spector, P. E. and E. L. Levine

1987   Meta-analysis for integrating study outcomes: A monte carlo study of its susceptibility to Type I and Type II errors. *Journal of Applied Psychology* 72:3–9.

Sterling, T. D.

1959   Publication decisions and their possible effects on inferences drawn from tests of significance—or vice versa. *Journal of American Statistical Association* 54:30–34.

Strike, K., and G. Posner

1983   Types of syntheses and their criteria. pp. 343–362. In Spencer Ward and L. Reed, eds., *Knowledge Structure and Use: Implications for Synthesis and Interpretation.* Philadelphia: Temple University Press.

Strube, M. J.

1985   Combining and comparing significance levels from nonindependent hypothesis tests. *Psychological Bulletin* 97:334–341.

———; W. Gardner; and D. P. Hartmann

1984   Limitations, liabilities, and obstacles in reviews of the literature: The current status of meta-analysis. *Clinical Psychology Review* 5:63–78.

Tesser, A.

1978   Self-generated attitude change. In *Attitudes in Experimental Social Psychology.* New York: Academic Press.

Tracz, S. M., and P. B. Elmore

1985   The effect of the violation of the assumption of independence when combining correlation coefficients in a meta-analysis. *Multiple Linear Regression Viewpoints* 14:61–80.

Tukey, J. W.

1979   Methodology and the statistician's responsibility for BOTH accuracy AND relevance. *Journal of the American Statistical Association* 74:786–793.

1980   We need both exploratory and confirmatory. *American Statistician* 34:23–25.

U.S. General Accounting Office

1983   *Evaluation Synthesis.* Washington, DC: U.S. General Accounting Office, Institute for Program Evaluation.

1986   *Teenage Pregnancy: 500,000 Births Yet Few Tested Programs.* Washington, DC: U.S. General Accounting Office, Program Evaluation and Methodology Division.

Uribe, O., and J. Schneider

1983   Background paper (unpublished). Washington, DC: National Institute of Education.

Walberg, H.

1984   Desegregation and educational achievement. In D. Armor, T. Cook, R. Crain, N. Miller, W. Stephan, H. Walberg, and P. Wortman, eds., *School Desegregation and Black Achievement.* Unpublished report. Washington, DC: National Institute of Education. ERIC, no. ED 241 671.

Weinberg, M.
   1970   *Desegregation Research: An Appraisal.* Bloomington, IN: Phi Delta Kappa.
   1977   *Minority Students: A Research Appraisal.* Washington, DC: National Institute of Education.

Wolf, F. M.
   1986   *Meta-Analysis: Quantitative Methods for Research Synthesis.* Beverly Hills, CA: Sage.

Wood, W.
   1982   Retrieval of attitude-relevant information from memory: Effects on susceptibility to persuasion and on intrinsic motivation. *Journal of Personality and Social Psychology* 42(5):798–810.

Wortman, P. M.
   1982   *School Desegregation and Black Achievement: An Integrative Review.* Ann Arbor: University of Michigan.
   1984   School desegregation and black achievement: An integrative view. In T. Cook, D. Armor, R. Crain, N. Miller, W. Stephan, H. Walberg, and P. Wortman, eds., *School Desegregation and Black Achievement.* Unpublished report. Washington, DC: National Institute of Education. ERIC, no. ED 241 671.
   ———, and F. B. Bryant
   1985   School desegregation and black achievement. *Sociological Methods and Research* 13:289–324.

Yeaton, W. H. and P. M. Wortman, eds.
   1984   Issues in data synthesis. *New Directions for Program Evaluation*, no. 24. San Francisco: Jossey-Bass.

Index

Abelson, R. P., 78
acute myocardial infarction (AMI), 51
agriculture, xvii
AID projects study, 113
alternate controls (ACT's), 51
Analytic Chemistry, 94
Andrews, 146
aphasia study, xiv, xv–xvi, 29–52, 173, 188; and "classical" vs. clinical approach, 31–32; completeness of, xx, xxi, 32–33
Armor, David J., 56, 58, 61–63; 67, 68, 69, 71, 107
astronomy, xvii
audience, 93, 96

background variables, in desegregation studies, 73, 74
bad studies, 126
Bailar, J. C., III, 186
Bakan, D., 19
balance, 105, 106
Bangert-Drowns, R. L., 140
Barnes, B. A., 71
Bayarri, M. J., 43
Becker, B. J., 23
Begg, C., 52, 187
beliefs, 77, 81, 87; ethics of, 186
Berkson, Joseph, 172
Berlin, 187
between-analyst variability, 109
bias, xviii, xxv, xxvii, 6, 11, 13, 126, 168, 187; and aphasia study, 42–43;

and comprehensive searches, 169–171; corrections for, 21; defined, 141; and desegregation studies, 69, 108–109; and limiting search, xxi, 171; methodological observations on, 139–151; nonsampling, 102–104; publication, 19–20; reporting, 17, 19–20; sampling, 102; undetected dependence and, 25–26
binomial effect size display (BESD), 128–131, 164
bioassay, xvii
"Blacks and *Brown*" (Stephan), 65
blinding, 48
Bozarth, H. D., 19
Bracht, G., 16
Bradburn, Norman M., xviii, 135–137, 156, 168–169
Bradley, G., 57
Bradley, L., 57
breast cancer, 52
Bridge, G., 56
Brody, N., 112
Bullock, R. J., 117
Bunker, J. P., 71
Byrk, A. S., 23

Campbell, D. T., 15
Carlson, Michael, 64–65
case studies, xv–xviii
central tendency, in desegregation studies, 68, 69, 71

study, 32–34, 43; for desegregation study, 58–60, 62, 63–64; and frame bias, 102
series of studies conducted by same investigators, 25
Shapiro, D. A., 111
sharing research data, standards for, 10
Sharing Research Data (Fienberg, Martin, and Straf), xvii, 10
Shulman, Lee, 75n
significance levels, 127–128, 150
Singer, Burt, 189
single values, overemphasizing, 124
Slavin, R. E., 16
Smith, M.L., xiii, 14, 16, 19, 21, 25, 30, 102, 117, 123, 126, 128, 129, 147
social psychology, of using research reviews, 75–87
socioeconomic status (SES), 56
sociologists, 78
Sonnefeld, L. J., 102
sources of information on study characteristics, 18–19
Spector, P. E., 151
stakeholders, multiple, 104–105, 116
standard deviations, choice of, 103
statistical assumptions, and bias, 146–147
statistically insignificant results, 19
Statistical Methods for Meta-Analysis (Hedges and Olkin), 6
Statistical Methods for Research Workers (Fisher), 4
statisticians, 30, 44, 47, 178, 186, 187
statistics, xiv–xv, xxii, xxv, 12
Stephan, Walter, 58, 65–66, 67, 68, 69, 71, 107
Sterling, T. D., 19
Straf, Miron L., xiii–xxviii, 10, 150, 171, 176–177, 182, 183, 184
Strube, M. J., 102, 117, 143, 148
Strike, K., 91, 92
structural modeling, xxiii
studies, too many, 127–128
study characteristics: for aphasia study, 34–36; missing data on, 18–19
study design, xxviii, 77, 164, 176–177; bias in, 142–143; flaws and study

results, 21; and informational utility, 76, 78–79; *see also* quality of studies
"study methods" approach, 20, 21
subcategorization, xxiii
subject matter specialist, 43, 47
substantive meaning, and effect sizes, 89
Sudman, 135, 136, 137
summarization, as goal, xxvii
surveys, 135–137
Svyantek, D. J., 117
systematic error, 102, 103, 108, 118

technical adequacy, 100–101, 108, 150–151
Tesser, A., 80
theoretical factors, 148
Thibodeau, 141
"threats-to-validity" approach, 20–21
tidying up bias, 147
timeliness, 104
topic familiarity, 83
Tracz, S. M., 151
treatment effects, assessment of, 14, 52; for aphasia study, 40
treatments; representative sampling of, 16; variations in, across studies, 21–22
true: effects, 157, 159, 160; value, 172
Tsutakowa, R.K., 26
Tukey, John, xxiii, 140, 148
type I errors, 147, 151
type II errors, 127, 151

U.S. Congress, 104, 105, 111, 173
unpublished sources, 19, 20, 48, 60
Uribe, O., 107, 112
utility, 92, 97, 100, 104, 109; informational, and experimental design, 76, 78–79

variables, number of, 178–179
variable error, 101–102, 108, 118
variability, 45, 103, 109–110, 112, 143, 145, 184; and desegregation studies, 180
variance component, 23, 24

variations: in treatments and controls across studies, 21–22; in precision, 13
von Euler, M., 56
vote counts, 6, 7

Wachter, Kenneth W., xiii–xxviii, 29, 49, 170–171, 172–174, 175, 176, 177, 178, 181–182, 188, 189
Walberg, Herbert, 58, 66–67, 71, 90–91, 107, 111
Ward, A. W., 150
Ward, Spencer, 75n
Ware, 141
Warren, Kenneth, 172
weighting studies, 136

Weinberg, M., 56
Whitla, D. K., 123
WIC program, 112
Wolf, Fredric M., xiii, xviii, xxiii, xxv, 117, 139–151, 156, 164, 168, 181
Wong, Wing, 24
Wortman, Paul, 57, 58, 62, 67, 68, 69, 71, 72, 107, 110, 114, 145, 182

X factors, 158, 162, 164

Yeaton, W. H., 71

Z factors, 158, 162, 164